SPURGEON

Yours ever heartily

C.H. Spurgeon

SPURGEON

A new biography by

Arnold Dallimore

THE BANNER OF TRUTH TRUST

THE BANNER OF TRUTH TRUST
3 Murrayfield Road, Edinburgh EH12 6EL, UK
P. O. Box 621, Carlisle, PA 17013, USA

*

First published in the U.S.A. by Moody Press
First Banner of Truth edition 1985
© The Banner of Truth Trust 1985
Reprinted 1988
Reprinted 1991
Reprinted 1995
Reprinted 1999
Reprinted 2005
Reprinted 2009

ISBN–13: 978 0 85151 451 2

*

Printed in the USA by
Versa Press, Inc.,
East Peoria, IL

In memory of
my mother,
Mabel Buckingham Dallimore,
who as a small child
was frequently taken by her father,
William Buckingham,
to the
Metropolitan Tabernacle
to hear
the preaching of
Charles Haddon Spurgeon

Contents

Preface

"Why would you write another biography of Spurgeon? Hasn't everything about him already been said and said a hundred times?" These questions and others like them have been asked as I wrote about Spurgeon's life.

Although Spurgeon is often discussed among evangelicals today, few people fully understand his person and his career. The lack of a suitable biography has been recognized by many. Dr. Wilbur Smith, writing in 1955, said, "I have tried to read again most of the autobiographical and biographical volumes on Charles H. Spurgeon, and in doing so I have come to the strong conclusion that the Christian church has not yet seen a fully adequate and definitive life of this great preacher of the grace of God."[1]

The reasons for this situation are evident. Following Spurgeon's death in 1892, for two years or more new biographies appeared at the rate of about one a month. At that time there was, of course, deep sorrow over his passing, and his memory was held in the highest admiration. The early accounts did little but emphasize that admiration. Certain areas that should have been presented—for instance, his ability as theologian and the methods he used in

---

1. In his *Treasury of Charles Haddon Spurgeon* (1955).

leading souls to Christ—were almost entirely overlooked. Likewise, the rugged, unbending strength of his character was not sufficiently depicted, and the concept of a personality somewhat weaker than the real Spurgeon was passed along to mankind.

The situation was remedied to some extent when in 1894 the six-volume *Life and Work of Charles Haddon Spurgeon* by G. Holden Pike appeared, and in 1897 when the four-volume work by Spurgeon's wife and secretary, entitled *C. H. Spurgeon's Autobiography,* began to be published. But both of those works were too large to receive wide circulation, and, although they provided a wealth of information, they did not present a vital story that made Spurgeon alive to their readers. Moreover, like the lesser biographies, the large accounts did not peer beneath the surface to reveal the heart and soul of the man—the essential Spurgeon.

Accordingly, many today think of him as merely a highly gifted orator who made his hearers laugh and cry and to whom the hour in the pulpit was a very pleasant activity. Because his burning earnestness and unyielding theological convictions are so little known it is assumed that he was much like the average evangelical of today. And someone has said that Spurgeon is regarded as a kind of grandfather of twentieth-century evangelism.

I trust that, at least to some extent, this book provides a more satisfactory account of the great Spurgeon. I have dealt with several matters on which the concept has long been inadequate, and the reader will find here a more definitive treatment given to his theology and preaching methods. I have endeavored to understand and present something of the inner man—Spurgeon in his praying, his sufferings and depressions, his weaknesses and strengths, in his triumphs, his humor, his joys, and his incredible accomplishments.

Here indeed was a mighty man of God, one of the greatest preachers of all Christian history. I confess the difficulty I have experienced in portraying so tremendous a personality. Nevertheless, I will have succeeded if many come to know him better and are both instructed and inspired by his powerful example.

Acknowledgments

I heartily express my gratitude to the following friends for their assistance:

To the Reverend Leroy Cole of Ottisville, Michigan, who placed at my disposal his large library on Spurgeon. I borrowed from him some forty books, most of which were biographies of Spurgeon, and without the volumes from Mr. Cole I could not have pursued this task.

To Bob Ross of Pilgrim Press, Pasadena, Texas. Mr. Ross has made me a gift of several works on Spurgeon published by Pilgrim Press. Particularly useful are those written by Eric W. Hayden.

To Dr. Peter Masters, pastor of the Metropolitan Tabernacle. Dr. Masters allowed me access to the record books of the Tabernacle from the days of Spurgeon's ministry. Also, in conversation he provided me with several points of information on the life of Spurgeon.

To the Reverend Gerald C. Primm of Greensboro, North Carolina, for several suggestions and for photocopying certain portions of Spurgeon's works.

To Phillip Borrè and Keith Lozon, both of Windsor, Ontario, each of whom loaned me various volumes of Spurgeon's *Sermons* and of *The Sword and the Trowel.*

Conditions in England During Spurgeon's Time

Spurgeon was born in 1834 and died in 1892. Conditions during that period were different in several regards from those of today, and a brief look at them will help us toward understanding his life.

Throughout those years Queen Victoria was on the throne. She exercised a strong influence for morality in government and in daily life. During her reign Britain greatly extended its empire, and the economy of the nation prospered markedly.

In London, horses, carriages, and carts were so many that traffic, which was governed by no rules of the road, was often brought to a standstill. The railroads were being steadily enlarged, but although England led the world in this regard, trains were slow and passenger travel was uncomfortable and often grimy.

Bathrooms with running water were gradually being installed in the homes of the wealthy and a few of the middle class. Among the poor they were entirely unknown. Heating was done largely through burning coal, and lighting was provided by oil and gas lamps, although the poorest still used candles.

During the years in which Spurgeon lived, great strides were made in medical knowledge. The existence of bacteria was discovered, a knowledge was acquired of antisepsis, and scientists realized that the drinking water supply could be contaminated if located too near sewage disposal, thus spreading cholera and other diseases. Surgery was performed without anesthetic until 1847, when chloroform was discovered, and in 1860, under the influence of Florence Nightingale, the first standards for nursing practice were set.

The class system generally prevailed. The upper class not only had wealth but also held privileges denied to all others. But the middle class was growing, and opportunities for men to acquire considerable possessions were steadily increasing. Still, there were many poor, and among them much ignorance, sickness, and need. The utterly destitute could apply for refuge at a workhouse, but conditions in those places were designed to be so bad that the inmates would make every effort to obtain some kind of employment and thus escape so terrible an existence. A large number of homeless children roamed the streets, and petty crime proved to be the only way they could keep themselves alive. We shall need to bear those circumstances in mind when we see Spurgeon creating an almshouse and an orphanage and providing education without charge for needy children and young men.

The Church of England was the state religion. It was supported by the government and was granted privileges that were denied to all who were not of its membership. The Nonconformist bodies— the Methodists, Congregationalists, Baptists, and Presbyterians— had made much growth as a result of the revival under Whitefield and the Wesleys during the preceding century, but by Spurgeon's time much of the fervor had died down, and a rather dreary formalism characterized a great deal of church life. The chief figures among the Congregationalists were Thomas Binney and Joseph Parker and, among the Baptists, John Clifford and Alexander MacLaren. The Brethren movement under John Darby began in the 1830s, and the Salvation Army under William Booth came into being during the 1870s.

One of the most important religious activities of the century was the Oxford Movement. Under the leadership of John Henry (later Cardinal) Newman, a large number of people left the Church of England to join the Roman Catholic Church, and that influence remained a strong factor in everyday English life.

Throughout this book the costs of buildings and other items are presented in the English money of those times. In order to translate the values into those of any other nation and any other age, the reader may use as a norm the wages paid to a workingman. A good wage for a skilled laborer was then about £100 a year.

Spurgeon was in many senses a typical Victorian Englishman. There was much that was good in society around him but also much that was evil. He devoted himself to one overwhelming task—the declaration of the life-transforming message of the gospel of Jesus Christ. And he saw its power displayed in the conversion of thousands.

THE PREPARATION OF THE MAN

1834—1854

The precocity of young Charles drew the attention of all around. He would astonish the grave deacons and matrons, who met at his grandfather's house on Sunday evenings, by proposing subjects for conversation and offering pertinent remarks upon them. And there were at that early period of his life palpable indications of that decision of character and boldness of address for which he became so remarkable.

Robert Shindler, *From the Usher's Desk to the Tabernacle Pulpit*, 1892

1

The Boy and the Books

"I would rather be descended from one who suffered for the faith than bear the blood of all the emperors in my veins." Spurgeon was referring to the fact that although there was a lineage from the valiant Norsemen in his blood, the chief factor in his inheritance was that some of the early Spurgeons had been among the seventeenth-century Protestants who fled from Catholic persecutions in Europe to find refuge in England.

One ancestor, a Job Spurgeon, "had to suffer both in purse and in person for the testimony of a good conscience."[1] Job, with three other men, was imprisoned for attending a Nonconformist meeting—a meeting of persons who refused to conform to the doctrines and practices of the Church of England. They suffered in jail throughout a winter that was "remarkable for the extremity of cold"; the three lay upon straw. Job Spurgeon was so weak he could not lie down and remained all the time in an upright position.

Charles stated, "I can cast my eye back through four generations and see that God had been pleased to hear the prayers of my grandfather's father, who used to supplicate with God that his chil-

1. *C. H. Spurgeon's Autobiography,* comp. Susannah Spurgeon and J. W. Harrald, 4 vols. (London: Passmore and Alabaster, 1897), 1:8.

dren might live before Him to the last generation; and God . . . has been pleased to bring first one and then another to love and fear His name."[2]

The background from which Charles Spurgeon came was therefore one in which standing for principle, whatever the cost, was prominent.

He was born June 19, 1834, in the Essex County town of Kelvedon. But at the age of fourteen months he was taken to the home of his father's parents, in the out-of-the-way village of Stambourne, and there he spent the following five years. His mother was only nineteen when he was born, and the arrival of another baby within the next year was probably the reason for the change.

The grandfather, the Reverend James Spurgeon, was the minister of Stambourne's Congregational (Independent) Church, a position he had filled for the preceding twenty-five years. He was a graduate of Hoxton College, London, and he possessed a deep knowledge of the Scriptures and of Puritan writings. His voice was strong, but exceptionally pleasant and widely expressive, and his preaching was both earnest and powerful. Into his work in the pulpit, as into his private conversation, there often crept a note of humor. His congregation was numerous for a village church, and the statement of one hearer, "I could mount on wings as eagles after being fed such heavenly food," was undoubtedly the feeling of many at the close of the sermon. He was loved by his people and also by those of Stambourne's Church of England, and he had not the slightest desire to move to a larger place.

The grandmother, Sarah, was a worthy partner to her husband. The home was happy and free from strife. The one statement about her that has come down to us is "She was a dear, good, kind soul."

James's and Sarah's youngest daughter, eighteen-year-old Ann, still lived with her parents. She was delighted to have little Charles in the home, and he became the special object of her love and care. She attended him in his baby needs, helped him as he learned to walk and to talk, and since she was full of fun she enjoyed many a romp with her young charge as he grew. She was also an earnest Christian and sought to promote his spiritual welfare by her devout life and her daily example.

The house in which the Spurgeons lived was a church manse that had originally been built as a gentleman's mansion. It was nearly

2. Ibid.

two hundred years old, and although its slanting walls and tilting floors revealed its age, it was still a comfortable home.

The front door opened into a wide hall, one wall of which held a huge fireplace with a large picture of David and Goliath. It had also a toy rocking horse—"The only horse," said Charles in adult life, "that I ever enjoyed riding." A winding stair led up to bedrooms above. The boy had a pleasant room with an old four-poster with chintz upholstery. He could lie and listen to the birds in the nearby eaves.

A well-kept garden lay at the rear and side of the house. It had an abundance of flowers and fruits and was bordered by a shaded grassy walkway, and here Charles's grandfather often came to meditate as he prepared for the labors of the Lord's day. In later times Charles proved very fond of a garden and freely used illustrations from plant life.

Immediately adjacent to the manse stood the chapel. In true Puritan fashion it was entirely unadorned, but it had a high box pulpit over which there hung a massive sounding board. It reminded young Charles, as he sat in church, of his toy jack-in-the-box, and he imagined the sounding board coming loose and falling upon his grandfather's head.

The chapel had also a unique feature—two large exterior doors in a side wall near the pulpit. If a carriage arrived carrying a sick person, those doors could be opened and the carriage—with the horses removed—could be pushed through, thus allowing the invalid a comfortable place to hear. Today there are "drive-in" and "wheelchair" services, but here was a combination of the two a century and a half ago.

Little Charles had the privilege of spending much time with his grandfather. James Spurgeon was an entirely unpretentious person, and though he was nearly sixty years of age there was still much about him that was young. It may have been for this reason that he was so attached to the boy, or it may have been that he already recognized his unusual qualities and wanted to guide them. Even when parishioners called to have their pastor advise and pray with them in their problems he often kept the lad at his side, and when he gathered with a company of ministers to discuss theological questions the boy remained, listening intently and doing his best to understand. Charles's introduction to the consideration of theological questions thus began very early.

Life in the Spurgeon home was built around the Scriptures. The

Bible was not only read, but it was also believed with unquestion-
ing assurance of its inerrancy. Likewise prayer was made in the full
realization that God heard and would answer according to His
sovereign will. The standards of the Bible were joyfully accepted,
and dishonesty or malice or any kind was entirely unknown. Life
was serious, but it was also marked by humor and happiness, and
"godliness with contentment [which] is great gain" characterized
both work and pleasure for the Spurgeons, old and young.

Charles was still a child when he first became aware of books.

One of the bedrooms in the manse led off into a small dark
chamber—dark because the window had been plastered over to
avoid the infamous "window tax," but this chamber held an old
Puritan library, and Charles was probably no more than three when
he began pulling volumes out into the light and looking at the
illustrations. We are told, "Even when a mere child, before his lips
had uttered an articulate word, he would sit patiently for hours,
amusing himself with a book of pictures."[3] It was during those very
early days that he came upon the illustrations in Bunyan's *Pilgrim's
Progress.* "When I first saw in it the woodcut of Christian carrying
the burden on his back I felt so interested in the poor fellow that I
thought I should jump for joy when, after he had carried it so long,
he at last got rid of it."[4] He also became acquainted with other
Bunyan personalities—Pliable, Faithful, and Talkative, for example—and learned their chief characteristics.

He made much of Foxe's *Book of Martyrs.* He sat gazing at its
pictures of the burning of the several Protestants during the reign of
Bloody Queen Mary, and the sufferings those men endured made a
lasting impression on him.

But Charles did more than merely look at pictures. He was still
young when he learned to read. Aunt Ann taught him at home, and
he also attended, he says, "a school for very juveniles," conducted
by "old Mrs. Burleigh." In turn, we find him when only five or six,
reading privately and also reading publicly during the time of family worship. One who terms himself "a contemporary" writes:
"Even at six years old, when some children have advanced no further in spelling than words of one syllable, he could read out with a
point and emphasis really marvellous in one so young."[5]

3. *Traits of Character* (London: n.p., 1860), 2:80.
4. Iain Murray, ed., *The Early Years* (London: Banner of Truth, 1962), p. 85.
5. *Traits of Character,* p. 80.

During those early days Charles also learned much about life in general. In later years he created a character he called "John Ploughman." Of this imagined person he told numerous tales, each with a pointed moral lesson. "John Ploughman" was patterned after both his grandfather and Will Richardson, a farmer he came to know during those days in Stambourne.

While yet a boy, Charles revealed a strong moral courage. For instance, learning that his grandfather was grieved over the behavior of one of his church members who had begun to frequent the tavern, he marched boldly into the place and confronted him. The man, Thomas Roads, said of the event,

> To think an old man like me should be took to task . . . by a bit of a child like that! Well, he points at me, with his finger just so, and says, "What doest thou here, Elijah? sitting with the ungodly; and you a member of a church, and breaking your pastor's heart. I'm ashamed of you! I wouldn't break my pastor's heart, I'm sure." And then he walks away. . . .
>
> I knew it was all true, and I was guilty; so I put down my pipe, and did not touch my beer, but hurried away to a lonely spot, and cast myself down before the Lord, confessing my sin and begging for forgiveness.[6]

The restoration of Thomas Roads proved real and lasting, and he became a zealous helper in the work of the Lord. At so early an age, Charles manifested the sense of righteousness and the strong stand against something he considered wrong that characterized him throughout his later life.

After five years at Stambourne, Charles was taken back to his parents. He had enjoyed an excellent childhood with his grandparents and was to visit them again during several forthcoming summers.

Charles's parents, John and Eliza Spurgeon, had now moved to Colchester, where John was employed as a clerk in a coal merchant's office. He was also the pastor of a Congregational church at Tollesbury, a village some nine miles away, and he made the journey each Sunday by horse and carriage. The two duties kept him much engaged and robbed him of time he would have liked to spend with his wife and children. He was a good preacher and possessed an exceptionally strong voice, but he did not have the pulpit power of his father.

There were now three other children in the home: a boy, James

6. *The Early Years*, p. 12.

Archer Spurgeon (nearly three years younger than Charles) and two still younger sisters, Eliza and Emily.

Charles immediately became their leader. This was not only because he was oldest but also because he possessed strong leadership qualities. For instance, his father found him on one occasion leading the other children in a game of church. He was standing in a hayrack pretending to preach, and he had the others seated on bundles of hay in front of him, listening to his sermon. Another time the two brothers were playing with toy ships on a creek; Charles had named his *The Thunderer,* a title he had chosen, he said, because he wanted one that sounded courageous and victorious.

In those days there was no system of free education, and large numbers of children remained illiterate. Schools were operated as personal businesses, so parents paid to have their children attend.

John Spurgeon wanted his boys to have the best education he could afford, and Charles was put under instruction immediately upon his return to Colchester. This was at a small school conducted by a Mrs. Cook, and he proved an excellent student. Moreover, as the months advanced it was evident he had a much greater desire for learning than for play, and his father stated:

> Charles was a healthy child and boy, having a good constitution, and he was of an affectionate disposition, and very studious. He was always reading books—never digging in the garden or keeping pigeons, like other boys. It was always books, and books. If his mother wanted to take him for a ride, she would be sure to find him in my study pouring over a book. He was clever, of course, and clever in most directions of study. He learned to draw very well.[7]

Despite, however, the parents' interest in their children's academic progress, they were more concerned about their spiritual welfare.

Since the father was so busy, the task of bringing up the family fell largely to the mother. She was an exceptionally devout and gracious woman, and the son James stated, "She was the starting point of all the greatness and goodness any of us, by the grace of God, have ever enjoyed."[8] Charles looked back on her with deep

---

7. G. Holden Pike, *The Life and Work of Charles Haddon Spurgeon,* 6 vols. (London: Cassel, 1898), 1:17.
8. G. Holden Pike, *James Archer Spurgeon* (n.p., n.d.), p. 20.

affection and gratitude, and he tells of her reading the Scriptures to her children and pleading with them to be concerned about their souls. "I cannot tell how much I owe of the solemn words of my good mother. . . ." he wrote. "I remember on one occasion her praying thus, 'Now, Lord, if my children go on in their sins, it will not be from ignorance that they perish, and my soul must bear a swift witness against them at the day of judgment if they lay not hold of Christ.' That thought of my mother's bearing a swift witness against me pierced my conscience. . . . How can I ever forget when she bowed her knee, and with her arms about my neck, prayed, 'Oh, that my son may live before Thee!' "9

He also tells of an occasion on which his father, while on his way to a church service, began to charge himself with neglecting his family and therefore turned back to his home. Finding no one in the lower floor, he went upstairs, and there he heard the sound of prayer. "He discovered," says Charles, "that it was my mother, pleading most earnestly for the salvation of all her children, and praying especially for Charles, her first-born and strong-willed son. My father felt that he might safely go about his Master's business while his dear wife was caring so well for the spiritual interests of the boys and girls at home."10

The interest Charles had begun to take in Foxe and Bunyan and other such writers while at his grandfather's was enlarged during the hours he now spent in his father's study. He became acquainted with several of the great Puritan authors and familiarized himself with their doctrinal convictions. Moreover, the opportunity of listening to strong theological discussions was available also at Colchester, for he was allowed to be present as his father and other ministers conferred on various biblical matters. He later stated, "I can bear witness that children *can* understand the Scriptures; for I am sure that, when but a child, I could have discussed many a knotty point of controversial theology, having heard both sides of the question freely stated among my father's circle of friends."11

Moreover, though his father possessed a number of theological books, Charles had many more available to him, as summer by summer he returned to his grandfather's home at Stambourne. He spoke of that upstairs chamber: "Out of that darkened room I

9. *The Early Years*, p. 44.
10. Ibid., p. 45.
11. Ibid., p. 46.

fetched those old authors . . . and never was I happier than when in their company." There can be no doubt that by the time he was nine or ten he was reading and understanding something of such mighty men as John Owen, Richard Sibbes, John Flavel, and Matthew Henry. He was already grasping the meaning of much of their theological argument and was reasoning out the pros and cons within his own mind.

Charles was still a child when, during one of his summers at Stambourne, he became the subject of a striking prophecy.

His grandfather brought to the church a former missionary, Richard Knill, for special meetings. Knill had spent many years in India and in Russia and was at that time serving in England. He became much taken with young Charles, quickly recognizing his unusual mental ability and his rare clarity of speech. For instance, Charles read the Scriptures each day at family worship, and in reporting the experience Knill stated, "I have heard old ministers and young ones read well, but never did I hear a little boy read so correctly before."[12]

Day by day the missionary spoke to Charles about his soul and prayed with him most earnestly. He believed the boy would assuredly become a minister, and when he was about to leave the home, with the family standing around, he set him on his knee and made the pronouncement, "This child will one day preach the Gospel, and will preach it to great multitudes, and I am persuaded he will preach it in the chapel of Rowland Hill."[13]

Rowland Hill's chapel was one of the largest in England at the time, and in later years Charles did preach there. Yet even on the occasion of hearing the prophecy he felt its effect and said, "I looked forward to the time when I should preach the Word: I felt very powerfully that no unconverted person might dare to enter the ministry; this made me . . . all the more intent upon seeking salvation."[14]

When he was ten, Charles was transferred to another school in Colchester, the Stockwell House School. Its academic standards were higher than most such institutions. A fellow student, writing in later years, reported: "Mr. Leeding was the classical and mathematical tutor; his teaching was very thorough, and in Charles Spurgeon he possessed a pupil of very receptive mind, especially

12. Robert Shindler, *From the Usher's Desk to the Tabernacle Pulpit* (London: Passmore and Alabaster, 1892), p. 31.
13. *The Early Years,* p. 27.
14. Ibid., p. 28.

with Latin and Euclid . . . in both of these subjects he was very advanced."[15]

Charles remained at this school for four years. They were years of much mental discipline and of excellent growth in knowledge. He was always at the head of his class, except during a week or two one winter, when he learned that by doing poorly he could be seated nearer to the fireplace. Upon discovering his scheme, the teacher reversed the seating order and arranged that the smartest boy should sit nearest the heat. Charles quickly improved in his work and retained the favored spot.

His parents removed him when he was fourteen to St. Augustine's Agricultural College in the town of Maidstone, a few miles southeast of London. The trial of being away from home was softened by the fact that he was not alone, for his brother James entered the school with him. Moreover, one of their uncles was the school's principal, and the boys boarded at his house.

During his year there Charles twice manifested something of his native audacity. The first instance was in a conversation he had with a Church of England clergyman who came regularly to the school to teach religion. The man led him into a discussion of baptism, and Charles replied with strong confidence and expressed an opinion quite different from that of the cleric. The second instance was in his action of correcting an error in mathematics made by his uncle—an action for which he was disciplined by being made to take his books out of doors—the weather was warm—and study beneath an oak tree beside the river. Nevertheless, the uncle recognized his mathematical ability and allowed him to make a set of calculations that proved of such benefit that a London insurance firm used them for half a century or more.

Thus Charles reached the age of fifteen. He was a lad of deep sensitivity but was by no means reticent and had never feared any man. He was a thoroughly good boy, entirely upright and honest; his imagination was lively and his memory unusually retentive. The extent of his reading was utterly amazing for one so young, and in the works of his favorite authors—the Puritan theologians—he was especially versed.

His brother James knew him better perhaps than anyone else.

> Charles never did anything else but study. I kept rabbits, chickens, and pigs and a horse; he kept to books. While I was busy here and there,

---

meddling with anything and everything that a boy could touch, he kept
to books and could not be kept away from study.

But though he had nothing to do with other things, he could have told
you all about them, because he used to read about everything, with a
memory as tenacious as a vice and as copious as a barn.[16]

16. Pike, *James Archer Spurgeon*, p. 23.

A spiritual experience which is thoroughly fla-voured with a deep and bitter sense of sin is of great value to him that hath it. It is terrible in the drink-ing, but it is most wholesome in the bowels, and in the whole of the after life.

Possibly, much of the flimsy piety of the present day arises from the ease with which men attain to peace and joy in these evangelistic days. We would not judge modern converts, but we certainly prefer that form of spiritual exercise which leads the soul by the way of Weeping-cross, and makes it see its blackness before assuring it that it is "clean every whit."

Too many think lightly of sin, and therefore think lightly of the Saviour. He who has stood before his God, convicted and condemned, with the rope about his neck, is the man to weep for joy when he is pardoned, to hate the evil which has been forgiv-en him, and to live to the honour of the Redeemer by whose blood he has been cleansed.

Spurgeon, c. 1890, *Autobiography*

2

Through Terrible
Conviction to Glorious
Conversion

In the summer of 1849 Charles entered still another school, this one in the town of Newmarket. Though he had just turned fifteen, he came not merely as a student but also as a part-time teacher—a position known as an "usher."

Not far before him lay the great transforming experience, his conversion. That event has long been common knowledge among evangelical Christians, often told from pulpits and reported in books and magazines.

But that event was preceded by a long and bitter conviction of sin and a longing for salvation, which is not usually mentioned. Yet Spurgeon considered that experience so important that not only did he frequently speak of it in his preaching, but in his *Autobiography* he devoted an entire chapter to it.

Moreover, in telling of it, this master of description seems almost at a loss to fix upon words severe enough to portray the agony he suffered. "I had rather," he says, "pass through seven years of the most languishing sickness, than I would ever again pass through the terrible discovery of the evil of sin."[1]

This bitter experience began when he was still very young. As we

1. Iain Murray, ed., *The Early Years* (London: Banner of Truth, 1962), p. 59.

saw, he was only three when he amused himself with the pictures of Bunyan's Pilgrim with the burden on his back, and before long he knew its meaning—that this was a burden of sin. As he learned to read, his reading material was largely the Bible and the works of some of the great Puritan writers. He listened acutely to theological discussions, and by the time he was ten or so he had acquired a remarkable knowledge of Christian doctrine. He was an honest and upright boy, yet he had seen something of what sin is in the eyes of God. He knew that, like Pilgrim, he was bearing the awful burden and that he himself could not remove it.

During one of his summertime visits to his grandfather's, the Scripture read one day spoke of "a bottomless pit," and Charles had interrupted, asking how there could be a place that was "bottomless." The grandfather made some reply, but it did not satisfy the boy, and from that point onward there was fixed in his mind the certainty that it was possible for an unjustified person to move, eternally, farther and farther away from God and away from all that was righteous and good.

Moreover, although he knew as well as anyone that "Christ died for our sins," he saw no application of this truth to himself. He tried to pray, but he says, "The only complete sentence was 'God be merciful to me, a sinner!' The overwhelming splendour of His majesty, the greatness of His power, the severity of His justice, the immaculate character of His holiness, and all His dreadful grandeur—these things overpowered my soul, and I fell down in utter prostration of spirit."[2]

Despite his many efforts, his conviction increased. He tells how, throughout several boyhood years, he was constantly conscious of the universal requirements of God's law. "Wherever I went," he says, "it had a demand upon my thoughts, upon my words, upon my rising, upon my resting." And amidst his struggles to overcome that dreadful realization he came face to face with its kindred truth, the spirituality of the law. Although he had never committed the sins *of the flesh* he felt himself guilty of them *in the spirit,* and he cried out, "What hope had I of eluding such a law as this, which every way surrounded me with an atmosphere from which I could not possibly escape."[3]

2. Ibid., p. 55.
3. Ibid., p. 62.

Frequently, upon awaking after a troubled night, he took up such books as Alleine's *Admonition to Unconverted Sinners* and Baxter's *Call to the Unconverted*. But the works that had been so helpful to others only enforced what he already knew—that he was lost and needed to be saved. They left him with a bitter longing to know how that great salvation was to be received, and he remained seeking and suffering.

In the midst of these circumstances, though he had seldom ever heard a blasphemy and much less uttered one, all manner of cursing God and man began to enter his mind. That was followed by severe temptations to deny the very existence of God, and those in turn led to an effort to tell himself he had become a Free Thinker and virtually an atheist. He even endeavored to doubt his own existence, but all such attempts were useless.

Finally he told himself, "I must feel something: I must do something." He wished he might give his back to be scourged or that he might make some difficult pilgrimage, if by such efforts he might be saved. Yet he admitted, "That simplest of all matters—believing in Christ crucified, accepting His finished salvation, being nothing and letting Him be everything, doing nothing, but trusting to what He has done—I could not get hold of it."[4]

This painful seeking went on throughout the years in which he attended school, both in Colchester and Maidstone, and it became still more fervent during his days at Newmarket. As we have seen, his academic work was always excellent, but he was inwardly in anguish. In later years, as he looked back upon this terrible time, he said, "I thought I would rather have been a frog or a toad than have been made a man. I reckoned that the most defiled creature . . . was a better thing than myself, for I had sinned against Almighty God."[5]

After going to Newmarket he attended services at first one church and then another, hoping he might hear something that would help remove his burden. "One man preached Divine sovereignty," he says, "but what was that sublime truth to a poor sinner who wished to know what he must do to be saved. There was another admirable man who always preached about the law, but what was the use of ploughing up ground that needed to be sown. Another was a practical preacher . . . but it was very much like a commanding officer

4. Ibid., p. 70.
5. Ibid., p. 59.

teaching the manouvers of war to a set of men without feet. . . .
what I wanted to know was 'How can I get my sins forgiven?' and
they never told me that."[6]

During December of 1849 there was an outbreak of fever at the
Newmarket school. The school was temporarily closed, and Charles
went home to Colchester to be there during the Christmas season.

This change in circumstances was used of God to bring the seeking lad to salvation. The story of Spurgeon's conversion is widely
known, but it may well be repeated, and it cannot be better told
than in the words in which he himself presented it.

I sometimes think I might have been in darkness and despair until
now, had it not been for the goodness of God in sending a snowstorm
one Sunday morning, while I was going to a certain place of worship. I
turned down a side street, and came to a little Primitive Methodist
Church. In that chapel there may have been a dozen or fifteen people. I
had heard of the Primitive Methodists, how they sang so loudly that they
made people's heads ache; but that did not matter to me. I wanted to
know how I might be saved. . . .

The minister did not come that morning; he was snowed up, I suppose. At last a very thin-looking man, a shoemaker, or tailor, or something of that sort, went up into the pulpit to preach. Now it is well that
preachers be instructed, but this man was really stupid. He was obliged
to stick to his text, for the simple reason that he had little else to say. The
text was—"LOOK UNTO ME, AND BE YE SAVED, ALL THE ENDS OF THE
EARTH."

He did not even pronounce the words rightly, but that did not matter.
There was, I thought, a glimmer of hope for me in that text.

The preacher began thus: "This is a very simple text indeed. It says
'Look.' Now lookin' don't take a deal of pain. It aint liftin' your foot or
your finger; it is just 'Look.' Well, a man needn't go to College to learn to
look. You may be the biggest fool, and yet you can look. A man needn't
be worth a thousand a year to look. Anyone can look; even a child can
look.

"But then the text says, *'Look unto Me.'* Ay!" he said in broad Essex,
"many on ye are lookin' to yourselves, but it's no use lookin' there. You'll
never find any comfort in yourselves. Some say look to God the Father.
No, look to Him by-and-by. Jesus Christ says, 'Look unto *Me.*' Some on ye
say 'We must wait for the Spirit's workin'.' You have no business with that
just now. Look to *Christ*. The text says, 'Look unto *Me.*' "

Then the good man followed up his text in this way: "Look unto *Me*; I
am sweatin' great drops of blood. Look unto Me; I am hangin' on the

6. Ibid., p. 87.

cross. Look unto Me, I am dead and buried. Look unto Me; I rise again. Look unto Me; I ascend to Heaven. Look unto Me; I am sitting at the Father's right hand. O poor sinner, look unto Me! look unto Me!"

When he had. . . . managed to spin out about ten minutes or so, he was at the end of his tether. Then he looked at me under the gallery, and I daresay, with so few present, he knew me to be a stranger.

Just fixing his eyes on me, as if he knew all my heart, he said, "Young man, you look very miserable." Well, I did, but I had not been accustomed to have remarks made from the pulpit on my personal appearance before. However, it was a good blow, struck right home. He continued, "And you will always be miserable—miserable in life and miserable in death—if you don't obey my text; but if you obey now, this moment, you will be saved." Then lifting up his hands, he shouted, as only a Primitive Methodist could do, "Young man, look to Jesus Christ. Look! Look! Look! You have nothing to do but look and live!"

I saw at once the way of salvation. I know not what else he said—I did not take much notice of it—I was so possessed with that one thought. . . . I had been waiting to do fifty things, but when I heard that word, "Look!" what a charming word it seemed to me. Oh! I looked until I could almost have looked my eyes away.

There and then the cloud was gone, the darkness had rolled away, and that moment I saw the sun; and I could have risen that instant, and sung with the most enthusiastic of them, of the precious blood of Christ, and the simple faith which looks alone to Him. Oh, that somebody had told me this before, "Trust Christ, and you shall be saved." Yet it was, no doubt, all wisely ordered, and now I can say—

"E'er since by faith I saw the stream
Thy flowing wounds supply,
Redeeming love has been my theme,
And shall be till I die. . . ."

That happy day, when I found the Saviour, and learned to cling to His dear feet, was a day never to be forgotten by me. . . . I listened to the Word of God and that precious text led me to the cross of Christ. I can testify that the joy of that day was utterly indescribable. I could have leaped, I could have danced; there was no expression, however fanatical, which would have been out of keeping with the joy of that hour. Many days of Christian experience have passed since then, but there has never been one which has had the full exhilaration, the sparkling delight which that first day had.

I thought I could have sprung from the seat in which I sat, and have called out with the wildest of those Methodist brethren . . . "I am forgiven! I am forgiven! A monument of grace! A sinner saved by blood!"

My spirit saw its chains broken to pieces, I felt that I was an emancipated soul, an heir of heaven, a forgiven one, accepted in Jesus Christ, plucked out of the miry clay and out of the horrible pit, with my feet set upon a rock and my goings established. . . .

Between half-past ten o'clock, when I entered that chapel, and half-past twelve o'clock, when I was back again at home, what a change had taken place in me! Simply by looking to Jesus I had been delivered from despair, and I was brought into such a joyous state of mind that, when they saw me at home, they said to me, "Something wonderful has happened to you," and I was eager to tell them all about it. Oh! there was joy in the household that day, when all heard that the eldest son had found the Saviour and knew himself to be forgiven.[7]

Spurgeon's conversion was the great turning point of his life. He was indeed a new creation. The long-experienced sense of terrible conviction was gone, and all was new before him.

The suffering through which he had passed, however, had a lasting effect upon him. A recognition of the awful evil of sin was deeply ingrained upon his mind and made him loathe iniquity and love all that was holy. The failure of preachers he had heard to present the gospel, and to do so in a plain, direct manner, caused him throughout his whole ministry to tell sinners in every sermon and in a most forthright and understandable way how to be saved.

Moreover, those lessons were not something merely for the future. His love for Christ was such that, although as yet he was only fifteen, he could not wait to do something for Him but must find ways in which to serve Him and must do so right away.

7. Ibid., pp. 87-90.

When my burden rolled from off my back it was a very real pardon . . . and when that day I said "Jesus Christ is mine" it was a real possession of Christ to me. And when I went up to the sanctuary in that early dawn of youthful piety, every song was really a psalm, and when there was a prayer, oh, how I followed every word! It was prayer indeed!

And so was it too, in silent quietude, when I drew near to God, it was no mockery, no routine, no matter of mere duty; it was real talking with my Father who is in Heaven.

And oh, how I loved my Saviour Christ then! I would have given all I had for Him! How I felt towards sinners that day! Lad that I was, I wanted to preach, and—

*"Tell to sinners round,
What a dear Saviour I had found."*

Spurgeon, *Autobiography*

3

Joyful First Efforts in Serving the Lord

A few days after his conversion Spurgeon returned to Newmarket and resumed his work in the school there.

But now everything was different. His spirit was alive with gladness, the Bible was ablaze with glory, and prayer opened for his approaching soul the very gates of heaven. He wanted above everything to be totally given over to God, and he wrote out and signed a covenant between himself and his Lord, solemnly declaring his determination:

> O great and unsearchable God, who knowest my heart, and triest all my ways; with a humble dependence upon the support of Thy Holy Spirit, I yield myself up to Thee; as Thine own reasonable sacrifice, I return to Thee Thine own. I would be forever, unreservedly, perpetually Thine; whilst I am on earth, I would serve Thee; and may I enjoy Thee and praise Thee for ever! Amen.
>
> Feb. 1, 1850.   Charles Haddon Spurgeon[1]

Having thus declared his determination, he immediately began to fulfill it. A woman who had distributed tracts each week to thirty-three homes was giving up the task, and with joy he accepted it. He

---

1. Iain Murray, ed., *The Early Years* (London: Banner of Truth, 1962), p. 125.

also wrote gospel texts on slips of paper and either gave them to persons he met or dropped them here and there in the hope someone would pick them up and read them. "I cannot be happy," he said, "unless I am doing something for God."

But he had some important lessons to learn, and the first was not long in arriving.

In the days immediately following his conversion, he believed that the devil would never bother him again.

Then came Satan's onslaught. The doubts he had experienced before his conversion came storming into his mind again, and with them came many of the old evil thoughts and blasphemies against God. He was sorely troubled and surprised.

But now the fight was different. He now experienced a power that strengthened him. Before long the doubts and evil thoughts were overcome, and Christ reigned supremely in his life again. The experience was bitter, but it was also highly beneficial, for he learned early that the Christian life is not "a flowery bed of ease" but is often a field of battle. And as he thought upon the temptation and trial he asserted, "This is one way in which Satan tortures those whom God has delivered out of his hands."[2]

In later pages we shall see Spurgeon refusing to have anything to do with a philosophy of "the victorious life" that was then coming into prominence. Although he constantly experienced a measure of victory above that known by most men, he also realized the Christian's daily strife. Frequently he cried out with Paul, "O wretched man that I am! Who shall deliver me from the body of this death?" Yet he could also assert with the apostle, "I thank God [that I am daily delivered] through Jesus Christ our Lord."

In his desire to serve the Lord, Spurgeon wanted to be publicly associated with the people of God, so he endeavored to join the Congregational Church at Newmarket.

Most ministers, of course, would have rejoiced to see such a youth come into their fellowship, but this pastor did not want him. Spurgeon called at the parsonage, but the minister refused to see him. He called a second time, and the result was the same. Twice more he called, but on each occasion there was some obstacle that prevented an interview. But he refused to be thus repulsed and wrote the minister a note, stating that at the next midweek meeting he would stand to his feet and propose himself as a candidate for

2. Ibid., p. 102.

membership. Thereupon the minister gave in, and Charles was received into the church.

There was a reason for the minister's reticence: Charles was not a Congregationalist at heart.

He had been brought up in that denomination, for, as we have seen, his grandfather and father were Congregational ministers. But although he rejoiced in the gospel they preached, he disagreed on the matter of baptism. They practiced the christening of infants, and he had been christened by his grandfather as a babe. But by now he had come to believe that biblical baptism was something very different—that it was being "buried with Christ"—the immersion of one who had believed on Christ unto salvation.

There had been leanings in this direction in Charles's mind during childhood, but he had come to a clearer conviction when, as a boy of fourteen, he had been led into a discussion of the subject by the Church of England clergyman who visited the school at Maidstone. The clergyman had told him that "faith and repentance" are prerequisites for baptism, and that because no infant possesses such qualifications, sponsors must supply them on the child's behalf till he grows up. He asserted that since his grandfather did not use sponsors, Charles was not truly baptized, and he went on to declare that "all persons spoken of in the Bible as being baptized were believers," and he gave the youth a week to search the Scriptures and learn this truth for himself.

At the end of the week Charles fully agreed that "faith and repentance" are necessary for baptism, but he also held that they must be found within the heart of the person being baptized—not in that of a sponsor. And he applied the principle to his own case, saying, "I resolved from that moment, that if ever Divine grace should work a change in me, I would be baptized."[3]

And now that the change had been wrought he put the determination into action.

He learned that the nearest Baptist minister was the Reverend W. W. Cantlow, of Isleham, a village some eight miles from Newmarket. He wrote to Mr. Cantlow, and we may well imagine the earnestness with which Charles would tell of his conversion and the enthusiasm with which he would declare his desire to be baptized. Mr. Cantlow, overjoyed at hearing from such a youth, gladly agreed to baptize him.

3. Ibid., p. 35.

Charles wrote to his parents, telling them of his conviction in this matter and asking their permission that he be baptized. His father was slow in replying but finally wrote and gave his somewhat reluctant consent. He even added a phrase that rather wounded the youth—a warning that he make sure he was not trusting in baptism as a help toward salvation, rather than trusting solely in Christ.

Mrs. Spurgeon also gave permission. But it was not fullhearted. "Ah, Charles, I often prayed the Lord to make you a Christian, but I never asked that you might become a Baptist." He replied, not without a note of pleasantry, saying, "Ah, Mother, the Lord has answered your prayer with His usual bounty, and has given you exceeding abundantly above what you asked or thought."[4]

The day appointed by Mr. Cantlow for the baptizing arrived. Here is Charles's own account of the solemnly joyful event.

I can never forget May 3, 1850; it was my mother's birthday, and I myself was within a few weeks of being sixteen.

I was up early, to have a couple of hours for quiet prayer and dedication to God. Then I had some eight miles to walk, to reach the spot where I was to be immersed. . . . What a walk it was! What thoughts and prayers thronged my soul during that morning's journey! It was by no means a warm day. . . . The sight of Mr. Cantlow's smiling face, was a full reward for that country tramp. I think I see the good man now, and the white ashes of the peat-fire, by which we stood and talked together about the solemn exercise which lay before us.

We went together to the Ferry, for the Isleham friends had not degenerated to indoor immersion in a bath made by the art of man, but used the ampler baptistry of the flowing river. Isleham Ferry, on the River Lark, is a very quiet spot, half a mile from the village. . . .

To me, there seemed a great concourse on that week-day [Friday]. Dressed, I believe, in a jacket, with a boy's turn down collar, I attended the service previous to the ordinance, but all remembrance of it has gone from me: my thoughts were in the water, sometimes with my Lord in joy, and sometimes with myself in trembling awe at making so public a confession.

There were first to be baptized two women . . . and I was asked to conduct them through the water to the minister, but this I most timidly declined. It was a new experience to me, having never seen a baptism before, and I was afraid of making some mistake.

The wind blew down the river with a cutting blast as my turn came to wade into the flood, but after I had walked a few steps, and noted the people on the ferry-boat, and in boats and on either shore, I felt as if

4. Ibid., p. 45.

Heaven, and earth, and hell, might all gaze upon me, for I was not ashamed, there and then, to own myself a follower of the Lamb. My timidity was washed away; . . . I have never felt anything of the kind since. Baptism also loosed my tongue. . . . I lost a thousand fears in that River Lark, and found that "in keeping His commandments there is great reward."[5]

Following the baptism service several people gathered with Mr. Cantlow in the vestry of his church. Spurgeon had previously begun the practice of leading in public prayer and at a meeting on the evening before his baptism he "was enabled," he said, "more than usual, to pour out [his] heart in prayer." Now, in this service in the vestry, experiencing a still greater measure of holy delight, he led the company in prayer. "The people," we are told, "wondered and wept for joy as they listened to the lad."[6]

Upon returning to Newmarket he partook of the Lord's Supper. This privilege he had thus far refused, feeling he could not scripturally accept it till he had been baptized.

Nearly four months had elapsed since his conversion, and during that time he had increased his labors for the Lord. "I have 70 people whom I regularly visit on Saturday," he wrote. "I do not give a tract and go away, but I sit down and endeavour to draw their attention to spiritual realities."[7] I trust the Lord is working among my tract people. . . . O that I could see but one sinner constrained to come to Jesus."[8]

Following his baptism Charles was asked to become a Sunday school teacher. So capable did he prove that he was shortly invited to address the whole school, and this effort was so successful that his task was enlarged to that of doing so each Sunday. His earnestness is manifest in his statement "I have endeavored to speak as a dying individual to dying individuals." And he did not address only the children, but several adults also began coming to hear him—a situation that aroused still further the dislike of the minister.

During those days Charles began to write a daily diary, recording his spiritual efforts and his innermost desires. He continued the diary for three months. Later (after he was married), he put the book into the hands of his wife. She treasured it throughout their

---

5. Ibid., pp. 145-50.
6. Robert Shindler, *From the Usher's Desk to the Tabernacle Pulpit* (London: Passmore and Alabaster, 1892), p. 46.
7. *The Early Years*, p. 119.
8. Ibid., p. 46.

married life, and following his death she published it as part of his *Autobiography.* In speaking of this precious little volume she said:

> How marked is his humility, even though he must have felt within him the stirrings and throes of the wonderful powers which were afterwards developed. "Forgive me, Lord," he says in one place, "if I have ever had high thoughts of myself"—early did the Master implant the precious seeds of that rare grace of meekness which adorned his after life. After each youthful effort at public exhortation, whether it be engaging in prayer or addressing Sunday School children, he seems to be surprised at his own success, and intensely anxious to be kept from pride and self glory. . . .
>
> So young in years when he wrote these thoughts, and yet so old in grace, and possessing an experience in spiritual matters richer and broader than most Christian attain to at an advanced age! . . .
>
> Perhaps of greatest price among the precious things which this little book reveals, is the beloved author's personal and intense love to the Lord Jesus. He lived in His embrace. . . . The endearing terms used in the Diary *and never discontinued,* were not empty words; they were the overflowing of the love of God shed abroad in his heart by the Holy Ghost.[9]

During those weeks Spurgeon saw before him a life spent in the work of the ministry. In the diary he made many expressions of which the following is representative: "Make me Thy faithful servant, O my God; may I honour Thee in my day and generation, and be consecrated for ever to Thy service."[10] His letters likewise reveal that intention, as in the following excerpts from his writing to his parents: "How I long for the time when it may please God, to make me, like you, my Father, a successful preacher of the Gospel,"[11] and, "I hope you may one day have cause to rejoice, should you see me, the unworthy instrument of God, preaching to others."[12]

His efforts in addressing the Sunday school revealed he had marvelous powers of public utterance. His statements about preaching make it evident he was experiencing an unmistakable call to the ministry. With these mighty gifts within him, and with his heart moved with a love for God and a love for the souls of mankind, it was inevitable that he should begin to preach.

9. Ibid., p. 124.
10. Ibid., p. 118.
11. Ibid., p. 116.
12. Ibid.

A man who has really within him the inspiration of the Holy Ghost calling him to preach, cannot help it—he must preach. As fire within his bones, so will that influence be, until it blazes forth. Friends may check him, foes criticize him, despisers sneer at him, the man is indomitable; he must preach if he has the call of Heaven. . . .

I think it is no more possible to make a man cease from preaching, if he is really called, then to stay some mighty cataract, by seeking, in an infant's cup, to catch the rushing torrent. The man has been moved of Heaven, who shall stop him? He has been touched of God, who shall impede him? . . .

And when a man does speak as the Spirit gives him utterance, he will feel a holy joy, akin to that of Heaven; and when it is over, he wishes to be at his work again, he longs to be once more preaching.

Spurgeon, *Autobiography*

4

The Boy Preacher of Waterbeach

In the summer of 1850 Spurgeon moved to the city of Cambridge. Mr. Leeding, under whom he had progressed so well at Colchester, now operated a school there, and Charles's father, seeking the best possible education for his son, had arranged for him to enter as a student-teacher. "I will readily engage," wrote Leeding, "to give him all the assistance in my power for the prosecution of his own studies, and his board and washing, in return for his [teaching] assistance."[1]

Desiring to be associated with the people of God in Cambridge, Spurgeon joined the St. Andrew's Street Baptist Church.

The first time he attended a service no one spoke to him. So, as the congregation was leaving the building, he said to a gentleman who had sat near him, "I hope you are well, sir?" This led to the following conversation:

Gentleman: "You have the advantage of me."

Spurgeon: "I don't think I have, for you and I are brothers."

Gentleman: "I don't quite know what you mean."

Spurgeon: "Well, when I took the bread and wine just now, in token of our being one in Christ, I meant it, did not you?"

1. Iain Murray, ed., *The Early Years* (London: Banner of Truth, 1962), p. 176.

By that time they had reached the street, and the man, placing both hands on the youth's shoulders, declared, "Oh, sweet simplicity! You are quite right, my dear brother, quite right. Come to tea with me."[2] The man soon found he had a most extraordinary guest and invited him to return on the following Sunday. Thereafter he wanted him every Lord's day, and a lasting friendship grew up between them.

As the weeks came and went Spurgeon made rapid advances in the Christian life. He increased in knowledge and revealed a spiritual maturity far beyond his years. In actions and words he often seemed more like a grown-up man than the youth that he was. For instance, in a letter to his mother, who apparently had been experiencing some feelings of depression, he wrote:

> The rapturous moments of enjoyment, the hallowed hours of communion, the blest days of sunshine in His presence, are pledges of sure, certain, infallible glory. Mark the providences of this year; how clearly you have seen His hand in things which others esteem chance! God, who has moved the world, has exercised His own vast heart and thought for you. . . . He who counts the hairs of our heads, and keeps us as the apple of His eye, has not forgotten you, but still loves you with an everlasting love. The mountains have not departed yet, nor the hills been removed, and till then we may have confidence that we, his own people are secure.[3]

Whatever Mrs. Spurgeon's feelings may have been, she could not have failed to rejoice in receiving such a letter from her son and must have marveled at the maturity he possessed at so early an age.

One of the activities of St. Andrew's was a lay preacher's association. It arranged for men to go out into various villages in the surrounding area to minister the Word. This work was under the direction of a James Vinter, and because of the wise manner in which he exercised his leadership he was known as "The Bishop."

Upon joining the church at Cambridge, Spurgeon was asked to address the Sunday school. Vinter immediately recognized his extraordinary powers of public speech and determined to thrust him out into the lay preaching. Feeling that a direct request might be refused, however, he adopted an adroit expedient. He asked Spurgeon to go to Teversham the following Sunday evening, explaining that "a young man was to preach there who was not much used to services and very likely would be glad of company."

Spurgeon agreed to go and, with the young man whom he assumed was to do the preaching, he set out on the Sunday evening for Teversham. As they walked he remarked to the companion that he hoped his preaching would be blessed of God. The companion was startled and cried out, "I have never done such a thing in my life! You're the one who is to preach! I'm here to keep you company!" Spurgeon was equally surprised and stated he was both inexperienced and unprepared for such a task. But the other countered that Spurgeon was accustomed to addressing the Sunday school and could easily repeat one of the talks he had given there.

Though amazed by what had happened, but also richly attracted by the opportunity, Spurgeon says, "I walked along quietly, lifting up my soul to God, and it seemed to me I could surely tell a few poor cottagers of the sweetness and love of Jesus, for I felt them in my own soul."[4]

The place of meeting was a thatched-roof cottage, and the audience was, in his language, "a few simple-minded farm-labourers and their wives." Spurgeon took as his text the Scripture "Unto you therefore which believe He is precious," and he spoke of Christ's glory and grace—that which he had himself received and which Christ offered to all who would come to Him.

The moment he finished preaching an elderly woman cried out, "Bless your heart, how old are you?" Spurgeon replied that there should be no interruptions in the service. But as soon as the last hymn was sung she burst forth again with her question, and this time he replied, "I am under sixty."

"Yes, and under sixteen!" she declared. Her enthusiasm was felt by the rest of the congregation, and they virtually demanded that he return and preach to them again as soon as possible.

Such was Spurgeon's first effort at preaching. It was for him a time of great joy, but it also caused him to feel he had begun an activity which, under the power of God, would be his great undertaking throughout the rest of his life.

During the weeks that followed Spurgeon was busy each day with his work at the school. He tutored several boys and also prosecuted

4. Ibid., p. 183.

his own studies under Mr. Leeding's direction. His brother James said, "He made such progress in his studies that I am sure there were few young men that were his equals."[5]

Charles soon preached again. The lay preachers' association regularly ministered at thirteen villages, and he took his turn with the other men in this work. But following his first visit to any place he was invariably urged to return as often as he could. This pleased Mr. Vinter and the other men too. Accordingly, evening after evening he was busy preaching the Word.

His joy was deep and abiding, and as he walked out to these preaching points he usually sang. He spoke especially of using on these occasions the grand hymn "Loved with Everlasting Love."

> I must have been a singular-looking youth on wet evenings, for I walked three, five and even eight miles out and back again on my preaching work, and when it rained, I dressed myself in waterproof leggings and a mackintosh coat, and a hat with a waterproof covering, and I carried a dark lantern to show me the way across the fields. . . .
>
> How many times I enjoyed preaching the Gospel in a farmer's kitchen, or in a cottage, or in a barn! Perhaps many people came to hear me because I was only a boy. In my young days, I fear that I said many odd things, and made many blunders, but my audience was not hypercritical, and no newspaper writers dogged my heels; so I had a happy training school, in which, by continual practice, I attained such a degree of ready speech as I now possess.[6]

Some may wonder how he could be so fully engaged in his work at the school all day and yet be ready to preach each evening. But the reading of theology now largely constituted the study of each day. "My quiet meditation during the walk helped me to digest what I had read. . . . I thought my reading over again while on my legs, and thus worked it into my very soul, and I can bear testimony that I never learned so much, or learned it so thoroughly, as when I used to tell out, simply and earnestly, what I had first received into my own mind and heart."[7]

Spurgeon spent one Sunday in October of 1851 at the Baptist church in the village of Waterbeach.

Here he was not only urged to return, but after a second Sunday

5. Ibid., p. 210 n.
6. Ibid., p. 186.
7. Ibid.

he was asked to become the regular pastor. Assured that God had called him into the ministry and knowing the village stood in great need of the gospel, despite the fact that he was only seventeen, he accepted the office.

Within a few weeks he resigned his work at the school. Although he continued to live at Cambridge, and also still spent many an evening ministering in the villages, he devoted himself to the pastorate in Waterbeach. Because of his youth he was known as "The Boy Preacher," but it must be pointed out he in no way referred to himself under this term or used it as a kind of gimmick to draw a crowd.

Nevertheless, he soon preached to a crowd and did so each Sunday. When he went to Waterbeach the congregation numbered about forty, but it grew with great rapidity. People came not only from the village itself but also from the surrounding countryside, till the attendance mounted regularly to four hundred and more. Of course, they could not all get into the little building, but doors and windows were left open, and people stood outside, listening to a preacher such as they had never heard before.

During his days at Waterbeach, Spurgeon manifested a gift for which he was to be preeminent throughout his later ministry—the gift of understanding and influencing people. He talked to men and women on the street, and he visited them in their homes; he knew them and their teenagers and their children by name. He recognized sin, and it was everywhere; he witnessed the people's manner of life; he prayed by the sick, comforted the suffering, and watched by the dying.

In public and in private he ever presented the gospel, and great was his joy when he heard the news of the first convert. This was a woman who came to tell him that under his preaching she had been brought into a deep conviction of sin, but that she had received the Savior and was now rejoicing. A great many others followed, till Waterbeach was virtually transformed.

Did you ever walk through a village notorious for its drunkenness and profanity? Did you ever see poor wretched beings, that once were men, standing, or rather leaning against the posts of the ale-house, or staggering along the street? Have you ever looked into the houses of the people, and beheld them as dens of iniquity, at which your soul stood aghast? Have you ever seen the poverty, and degradation, and misery of the inhabitants, and sighed over it? "Yes," you say, "we have."

But was it ever your privilege to walk through that village again, in after years, when the Gospel had been preached there? It has been mine. I once knew just such a village as I have pictured—perhaps in some respects one of the worst in England—where many an illicit still was yielding its noxious liquor . . . and where in connection with that evil, all manner of riot and iniquity was rife.

There went into that village a lad, who had no great scholarship, but who was earnest in seeking the souls of men. He began to preach there and it pleased God to turn the whole place upside down. In a short time the little thatched chapel was crammed, the biggest vagabonds in the village were weeping floods of tears, and those who had been the curse of the parish became its blessing. Where there had been robberies and villainies of every kind, all round the neighbourhood, there were none, because the men who used to do the mischief were themselves in the house of God, rejoicing to hear of Jesus crucified.

I am not telling an exaggerated story, nor a thing I do not know, for it was my delight to labour for the Lord in that village. It was a pleasant thing to walk through that place, when drunkenness had almost ceased, when debauchery in the case of many was dead, when men and women went forth to labour with joyful hearts, singing the praises of the ever-living God; and when, at sunset, the humble cottager called his children together, read them some portion of the Book of Truth, and then together they bent their knees in prayer to God. I can say, with joy and happiness, that almost from one end of the village to the other, at the hour of eventide, one might have heard the voice of song coming from nearly every roof-tree. . . .

I do testify, to the praise of God's grace, that it pleased the Lord to work wonders in our midst. He showed the power of Jesu's name, and made me a witness of that Gospel which can win souls, draw reluctant hearts, and mould afresh the life and conduct of sinful men and women.[8]

Spurgeon's pastorate at Waterbeach continued until he was nineteen. During that period, although he manifested a rare maturity, he also had much to learn about the day-by-day conducting of the ministry.

That experience was evident, for instance, in his sermon preparation. He sought to be led by God to some passage of Scripture, endeavoring in prayer and study to understand it thoroughly. After filling his soul with its message, he marshaled its truths into organized form in readiness for delivery. He found the main points and then the secondary points that the chosen Scripture contained,

8. Ibid., pp. 193-94.

wrote them out in two or three pages of notes, and carried those into the pulpit with him.

Some two hundred or so Waterbeach sermon outlines are still extant, and they manifest the nature of his early preaching. He did not, like most men during their first few years in the ministry, merely touch the surface of gospel truths. On the contrary, the great system of doctrine that he had been weighing in his mind since childhood and that had largely constituted the body of his study, underlay virtually all he said and provided the strength of his ministry.

Spurgeon's experience also grew in his handling of people during those days.

When the town scourge unloosed her tongue upon him one day, he replied as though he had barely heard her and incorrectly understood her words. After two or three outbursts she hurried away, saying, "The man is as deaf as a post!"

A certain minister who invited him to come and preach, upon seeing how boyish he looked, treated him with contempt. But Spurgeon, in his sermon, replied by quoting a verse from Proverbs that rebuked the man's uncivil behavior, and then he went on to preach so powerfully that when the service was over the man patted him on the back and said, "You're the sauciest dog that ever barked in a pulpit!" The occasion marked the beginning of a warm friendship between them.

There was a woman who, though a true saint, constantly lacked Christian confidence. She told Spurgeon she was such a hypocrite that she ought not to attend church and that she had no Christian hope whatsoever. Knowing her true earnestness and desiring to help her, he offered to buy her hope for £5, to which she exclaimed, "Oh, I would not sell my hope in Christ for a thousand worlds!"

During those teenage days in Waterbeach, Spurgeon revealed much of the character that later shone in him so prominently. Admittedly, he was audacious and fearless, and any who saw this feature alone could well assume he was impudent. But he was also very real—he had not the slightest element of pretense, and in both his public ministry and his pastoral relationships his unrelenting earnestness was manifest to all. His extraordinary preaching powers were also evident—a voice of tremendous strength together with the sweetest, moving tones and all under constant control.

Spurgeon exercised an unyielding self-discipline. To him the Christian life must be fully governed, and he put that ideal into steady practice. Rising early, he filled the day with labor, studying and visiting, praying and preaching. He gave no attention to sports and had no personal friendships with members of the opposite sex, but all his time and thought were given to the Lord.

In many senses, though yet so young, he was far ahead of many older ministers in knowing and doing the work of that office. As his brother James expressed it, "He was a marvellous example of a preacher leaping at a bound, full grown into the pulpit."[9]

Charles's extraordinary advancement in the work of the ministry was not understood, however, by his father.

John Spurgeon, wanting the best for his son, made plans to put him into Stepney College, the Baptist ministerial training school. (The universities had long been closed to all who were not members of the Church of England.) Charles was not happy about his father's idea, but he was willing to go along with it, if necessary, and he agreed to meet the college principal, Dr. Joseph Angus. The interview was to take place at a home in Cambridge—that of Daniel McMillan, the prominent publisher. Charles arrived at the appointed hour and was shown by a maid into a sitting room, and there he waited for Dr. Angus to arrive. But at the end of two hours he called for the maid, only to discover she had shown the gentleman into a room at the other side of the house. He too had waited all that time but having to catch a train he had left the house some moments earlier.

Later that day Spurgeon was walking through the fields on his way to a village service. As he thought of the strange event of the afternoon there came an overwhelming impression on his mind, almost as though he actually heard a voice that said, very distinctly, "Seekest thou great things for thyself? Seek them not!" He immediately rejoiced in this counsel, and then and there he determined not to enter the college. He knew God had already made him a minister, and he purposed to continue the manner of life that had been his for the past two years. The decision allowed no room for earthly ambition. It marked another step forward in the mortification of self and in the growth of his soul's devotion to the Lord.

In later years Spurgeon referred to the event of his missing Dr. Angus as "the Lord's hand behind the maid's mistake." The college gave its students valuable knowledge of the Bible and of general theological subjects. It provided classroom instruction in how to prepare sermons and how to deliver them, and it endeavored to lead

9. G. Holden Pike, *The Life and Work of Charles Haddon Spurgeon*, 6 vols. (London: Cassel, 1898), 1:59.

the young men into a well-ordered and disciplined manner of life. But those things were hardly necessary to Spurgeon.

He was already far beyond the college's students and undoubtedly beyond most of its faculty in theological knowledge and preaching ability, and he already possessed a wide pastoral experience. Moreover, though strictly subject to all that was righteous and true, he was in some senses a free spirit, without fear of man and entirely unfettered by human conventions. He had received in birth a unique genius of spirit, and that would surely have suffered had he entered an environment where efforts would have been made to force it into the mold of ordinary individuals. He had been prepared for a divinely ordered ministry and did not need the usual shaping by the hands of man.

After Spurgeon had been in Waterbeach two years an event took place which, in the plan of God, drew his ministry there to its close.

In November 1853 he spoke at a meeting of the Cambridge Sunday School Union. He was followed by two other ministers, each of whom referred belittlingly to his youthfulness. One, in fact, was particularly nasty and stated, "It is a pity boys do not adopt the Scriptural practice of tarrying at Jericho till their beards are grown, before they try to instruct their seniors."

When the speaker had concluded Spurgeon secured the chairman's permission and made a reply. "I reminded the audience," he says, "that those who were bidden to remain at Jericho were not boys, but full-grown men whose beards had been shaved off by their enemies, as the greatest indignity they could be made to suffer, and who were, therefore, ashamed to return home until their beards had grown again. I added that the true parallel to their case could be found in a minister who, through falling into open sin, had disgraced his calling and needed to go into seclusion . . . till his character had to some extent been restored."[10]

Spurgeon knew nothing of the man who had attacked him, but he had unwittingly described his condition—the poor man had fallen into sin, and since his behavior was known to the people, one can but imagine his embarrassment.

This meeting, however, though of no special importance in itself, proved of pivotal significance in Spurgeon's life. It led in an indirect way to the placing before him of the supreme opportunity of his career—the opening of "a great door and effectual,"—a call to the pastorate of the New Park Street Baptist Church in London.

10. Ibid., 1:245.

THE FIRST YEARS
IN
LONDON

1855—1864

To what, then, was Spurgeon's swift and decisive promotion due? We infer it was due to this fact— that there was nothing in him necessitating delay. He could be placed in the seat of honour, for he had the spiritual grounding requisite. He could serve the relative end, for the basis of it had been laid in his own heart.

The light was there; it needed but a stand adequate to its power of illumination.

And specially should be instanced this point— that he had the true Christian foil in respect of honour, namely, humility. He had, as we have just seen, foresworn the search of great things for himself. And what is this, in the economy of grace, but the forerunner of promotion? He had no great stalking ambition . . . the role of a country village pastor was as ample as his heart's desire. . . . London might make him greater; it could hardly make him happier.

James Douglas, *The Prince of Preachers*, 1894

5

"A Great Door and Effectual Is Opened"

A man named George Gould was present at that meeting in Cambridge. He was deeply impressed by Spurgeon's ministry and gave a London friend, William Olney, a glowing report of the young Waterbeach preacher. Olney was a deacon of the New Park Street Baptist Church, and since it was without a pastor at the time, Gould urged that it seriously consider this remarkable youth.

The New Park Street church invited Spurgeon to supply its pulpit for a Sunday. He was amazed at the request and replied to their letter saying they must have the wrong Spurgeon, for he was merely a youth of nineteen. They replied that he was the one they had intended, so he agreed to spend Sunday, December 18, 1853, with them.

Reaching London on Saturday, he went, as they had arranged, to a boardinghouse in the Bloomsbury district. Several young gentlemen lived at this house, and as they looked upon the visitor—his clothes anything but stylish, his hair unkempt, and his whole appearance countrified—they were much amused. At the supper table they told him of the extraordinary abilities of many of the London preachers—men, they said, of thorough scholarship and rare oratorical powers—and the suggestion was that Spurgeon was entirely out of place in one of the city's most prominent Nonconformist churches.

Spurgeon felt that much would be expected of him in this pulpit, especially because of the personal greatness and lengthy ministries of three of the men who had filled it.

The first of those was Benjamin Keach, an outstanding preacher and author who had suffered in the pillory for his faith during the seventeenth century. The second was John Gill, a man of tremendous learning, the author of ponderous volumes of theology and biblical commentary, who had exercised his ministry there for fifty-one years. The third, John Rippon, had proved himself an able preacher and had edited a widely-used hymn book, and his ministry in this pulpit had lasted for the amazing length of sixty-three years.

These men were yet highly revered, especially by Baptists, throughout England, and their greatness served all the more to discourage Spurgeon as he came now to spend the Sunday in their pulpit.

After having supper with the young gentlemen Spurgeon went to his room. It was not actually a room—merely a kind of cupboard over the stairs and so small he could barely kneel beside the bed. Throughout the night there was almost constant noise from horses and carriages on the street below, and he found it difficult to sleep. As he awoke in the morning he felt lonely and friendless, the great city seemed forbidding, and he longed for his flock in Waterbeach who would that day be meeting without him.

Nor were matters improved when he made his way to the church.

The building had been a rather grand place. It was of stone and brick construction, now much blackened by the city's grime. Nevertheless, it remained one of the largest Baptist chapels in Britain, and he says that upon first viewing it, "I felt for a moment amazed at my own temerity, for it seemed to my eyes to be a large, ornate and imposing structure, suggesting an audience wealthy and critical, and far removed from the humble folk to whom my ministry had been sweetness and light."[1]

But although the building was imposing, the location was deplorable. It lay south of the Thames, and the only immediate access from the other side of the river was by a toll bridge. The area was low and flooded easily, and smoke and soot were everywhere. Around the chapel stood a brewery, warehouses, and factories: The only homes close by were impoverished hovels.

Among the members of the church, however, were several very earnest Christians. Some were men of professional status, and oth-

1. Iain Murray, ed., *The Early Years* (London: Banner of Truth, 1962), p. 248.

ers operated their own businesses, and in general the congregation was composed of very respectable middle-class people.

During the months without a pastor the church had heard several supposedly capable men. But "they had never asked one of them twice, for they gave them such philosophical, or dry learned sermons, that once was enough."[2] As a result attendances had decreased, the work was at a low ebb, and the people were discouraged.

As Spurgeon entered the pulpit that morning, though the church had seats for twelve hundred, he saw a congregation estimated by some as high as two hundred and by others as low as eighty.

All feelings of depression vanished from his mind before the responsibility that was now his—that of preaching the Word. The people saw a man strong in confidence in God, and they listened to a voice the like of which they had never heard before. Taking as his text "Every good and every perfect gift is from above, and cometh down from the Father of lights, with whom is no variableness, neither shadow of turning," he spoke of God as described in the term *the Father of lights*. He enlarged upon the divine attributes, especially God's unchangeableness, and closed by declaring His giving of gifts, even the gift of His Son, the Lord Jesus.

The sermon was not in any way an effort to produce something profound to win the favor of the London audience. It was simply the kind of sermon he would have delivered to his rustic congregation in Waterbeach.

But the result was extraordinary. A few hearers knew not what to think of him, for he was so young, yet seemed so mature, and he was entirely different from any preacher they had ever heard. But most were excited and could hardly find words to express their delight.

During the afternoon several of them called on members who had been absent in the morning and on various neighbors and friends, telling them of the marvelous youth from the country and declaring they must come and hear him in the evening.

Accordingly, the evening congregation was much larger than that of the morning. Spurgeon was more at home in his surroundings as well, and as he preached on "They are without fault before the throne of God," the people were lifted to new heights of understanding and to new raptures of feeling.

When the service closed, most were unwilling to leave the

2. Ibid.

church. They stood around in clusters greatly moved, overwhelmed by the glory of what they had heard, and urging the deacons to make sure this amazing preacher returned.

The deacons were equally enthusiastic. They asked Spurgeon to set dates to minister to them again, and they declared that if he were in the pulpit for three Sundays the building would be filled. They were spiritually "so starved that a morsel of Gospel was a treat for them."[3] Deeply affected by the need and assured that this door was being divinely opened, he agreed to return on three Sundays the following month, January of 1854.

During the conversation he informed the deacons he was not a college man. But they had heard so many college graduates and had been wearied with their preaching that they replied, "That is to us a special recommendation, for you would not have much savour or unction if you came from college."[4]

Spurgeon walked back to the boardinghouse a different man. "I wanted no pity from anyone," he says. "I did not care a penny for the young gentlemen lodgers and their miraculous ministers, nor for the grind of the cabs, nor for anything else under the sun."[5] God had anointed his ministry, the people had been delighted, and he was to come again!

After two weeks he again spent a Sunday at New Park Street. He returned immediately to Waterbeach, but the London church would not wait for him to fulfill the arrangement he had made with them. The deacons wrote immediately, expressing the people's unbounded satisfaction with his ministry and extending him a call to become the pastor right away. The Sunday school superintendent wrote separately and told him, "I never saw such a desire . . . toward a minister as there is at the present time toward you. . . . You will find a great many faithful friends: and should the Holy Spirit lead you to decide for New Park Street . . . I hope and pray you will prove a blessing to thousands."[6]

Spurgeon had apparently mentioned his sense of the awesome spiritual responsibility of this task. The letter from the deacons suggested that he might want to accept the pastorate on a trial basis; they added that at the end of six months he might reconsider the matter, if he then felt it necessary. But he replied that he would

3. Ibid., p. 249.
4. Ibid.
5. Ibid.
6. Ibid., p. 253.

come on three months' trial and concluded by stating his urgent request that all the people pray for him. "One thing is due," he declared, ". . . namely, that in private as well as public, they must all wrestle in prayer . . . that I may be sustained in the great work."[7]

His parting from his people in Waterbeach was sad for him and sad for them. Some had realized they could not long hope to keep such a man in so small a place, but now that the removal was imminent, though they rejoiced in the prospect before him, they shed many tears at the thought of seeing him go. He had loved them, and they had loved him, and the bonds of affection could not easily be broken. Throughout the rest of his life some of the warmest friends he had anywhere were to be found in the Baptist chapel at Waterbeach.

In February 1854, at the age of nineteen, Spurgeon entered his ministry in London. He came on three months' trial, but his labor there was to last till his death nearly forty years later.

As the people had expected, the New Park Street attendance jumped immediately. Within a month the chapel was crowded, with the seats filled, the aisles packed, and people sitting in the windows and standing shoulder to shoulder in the Sunday school area. All manner of reports about this ministry spread across London.

In the midst of this happy situation the deacons brought up the matter of ordination. During his days at Waterbeach, Spurgeon had been unordained, but he was assured he was ordained of God and as far as he was concerned that was all that mattered. But human ordination was everywhere practiced by Baptists, and among the New Park Street people there were several who felt the church should now call an ordination service.

Spurgeon told them he did not believe this was a scriptural practice and that he did not need it to validate his ministry. The blessing of God, he declared, was the divine seal upon his holding of the office. Man could add nothing to it. Nevertheless, he was willing to go through with the ceremony if the church thought it necessary, and although it would do him no harm neither would it do him any good. And there the matter rested.

Similarly Spurgeon rejected the title *Reverend*. He said it was a remnant of Romanism that the Reformers ought to have dropped. But his publishers inserted it before his name at the head of his printed sermons, and the fact that for some years he did not forbid

7. Ibid., p. 256.

it was probably a concession to those who felt they were honoring him by using it. Finally, in 1865 he had the practice stopped. He urged his students to use instead the scriptural term *Pastor*.

The lack of the title, however, did not hinder—it probably helped Spurgeon's acceptance by the common man. The crowd came every time he preached, and for this reason he was constantly spoken of as "a second Whitefield."

But, like Whitefield, Spurgeon did not make the gathering of a crowd his first interest. In view of the spiritual warfare in which the Christian is placed, he was concerned first of all that his people learn truly to pray.

Of course, during previous months the New Park Street people had prayed. But their prayers were little more than nicely worded phrases, unctionless petitions uttered in a rather formal manner.

To Spurgeon prayer was something far superior to mere surface activity. He talked with God in reverence but with freedom and familiarity. In his prayers there were none of the tired expressions many ministers use, but he spoke as a child coming to a loving parent. A fellow minister declared, "Prayer was the instinct of his soul and the atmosphere of his life. It was his 'vital breath' and 'native air.' He sped on eagle wings into the heaven of God," as he prayed.[8]

So real was Spurgeon's praying that the formal effort showed in glaring contrast beside it. "I can readily tell," he stated, "when a brother is praying, or when he is only performing, or playing at prayer. . . . Oh for a living groan! One sigh of the soul has more power in it than half an hour's recitation of pretty pious words. Oh! for a sob from the soul, or a tear from the heart!"[9] And he was equally opposed to the "Hallelujah!" or "Praise the Lord!" that was only a formality and arose not from the inner man.

Spurgeon truly expected to see God answer prayer, both in the individual life and in the life of the church. He recognized unanswered prayer beyond human understanding, but he also experienced numerous instances in which God moved in response to his cry. He knew that God's power was manifested in the services in proportion as God's people truly prayed, and that in such proportion also souls were brought under conviction and drawn to Christ.

Spurgeon's own praying proved of great influence upon his people. Deeply moved by the reality of his intercession, many of them

8. Dinsdale T. Young, *C. H. Spurgeon's Prayers* (New York: Revell, 1906), p. vi.
9. Iain Murray, *The Forgotten Spurgeon* (London: Banner of Truth, 1966), p. 33 n.

became ashamed of their own "pretty pious words." Some of them undoubtedly had a difficult struggle to overcome the formal practices of previous years, but they persisted, and little by little they began to wrestle with God in true prayer.

> I can never forget how earnestly they prayed. Sometimes they seemed to plead as though they could really see the Angel of the covenant present with them. . . .
> More than once we were all so awe-struck with the solemnity of the meeting, that we sat silent for some moments while the Lord's power appeared to overshadow us. . . . We had prayer meetings in New Park Street that moved our very souls. Each man seemed like a crusader besieging the New Jerusalem, each one appeared determined to storm the Celestial City by the might of intercession, and soon the blessing came down upon us in such abundance that we had not room to receive it.[10]

As we go on to consider the rest of Spurgeon's life we must bear in mind the manner in which his people prayed. Numerous men and women were converted, several institutions developed, various buildings were erected, and their work had its effect to the ends of the earth. All the time true prayer rose to God. When someone once asked Spurgeon the secret of his success, he replied, "My people pray for me." He meant not prayer in the usual formal and unexpectant manner but wrestling with God in living faith that He would answer.

The arrangement under which Spurgeon had come to London was soon overruled by the members of the church. Well before that period had elapsed a business meeting was held, and the people urged him to receive the pastorate on a permanent basis. He replied, "There is but one answer to so loving and cordial an invitation. I ACCEPT IT." But he continued: "I entreat of you to remember me in prayer, that I may realize the solemn responsibility of my trust. Remember my youth and inexperience, and pray that these may not hinder my usefulness. I trust also that the remembrance of these will lead you to forgive mistakes I may make, or unguarded words I may utter. . . . Oh, that I may be no injury to you, but a lasting benefit."[11]

In April 1854, at the age of nineteen, Spurgeon fully undertook the pastorate in London.

10. *The Early Years*, p. 263.
11. Ibid., pp. 259-60.

The crowds soon created a problem. Sunday by Sunday, morning and evening, every foot of space in the chapel was filled. In turn, the place became unbearably hot, and the oxygen was used up, yet there was no possibility of fresh air, for the windows had not been constructed to open. Spurgeon repeatedly suggested to the deacons that the small upper panes of glass be removed, but they did nothing about it.

One morning it was discovered that the panes had been smashed out. Spurgeon was delighted and proposed that "a reward of five pounds should be offered for the discovery of the offender, who when found should receive the amount as a present." Of course, he had removed the glass himself. "I have walked with the stick which let the oxygen into that stifling structure." Thus he made a bit of a game of doing what the deacons ought to have engaged a workman to do.

The additional air was a help, but it was evident a much larger seating capacity was needed. After the church had put up with the difficulty of the overcrowding for a few more months, construction operations were begun to enlarge the building.

While this work was in progress the services were held at Exeter Hall. This was a large auditorium in the heart of the city, but despite its 4,000 seats and standing room for another 1,000 it proved much too small, and hundreds were turned away.

Upon completion of the enlargement at New Park Street the services were again held there. It now seated 1,500, and with the filling of the Sunday school hall and other rooms, a total of 2,000 could be squeezed in. But numerous persons who had heard Spurgeon at Exeter Hall now came to hear him at the chapel, and the crowding was worse than ever. The only recourse was to move the evening service to the hall again and to try to make do with the chapel in the morning.

Thereafter, evening by evening the hall was crowded to its utmost capacity. Thousands who arrived, hoping to get in, failed to do so and remained outside—a noisy, milling multitude that blocked the movement of traffic on the street.

News of this activity spread throughout London and even to much of the British Isles. Exeter Hall was normally used for musical concerts and educational lectures, but it was almost unheard of for such a place to be used for religious services. Many persons looked on the whole procedure with strong disapproval and, knowing that Spurgeon was not a college graduate and that he was unordained, they quickly assumed he must be a charlatan, a man who knew how to attract and sway an audience and get them to give their money.

But circumstances arose in which Spurgeon gave evidence of his love of mankind and of his willingness to devote himself to comforting those in need.

An epidemic of Asiatic cholera at that time began to rage in London, particularly in the area south of the Thames. Spurgeon canceled all out-of-town engagements and gave his time to visiting the sick. The disease entered numerous homes. Almost everywhere there was suffering, and often there was death. "Family after family," he says, summoned me to the bedside of the smitten and almost every day I was called to visit the grave." With lovingkindness to the sick and in heart-felt sympathy with the bereaved he conducted this labor, and at any hour of the night he might be awakened with an urgent request to come and pray with someone who seemed about to pass into eternity.

Under this unremitting labor he soon became utterly exhausted. He was not only tired but was becoming sick himself.

In this condition, as he returned one day from a funeral, he noticed a piece of paper pasted up in a shoemaker's window. To his delight he found it carried a verse of Scripture: "Because thou hast made the Lord, which is my refuge, even the Most High, thy habitation; there shall no evil befall thee, neither shall any plague come nigh thy dwelling."

As Spurgeon read this verse his outlook was suddenly lifted. "Faith appropriated the passage as her own," he says. "I felt secure, refreshed, girt with immortality. I went on with my visitation of the dying in a calm and peaceful spirit, and I suffered no harm."[12]

Thus passed Spurgeon's first year in London, and as month succeeded month his fame increased. Although he was cruelly attacked in much of the press, he was greatly loved by his own people and had a host of admirers among the population at large. A former actor, Sheridan Knowles, had been converted at Bloomsbury Baptist Church, and his life had been changed. He was asked to speak at the Stepney College, and a student wrote:

> Immediately upon entering Mr. Knowles exclaimed, "Boys, have you heard the Cambridgeshire lad? . . .
>
> "Go and hear him at once if you want to know how to preach. His

12. Ibid., p. 272.

name is Charles Spurgeon. He is only a boy, but he is the most wonderful preacher in the world. He is absolutely perfect in his oratory; and, beside that, a master in the art of acting. He has nothing to learn from me, or anyone else. . . .

"I was once lessee of Drury Lane Theatre; and were I still in that position I would offer him a fortune to play for one season on the boards of that house. Why, boys, he can do anything he pleases with his audience! He can make them laugh, and cry, and laugh again, in five minutes. His power was never equalled.

"Now mark my words, boys, that young man will live to be the greatest preacher of this or any other age."[13]

Statements equally praiseful from many other persons raise the question as to what effect such admiration had upon him. Many a man has been ruined by a mere fraction of the adulation Spurgeon received, and he was conscious of the temptation to self-esteem it provoked. He paid a visit to Scotland, and although he won the favor of numerous ministers there, some of the Scottish divines thought his strong confidence manifested a somewhat proud spirit. In England he was more than once spoken of as "impudent," and there were occasions when he conducted himself with a boldness and an authority that seemed to support that view.

Nevertheless, we must remember that he was merely twenty and twenty-one. During such immaturity some measure of over-confidence was to be expected.

Yet the very reason for the praise lay to some extent in his humility. More than most men, he knew a deadness to self and was concerned above all things with bringing glory to God. What he was at heart is manifest in a statement that he wrote later.

When I first became a pastor in London, my success appalled me, and the thought of the career which it seemed to open up, so far from elating me, cast me into the lowest depths.

Who was I that I should continue to lead so great a multitude? I would betake myself to my village obscurity, or emigrate to America, and find a solitary nest in the backwoods where I might be sufficient for the things which would be demanded of me. It was just then that the curtain was rising upon my life-work, and I dreaded what it might reveal.[14]

13. Ibid., pp. 260-61.
14. Ibid., p. 263.

Spurgeon needed someone in whom he could confide, someone who could comfort and encourage him, who could share his innermost desires and feelings. In the divine workings such a one now entered his life and became his magnificent help "till death did them part."

The fact is, that Mrs. Spurgeon's aid and sympathy were invaluable in the moulding of her husband's character and life, so that he never could have been what he was without her. His mind was finely balanced, so was hers. His common sense was large, hers was equally so. His heart throbbed with love to God and mankind, and hers glowed in fully as warm a flame. He was equal to the perfecting and execution of every form of benevolence, and in this she was a true yoke-fellow at every step. While at every turn in his public life he was the target for many a rude attack, she, next to God, was his shield and helper.

No two souls on earth from the first fair dawn were more perfectly adapted to each other than Charles and Susannah Spurgeon.

H. L. Wayland, *Charles H. Spurgeon, His Faith and Works*, 1892

6

Spurgeon's Marriage— This One Truly Made in Heaven

Although most boys during their late teen years are busy seeking the company of girls, Spurgeon had thus far given no attention to the opposite sex. Till the age of nineteen he had devoted himself totally to studying and preaching.

But now all became changed.

A young lady, Susannah Thompson, was present at the evening service of his first Sunday at New Park Street. On this occasion she viewed him as something of an oddity.

> I was not at all fascinated by the young orator's eloquence, while his countrified manner and speech excited more regret than reverence. . . . I was not spiritually minded enough to understand his earnest presentation of the Gospel, and his powerful pleading with sinners, but the huge black satin stock, the long badly-trimmed hair and the blue pocket-handkerchief with the white spots . . . these attracted most of my attention, and, I fear, awakened some feelings of amusement.[1]

Those first impressions did not last long. Susie was a close friend of the Olney family, and Spurgeon was often in the Olney home. In this frequent crossing of their paths she began to see something of

1. Iain Murray, ed., *The Early Years* (London: Banner of Truth, 1962), p. 280.

his qualities, and he began to be attracted to her. By the time he had been in London merely two and a half months he sent her a gift. It was a copy of *Pilgrim's Progress,* and in it he had written:

Miss Thompson
with desires for her progress
in the blessed pilgrimage
From
C. H. Spurgeon
Ap. 20, 1854.

From that point he became her spiritual guide. Susannah had earlier believed in Christ for salvation, but had not grown during the period the church was without a pastor. Now, as the days passed, "he gently led me," she says, "by his preaching, and by his conversations . . . to the cross of Christ for the peace and pardon my weary soul was longing for."[2]

Their friendship soon became more personal. On June 10 of that year there was a gala event in London—the opening of the Crystal Palace. This was a great exhibition hall that housed displays of goods from the ends of the earth, and it had its own walks and planted areas. Charles and Susannah attended with a party of friends, and he saw to it that he sat next to her. During a lull in the proceedings he pointed out some lines in a book he had brought with him—lines that admonished any young man seeking a wife "to pray for her weal." As she read them he asked, "Do you pray for him who is to be your husband?" She was strangely excited, even by the mere reference to marriage, although she made no reply.

When the ceremonies were ended, "the same low voice whispered again, 'Will you come and walk round the Palace with me?' " Thereupon, leaving the rest of the party they walked away by themselves, and she later wrote, "We wandered together for a long time, not only in the wonderful building itself, but in the garden and even down to the lake. . . . During that walk, on that memorable day in June, I believe God Himself united our hearts in indissoluble bonds of true affection. . . . From that time our friendship grew apace, and quickly ripened into deepest love."[3]

Within a few more weeks (on August 2), they were at her grandfather's home and walked together into the garden. There, in solemn joy, he pledged his love and asked her to marry him.

2. Ibid., p. 282.
3. Ibid., p. 283.

I think of that old garden as a sacred place, a paradise of happiness, since there my beloved sought me for his very own, and told me how much he loved me. Though I thought I knew this already, it was a very different matter to hear him say it, and I trembled and was silent for very joy and gladness. The sweet ceremony of betrothal needs no description. . . . To me, it was a time as *solemn* as it was sweet, and with a great awe in my heart, I left my beloved, and hastening to the house and to an upper room, I knelt before God, and praised Him with happy tears, for His great mercy in giving me the love of so good a man.[4]

During the months that followed, Susannah became spiritually stronger. Early in the new year (1855) she applied to be baptized. Spurgeon had tried to keep their relationship a private matter, but the news had apparently leaked out. As the list of candidates for baptism was being read to the church, the name immediately preceding hers was that of an elderly man, Johnny Dear. Two maiden ladies sitting at the back of the room were overheard to say, "What was that man's name?"

"Johnny Dear."

"Oh, I suppose the next will be 'Susie dear,' then!"[5]

Throughout this period Spurgeon was enduring bitter attacks in much of both the secular and religious press. They were distorted, false, and cruel, and although he bore up well, he was often sorely wounded. He needed help and encouragement and these, with marvelous understanding and sympathy, Susannah provided.

The time they were able to spend together was very limited. He usually came to her home each Monday morning, yet he had no choice but to bring with him the secretary's transcript of one of the Sunday's sermons, which he edited. The sermon, when printed, had to fill eight pages. He might need to remove or add a portion, and there was also paragraphing to be introduced and various changes to be made. He hastened to have it ready for a messenger boy who would arrive on a bicycle at a given time in the afternoon and would hasten with it to the printer, who would immediately set about putting it into print, that it might be in the hands of the readers by Thursday morning. This labor marked—or marred—his Monday visits to Susie.

They also sought to have an hour or two together on Friday afternoons. The Crystal Palace, which always had displays of an interesting and instructive nature with its walks and botanical life,

4. Ibid., p. 284.
5. Ibid., p. 285.

was usually their trysting place. This afforded him a temporary rest
from his tremendous round of activity and gave him relaxation in a
quiet atmosphere and in company he loved the best.

But all was not ideal in their relationship. There were times when
he wounded Susie by forgetting all about her.

This happened once when he took her as he went to preach on a
certain afternoon in a large London auditorium. She says:

> We went together . . . in a cab, and I well remember trying to keep
> close by his side as we mingled with the mass of people thronging up
> the staircase. But by the time we had reached the landing, he had
> forgotten my existence; the burden of the message he had to proclaim to
> that crowd of immortal souls was upon him, and he turned into the small
> side door where the officials were awaiting him, without for a moment
> realizing that I was left to struggle as best I could with the rough and
> eager throng around me.
>
> At first, I was utterly bewildered, and then . . . I was *angry*. I at once
> returned home, and told my grief to my gentle mother. . . . She wisely
> reasoned that my chosen husband was no ordinary man, that his whole
> life was absolutely dedicated to God and His service, and that I must
> never, *never* hinder him by trying to put myself first in his heart.
>
> Presently, after much good and loving counsel, my heart grew soft and
> I saw I had been very foolish and wilful; and then a cab drew up at the
> door, and dear Mr. Spurgeon came running into the house, in great
> excitement calling, 'Where's Susie? I have been searching for her every-
> where, and cannot find her; has she come back by herself?' My dear
> mother went to him . . . and told him all the truth; and I think when he
> realized the state of things, she had to soothe him also, for he was so
> innocent at heart of having offended me in any way, that he must have
> felt I had done him an injustice in thus doubting him.
>
> Quietly he let me tell how indignant I had felt, and then he repeated
> mother's little lesson, assuring me of his deep affection for me, but
> pointing out that, before all things, he was God's *servant,* and I must be
> prepared to yield my claims to His.
>
> I never forgot the teaching of that day; I had learned my hard lesson *by
> heart,* for I do not recollect ever again seeking to assert my right to his
> time and attention when any service for God demanded them.[6]

There were occasions when Susie walked into his vestry at the
chapel just before he was to go out to preach and so intent was he
on the task ahead of him that he stood and shook hands with her as
though she was a stranger. Upon noticing his error he immediately

6. Ibid., p. 289.

apologized, but the mistake manifests the concentration of his mind in anticipation of the tremendous responsibility he felt in preaching.

Charles and Susannah had been engaged for eighteen months when she wrote, "The year 1855 was now drawing to a close, and we were looking forward, with unutterable joy, to having a home of our own, and being united by the holy ties of a marriage 'made in heaven.' "[7]

On January 8, 1856, the two lives were joined. The ceremony was held at New Park Street and was conducted by a neighboring pastor, Dr. Alexander Fletcher. For some hours before the event people were waiting at the church, and although by this date it had been much enlarged it was filled to overflowing. A whole detachment of police arranged themselves outside to control the great number who remained there.

The wedding was followed by a ten-day trip to Paris. Susannah had been to France earlier and could now point out to Charles various important sights. They visited art galleries, palaces, and museums and even went to see the working of the stock market.

Upon returning to London they settled into married life in a very modest home on New Kent Road.

Of course, Charles was very busy. Besides the multiple labors associated with New Park Street he was now preparing for the publication of his first book, *The Saint and His Saviour.* There were also numerous calls to preach at other churches, some in London and some in distant cities. Most evenings he was away ministering somewhere, and on occasion he was absent for a day or more at a time. He frequently returned home utterly exhausted, but invariably found loving arms awaiting him amid every possible kindness and comfort.

Susannah and Charles were very well suited. Though Spurgeon was militant and fearless in his stand for the truth of God, he was also a very tender and sensitive man, and he needed kindness and understanding in a wife. This he found in Susannah. Russell H. Conwell, the founder of Temple University in Philadelphia, who later visited the Spurgeons and became close friends with them, commented on the loveliness of their married life.

> Had he married a silly wife, who would have regarded him as the perfection of sainthood, or a devotee of fashion who would have dis-

7. Ibid., p. 299.

couraged him with her corrections, he could never have attained the eminence he reached. Had he allied himself with a wife who was less pious and sincere, or who would have maintained her hold upon the affections and esteem of his congregation, she would have served to injure his reputation. . . .

But she worked with him, prayed with him, believed in him and affectionately loved him through his many years of work. The thought of her, even when he was absent from home, was to him a subtle rest of spirit. He could travel many days, and preach several times a day, finding a rest in the thought that at home she was hourly praying for him, and was awaiting him with a welcome he could anticipate with a sense of divine peace.[8]

Spurgeon's affection for Susannah and hers for him never waned. Both endured much sickness as their days wore on, but they exercised toward each other a beautiful patience. Their unchanging affection is manifest in some poetic lines that he wrote while away from home at a time when he had been married for several years. They read, in part:

> Over the space that parts us, my wife,
>   I'll cast me a bridge of song;
> Our hearts shall meet, O joy of my life,
>   On its arch, unseen, but strong.
>
> The wooer his new love's name may wear
>   Engraved on a precious stone,
> But thine image within my heart I bear,
>   The heart that has long been thine own.
>
> The glowing colours on surface laid,
>   Wash out in a shower of rain;
> Thou need'st not be of rivers afraid,
>   For my love is dyed ingrain.
>
> The glittering dew drops of dawning love
>   Exhale as the day grows old;
> And fondness, taking the wings of a dove,
>   Is gone like a tale of old.
>
> But mine for thee, from the chambers of joy,
>   With strength came forth as the sun,
> Nor life nor death shall its force destroy,
>   Forever its course shall run.

8. Ibid., p. 233-34.

> Though He who chose us all worlds before,
> Must *reign* in our hearts alone,
> We fondly believe that we shall adore,
> *Together* before His throne.[9]

It is impossible to imagine anyone who would have been so suitable a wife for Charles Spurgeon as was this extraordinary woman, Susannah Thompson. They were molded for each other by the divine hand, and their union can only be considered as a fulfillment of Susannah's anticipation—it was indeed "a marriage made in heaven."

---

9. *C. H. Spurgeon's Autobiography,* comp. Susannah Spurgeon and J. W. Harrald, 4 vols. (London: Passmore and Alabaster, 1897), 2:298-99.

The tongue of the wicked has assailed Mr. Spurgeon with the most virulent abuse and lying detraction. His sentiments have been misrepresented, and his words perverted. His doctrines have been impugned as "blasphemous," "profane," and "diabolical." Nevertheless, the good hand of the Lord has been upon him, and he has not heeded the falsehood of the ungodly.

Passmore and Alabaster, Spurgeon's publishers,
August 1856

7

Conflict

When Spurgeon flashed upon the scene in London he disturbed the complacency of the religious life of the day.

Most Baptist and Congregational churches were quiet and subdued, and even the Methodists had largely lost their original fire. Those bodies in general still held to the evangelical faith, but the preaching lacked fervor, the churches possessed little vitality, and most were happy merely to "keep the even tenor of their way."

But this situation was challenged by the vitality and power that radiated from Spurgeon's ministry and personality.

Spurgeon had intellectual abilities of a very rare order. The constant reading he began as a boy continued, and by the time he came to London the knowledge he had amassed could virtually be termed "encyclopedic."

When he stood to preach he had that vast learning at his disposal. He could quote at will from any book of the Bible, using a most apt selection and repeating it exactly. He had memorized an immense number of hymns, and from those too he could in an instant repeat a verse or several verses. He could refer by way of illustration to incidents from the history of the ancients, the Reformers, and the Puritans, and he made much use of events in the lives of Whitefield and Wesley and others of their times.

He was ever reading literature about the Bible—a breadth of study that enabled him less than twenty years later to write his volume *Commenting and Commentaries.* In the preparation of this book he "passed under review," he said, "some three or four thousand volumes." His one hobby, if it can be so termed, was that of scouting out and buying second-hand books, and his personal library grew till its volumes numbered more than ten thousand.

We must recognize that Spurgeon was, above everything, a theologian. He had given thought to the great doctrines of the Bible from the time he had begun to read, and from that point he had been steadily building in his mind and heart a knowledge of the vast system of theology that is revealed in the Scriptures. Londoners were startled as much by what he said as by how he said it, and this system of doctrine was the pervading quality of all his ministry.

Nevertheless, his voice possessed not only a carrying quality but also an indefinable character that made many a hearer feel the preacher had singled him out and was speaking only to him. The voice was in perfect control, and though it could thunder with startling force it could also speak in the most moving, gentle tones. The phrase often used of it was "like a chime of silver bells."

Above all, in his delivery Spurgeon was entirely natural. There was nothing "put on" about him, and although a note of humor often crept into what he was saying, the whole of his preaching was overshadowed by his tremendous earnestness.

Although a vast host of Londoners became Spurgeon's hearers and admirers, there were numerous others of a different mind. Many, knowing only that he was very young, was not college trained, and not ordained, jumped to the conclusion that he could not be a qualified minister and therefore must be a ministerial quack.

This was true of several newspaper editors. Spurgeon was so much in the public eye that they could not avoid mentioning him, and since they regarded him as a charlatan, they set out upon a campaign of bitter denunciation. Some of their statements were too crude or blasphemous to be repeated, but there were others. An *Ipswich Express* correspondent reported under the title *A Clerical Poltroon:*

> As his own chapel is under repair, he preaches in the Exeter Hall . . . and the place is crammed to suffocation.
>
> All his discourses are redolent of bad taste, are vulgar and theatrical, and yet he is so run after that, unless you go half an hour before the time,

you will not be able to get in at all. . . . One leading minister of the Independent denomination, after hearing this precocious youth, said that the exhibition was "an insult to God and man."

. . . The gifted divine had the impudence, before preaching, to say, as there were many young ladies present, that he was engaged—that his heart was another's, he wished them clearly to understand that—that he might have no presents sent to him, no attentions paid him, no worsted slippers worked for him by the young ladies present. I suppose the dear divine has been rendered uncomfortable by the fondness of his female auditors.[1]

These remarks brought protests from numerous readers. In response the *Express* rather flippantly admitted it now believed the report about the slippers to be untrue. But in the meantime the statement had been copied by several other papers, and those allowed it to stand without correction. In fact, the *Lambeth Gazette* declared, "The young sisters are dancing mad after him. He has received slippers enough from these lowly-minded damsels to open a shoe-shop."[2]

Another paper that had much to say about Spurgeon was the *Essex Standard*. The following passage is typical:

His style is that of the vulgar colloquial, varied by rant. . . . All the most solemn mysteries of our holy religion are by him rudely, roughly and impiously handled. Mystery is vulgarised, sanctity profaned, common sense outraged and decency disgusted. . . . His rantings are interspersed with coarse anecdotes that split the ears of groundlings; and this is popularity! this is the "religious furor" of London![3]

The *Patriot* pointed out various elements of Spurgeon's ability, but then went on to criticize him.

All, in turn, come under the lash of the precocious tyro. He alone is a consistent Calvinist; all besides are either rank Arminians, licentious Antinomians, or unfaithful professors of the doctrines of grace. . . . The doctrine of election is, "in our age, scorned and hated." "The time-serving religion of the present day is only exhibited in evangelical drawing rooms." He never hears his brother ministers assert the positive satisfaction and substitution of our Lord Jesus Christ.

1. Iain Murray, ed., *The Early Years* (London: Banner of Truth, 1962), p. 311.
2. Charles Ray, *The Life of Charles Haddon Spurgeon* (London: Passmore and Alabaster, 1903), p. 174.
3. *The Early Years*, p. 316.

Still rougher, if possible, is Mr. Spurgeon's treatment of theologians not of his own especial school. "Arminian perversions, in particular, are to sink back to their birthplace in the pit." Their notion of the possibility of a final fall from grace "is the wickedest falsehood on earth."[4]

Another publication linked together the names "Tom Thumb, the Living Skeleton, and C. H. Spurgeon," thus suggesting that his right place was in a circus. Still another said that his ministry was a reviving of the ancient "Feast of the Ass," and a third asserted:

> We had thought that the day for dogmatic, theological dramatising was past—that we should never more see the massive congregation listening to outrageous manifestations of insanity—no more hear the fanatical effervescence of ginger-pop sermonizing, or be called upon to wipe away the froth, that the people might see the colour of the stuff.
> . . . It is not Christian-like to say, "God must wash brains in the Hyper-Calvinism a Spurgeon teaches before man can enter Heaven." . . . When the Exeter Hall stripling talks of Deity, let him remember that He is superior to profanity, and that blasphemy from a parson is as great a crime as when the lowest grade of humanity utters the brutal oath at which the virtuous stand aghast.[5]

Several newspaper cartoonists made Spurgeon their subject. Most derided him, but two or three could not refrain from recognizing that he proclaimed a clear and positive message, and they made him look superior to various others of the nation's religious leaders.

To all the attacks Spurgeon made no reply. In his preaching, however, he sometimes made reference by way of illustration to something the papers had said about him. When writing to his parents he more than once assured them that several statements—for instance, the one about the slippers—were untrue and urged them not to be alarmed about the opposition he was receiving.

Nevertheless, he was wounded in seeing himself thus accused and held up to ridicule. Mrs. Spurgeon gathered all the defamatory statements and pasted them in a scrapbook, till it finally became a huge volume. She also framed a text and hung it on the wall. It read: "Blessed are ye, when men shall revile you, and persecute you, and shall say all manner of evil against you falsely, for My sake.

4. G. Holden Pike, *The Life and Work of Charles Haddon Spurgeon*, 6 vols. (London: Cassel, 1898), 2:196.
5. *The Early Years*, p. 320.

Rejoice, and be exceeding glad: for great is your reward in Heaven: for so persecuted they the prophets which were before you."

Spurgeon met opposition not only from the secular press but also from certain religious papers because of his Calvinism.

Spurgeon wrote "A Defence of Calvinism," which constitutes an entire chapter in his *Autobiography*.[6] He says, "We only use the term 'Calvinism' for shortness. That doctrine which we call 'Calvinism' did not spring from Calvin; we believe that it sprang from the great founder of all truth."[7] He termed this theological system "the doctrines of grace," and he used the two terms interchangeably.

He had long been familiar with these views, for they had composed the discussion he had heard in the homes of his grandfather and father. These were the doctrines presented by Bunyan and other Puritan writers. It was these in which he was vigorously instructed by Mary King, the housekeeper of the school he attended at Newmarket.

> She liked something very sweet indeed, good strong Calvinistic doctrine, but she lived strongly as well as fed strongly. Many a time we have gone over the covenant of grace together, and talked of the personal election of the saints, their union to Christ, their final perseverance and what vital godliness meant; and I do believe that I learnt more from her than I should have learned from any six doctors of divinity of the sort we have nowadays.[8]

When he came to London, Spurgeon looked upon his ministry as that of a reformer—he was laboring to bring men back to the truths they had left. The generality of the Protestant ministers were basically evangelical, but their preaching was very short on doctrine, and he felt himself largely alone in the theological system he held and declared. In sermon after sermon during his first years in London he asserted the doctrines of human depravity and divine election, and he did so with strong emphasis and much instruction. "My daily labour," he stated, "is to revive the *old* doctrines of Gill, Owen, Calvin, Augustine and Christ."[9]

Spurgeon spoke out against the unthinking manner in which some Calvinists talk about a "limited atonement." He much pre-

6. Ibid., p. 162.
7. Ibid., p. 163.
8. Ibid., pp. 38-39.
9. Iain Murray, *The Forgotten Spurgeon* (London: Banner of Truth, 1966), p. 58.

ferred the term "particular redemption"—the belief that Christ did
not merely make salvation possible and leave it to man to do the
rest, but that He accomplished the redemption of each of His elect
ones and thus assured their salvation.

But although he declared "Salvation is of the Lord!" Spurgeon also
preached "Whosoever will may come." Into the New Park Street
Chapel and into Exeter Hall came hundreds of men and women
who did not know the Lord. In virtually every sermon he pleaded
with them to recognize their lost condition, to know that Christ
could save them, and to believe on Him then and there. His preaching abounded with the free offer of the gospel to all mankind and
was fruitful in the conversion of a great number.

Spurgeon recognized that the two concepts seemed contradic-
tory. But he declared the Scripture taught both—that God would
save His elect ones, but also that man was responsible concerning
his soul. Therefore he constantly urged, "Believe on the Lord Jesus
Christ, and thou shalt be saved."

This free offer of the gospel to all who would believe brought
upon Spurgeon the attack of the hyper-Calvinists.

The hyper-Calvinists believed everything held by other Calvinists, except that they also believed the gospel offer ought not to be
extended before an audience composed of saved and unsaved. They
declared the gospel was only to be presented to "sensible sinners"— persons conscious of their need of Christ.

Spurgeon frequently spoke against this form of Calvinism because it did nothing to awaken sinners to their need of Christ. The
"hypers" were not evangelistic—they did not go out to seek the
lost, and they virtually rejected Christ's command "Go ye into all
the world and preach the gospel to every creature."

But although these people did not go after the lost themselves,
they were not lax in going after the man who did. Their chief
spokesman was James Wells, the minister of a fairly large congregation, and in the hyper-Calvinists' paper *The Earthen Vessel* he severely attacked Spurgeon. To him and his people Spurgeon's soul-
winning activity was anathema. God would save His elect without
the interference of this young upstart. Wells took the stand of a very
righteous man, one who was contending for the faith, and in a
lengthy assessment of Spurgeon and his ministry he stated he could
find not the least evidence of saving grace in him and concluded
that he probably had never been converted.

In his preaching Spurgeon frequently struck out at the hyper-

Calvinists.[10] But his strongest reply to them was the glory of the gospel that he preached and the fact that he saw it used of God in the transformation of a multitude of lives.

Other religious journals also found fault with Spurgeon during his first years in London. *The Baptist Reporter, The United Presbyterian Magazine, The Critic,* and *The Christian News* are examples of those that attacked him.

The opposition from the world brought on a terrible tragedy.

He was denied the continued use of Exeter Hall, and therefore he considered obtaining the Surrey Gardens Music Hall. This was a very large auditorium that, besides its main floor area, had three galleries, and the total seating capacity was spoken of as 10,000. It seemed an impossible scheme for him to try to use such a place, for although Whitefield had preached to 20,000 and more, that was in the open air, and probably no one in all history had ever reached so immense a crowd indoors.

Nevertheless, Spurgeon determined to attempt the gigantic task. Knowing that as long as he was limited to his chapel, hundreds of people who wanted to hear the gospel were turned away each Sunday, he felt he had no choice but to try to use this hall.

The news that Spurgeon would preach in the Surrey Gardens Music Hall spread quickly throughout much of London. It excited his own people with joyful anticipation, it aroused many outsiders with a desire to attend, but it also moved some whose motives were evil to plan to disturb so significant an event.

The opening service at the hall was planned for the evening of Sunday, October 19, 1856. The preceding days were a time of much activity in the Spurgeon household, for on September 10 they moved to a new home, Helensburgh House, and just ten days later Susannah gave birth to two babies, twin sons, whom they named Charles and Thomas.

The crowd that gathered exceeded all expectations. The hall was set in a kind of park that was surrounded by a large ornamental iron railing, and people began to assemble within it not long after the noon hour. Their numbers steadily increased, and when early in the evening the building was opened, they flooded in. They filled every seat, packed the aisles, and crowded the stairways, while

10. Spurgeon sometimes referred to Hyper-Calvinists as merely "these Calvinists." Although the context clearly indicates his meaning, some have incorrectly assumed he was denouncing Calvinism itself.

thousands of others stood outside, refusing to go away and hoping to hear something of the sermon through the windows.

When Spurgeon arrived, upon witnessing this vast concourse of humanity, he was almost overwhelmed. He was yet but twenty-two, and to stand before this audience, conduct the service and preach, making himself heard and understood by such a multitude, seemed truly an impossible task. But in the assurance of divine strength he went before the multitude and began the service.

For the first moments everything proceeded with the decorum of any ordinary Sunday service, and the singing seemed particularly reverent and joyous.

But just after Spurgeon began to pray the place was suddenly thrown into consternation. Someone in a gallery shouted, "Fire!" and that was followed by a cry from the ground floor, "The galleries are falling!" Then a third voice was heard, "The whole place is collapsing!" Immediately much of the hall was in a panic, and people began rushing for the stairs and pressing to get out of the doors.

Under the extreme pressure a stair railing gave way, and several fell with it onto the crowded floor beneath. Some jumped from the gallery, and others lost their footing on the stairs. Falling to the floor, they were trodden down by the many who attempted to pass over them. A stream of people pushed their way out of the doors, but as they did so, others thrust themselves in, intent on securing the seats they had left.

From his place on the platform Spurgeon could not see all that was going on at the far end of the hall, where the stairs and doors were located. He tried to calm the audience and attempted to preach, but it soon became evident the service could not be continued, and he requested the congregation to leave in an orderly manner.

He went into a side room, so overcome that he fell to the floor, almost unconscious. Before he left he learned that seven persons had died and twenty-eight others had been removed to the hospital, many of them severely wounded.

He was taken to his home and had the comfort and consolation of his wife. But the trouble had come at a time she was not as able to help as she normally would have been, for less than a month had passed since she had given birth, and she was still weak and unwell.

The deacons realized that his home would not be the best place for him under the present circumstances. There would be numerous visitors—friends who wished to help and foes who wanted to blame—and there would assuredly be reporters. Knowing the extreme sensitivity of his nature and the extent of his compassion for the sufferers, the deacons whisked him away to a home in the suburbs. Here he would largely escape from visitors, and they hoped that in the quietness he would recuperate.

Providentially, hidden away in the peaceful retreat, Spurgeon did not see the reports carried in the papers. Some were sympathetic, but others were cruel. The following is an example of what his opposers wrote:

> We are neither straight-laced nor Sabbatarian in our sentiments, but we would keep apart, widely apart, the theatre and the church; above all, we would place in the hand of every right-thinking man a whip to scourge from society the authors of such vile blasphemies as on Sunday night, above the cries of the dead and the dying, and louder than the wails of misery from the maimed and suffering, resounded from the mouth of Spurgeon. . . . And lastly, when the mangled corpses had been carried away from the unhallowed and disgraceful scene—when husbands were seeking their wives and children their mothers, in extreme agony and despair—the clink of money as it fell into the collection-boxes grated harshly, miserably, on the ears of those who, we sincerely hope, have by this time conceived for Mr. Spurgeon and his rantings the profoundest contempt.[11]

It is well this report and the others like it were kept from Spurgeon. Of course, the statement about the use of the money-boxes was an entire fabrication, and to portray him as heartless amidst the tragedy was as cruel as it was false. We must assume, however, that Susannah saw the papers.

Spurgeon continued in his broken condition for seven or eight days. Then, as he walked in his friend's garden, a verse of Scripture about Christ flashed into his mind. He saw it afresh—"Wherefore God also hath highly exalted Him and given Him a name which is above every name," and as he fed his soul upon its truth he began to improve. His burden was gradually lifted so he could return to his home. On the following Sunday he ministered again at New Park Street. He had been out of his pulpit for but one Sunday.

Spurgeon immediately set about helping the sufferers. A fund was raised toward meeting their needs, and Spurgeon, the deacons, and

11. Pike, 2:247.

others visited hospitals and homes and the relatives of those who had died. Yet although he resumed his general labors, the terrible event had severely affected his nervous system. Throughout the rest of his days the sight of an overcrowded building placed him under an immediate strain, and, even years later, upon being reminded of the event at the Surrey Gardens he easily became weak and sometimes seemed about to faint.

Whatever the motive behind the tragedy, it joined with the printed opposition in furthering Spurgeon's ministry. The news of what had happened became known throughout Britain, and despite the evil reports, many persons could not help but feel sympathetic toward him. Moreover, the New Park Street people had already appointed a committee to make plans for the construction of a new and very large church, and the catastrophe moved them to work and pray to see the planning completed and the actual construction begun.

And Spurgeon benefited within himself. The opposition taught him to sacrifice even his reputation for Christ. "If I must lose that too," he wrote, "then let it go; it is the dearest thing I have, but it shall go too, if, like my Master, they shall say I have a devil and am mad."[12] The experience, heartrending though it was at the time, brought him into an increased maturity, and it was a wiser Spurgeon who led his church forward.

Undoubtedly, some would like to think of Spurgeon as a man who seldom disagreed with anyone and who was always widely loved and admired. But in his doctrinal emphasis he ran contrary to many, and for this reason, in addition to his unusual zeal, he became an object of ridicule and reproach, and some years were to elapse before the nation began to recognize his true qualities and to know his extraordinary worth.

12. *The Early Years*, p. 304.

There was a specimen before me of the plough-man who overtook the reaper, of one who sowed the seed who was treading on the heels of the men who were gathering in the vintage.

And the like activity we have lived to see in the Church of Christ. Did you ever know so much doing in the Christian world before? There are grey-headed men around me who have known the Church of Christ sixty years, and they can bear me witness that they never knew such life, such vigour and activity, as there is at present.

Spurgeon, January 1860

8

Revival in London

For three years Spurgeon used the Surrey Gardens Music Hall as the site of his morning service, and the evening congregation continued to meet, though terribly overcrowded, in the New Park Street Chapel. These were years of tremendous labor and also of great blessing.

A congregation of an unusual nature was drawn to the great hall. Among them were many persons of learning and position, and a large number were middle-class citizens—people whose possessions were sufficient to afford them a very comfortable manner of life. But there were numerous poor in London in those days, and among them poverty was the daily lot, sickness was frequent, and drunkenness, immorality, and thievery abounded. Life was hard, suicides were not uncommon, and most had long been forced to say, "No man careth for our souls." Hundreds from this poor class came to hear Spurgeon.

The first experience many of these people had with Spurgeon was during the cholera epidemic. He had not tried to escape the contagion but had gone freely to the homes of the sick. He had shown kindness, prayed for the suffering, comforted the mourners, and buried the dead. News of his actions had spread around the entire area, and people recognized that here was a preacher who truly cared about them.

The attention thus drawn to Spurgeon was increased by the campaign of opposition against him. His name was on many tongues, and it was spoken so frequently in contempt and with such bitter accusations that many people were moved by curiosity to go to hear him. Moreover, going to the hall did not seem like going to so forbidding a place as a church.

And as they listened they found he did not speak in some difficult style, but he spoke their language, the tongue of the common man. He used words they knew well and illustrations they could understand, and he seemed to be talking to each one personally. Above all, he had a message that reached many hearts as he told of the new life that could be had in Christ.

In seeking to reach these people—indeed, in every aspect of his ministry—Spurgeon was characterized by an earnestness that almost defies description.

Some authors have assumed that he was little more than an entertainer. They picture him as a man who entered the pulpit in a jovial manner, made people laugh and feel good, and who regarded preaching as something of a casual pastime. Nothing can be further from the truth.

Certainly, Spurgeon had a gift of humor, and at times it came into play as he preached. A Scottish minister, after hearing him, said his speaking was enlivened here and there with a flash of wit that was "like the gleam of sunshine on the ripples of a river." But to suppose that Spurgeon told jokes in the pulpit or treated the work of preaching lightly is to reveal an utter ignorance of the man and of his concept of the ministry. In speaking to his students on how the pulpit's power for good may be destroyed, he said, "It may be done by putting empty-headed men in the pulpit, men who have nothing to say, and say it; or frothy, feathery men who introduce a joke in the pulpit for joking's sake."[1]

Clowning in the pulpit called down his strongest denunciations.

In his regular Sunday work, he spent some time before the beginning of the services alone with God, feeling the awesome responsibility of preaching the gospel to lost mankind and pouring out his soul in prayer. On some occasions he seemed unable to go out and stand before the people, and the deacons found it necessary almost

---

1. G. Holden Pike, *The Life and Work of Charles Haddon Spurgeon*, 6 vols. (London: Cassel, 1898), 3:185.

to lift him from his knees as the moment for commencing the service drew near.

Yet he went forth—always right on time—and as he stood before the congregation he experienced a great sense of "power from on high." He preached with confidence, with clear instruction and heart-felt pleading, but as soon as the service was concluded he hastened away to his vestry, there to groan out before God his sense of failure. He could not be alone for long, for people came lining up before the vestry door, some coming as visitors from afar to greet him, but others coming to tell him they were in sore spiritual need and wanted him to show them the way to the Savior.

Spurgeon spoke out against the kind of minister who before preaching can be a jolly fellow, happily greeting the people, and who after the service can gather jovially with them at the door, having fair words for all. His place at such a time, he declared, is with God, weeping out the failure of his preaching and pleading that the seed sown in hearts might take root and bring forth fruit unto eternal life.

This earnestness characterized the whole service—the singing, the Scripture reading, and the preaching—but it was especially evident as Spurgeon led the congregation in prayer. Throughout his entire ministry many hearers remarked that, moved as they were by his preaching, they were still more affected by his praying. D. L. Moody, after his first visit to England, being asked upon his return to America, "Did you hear Spurgeon preach?" replied, "Yes, but better still, I heard him pray."

Spurgeon asked that no one take down his prayers in shorthand, declaring prayer was too solemn an activity to be subjected to reporting. But at times the request went unheeded; his prayer at the watchnight service in 1856 was recorded, and we may sense something of his tremendous earnestness as we read it:

> O God, save thy people! Save thy people! A solemn charge hast thou given to thy servant. Ah! Lord, it is all too solemn for such a child. Help him, help him by thine own grace, to discharge it as he ought. O Lord, let thy servant confess that he feels his prayers are not as earnest as they should be for his people's souls; that he does not preach so frequently as he ought with that fire, that energy, that true love for men's souls. But O Lord, damn not the hearers for the preacher's sin. O destroy not the flock for the shepherd's iniquity. Have mercy on them, good Lord, have mercy on them, O Lord have mercy on them!

There are some of them, Father, that will not have mercy on themselves. How have we preached to them and laboured for them. O God, thou knowest that I lie not. How have I striven for them that they might be saved! But the heart is too hard for man to melt, and the soul made of iron too hard for flesh and blood to render soft.

O God, the God of Israel, thou canst save. There is the pastor's hope, there is the minister's trust. He cannot, but thou canst, Lord. They will not come but thou canst make them willing in the day of thy power. They will not come unto thee that they may have life; but thou canst draw them and then they shall run after thee. They cannot come; but thou canst give them power; for though "no man cometh except the Father draw him," yet if he draw him, then he can come.

O Lord, for another year has thy servant preached—thou knowest how. It is not for him to plead his cause with thee. . . . But now, O, Lord, we beseech thee, bless our people. Let this our church, thy church, be still knit together in unity; and this night may they commence a fresh era of prayer. They are a praying people, blessed be thy name, and they pray for their minister with all their hearts. O Lord, help them to pray more earnestly. May we wrestle in prayer more than ever, and besiege thy throne until thou makest Jerusalem a praise, not only here, but everywhere.

But, Father, it is not the church we weep for; it is not the church we groan for; it is the world. O Faithful Promiser, hast thou not promised to thy Son that he should not die in vain? Give him souls, we beseech thee, that he may be abundantly satisfied. Hast thou not promised that thy church shall be increased? O increase her, increase her. And hast thou not promised that thy ministers shall not labour in vain? For thou hast said, "as the rain cometh down and the snow from heaven, and returneth not thither, but watereth the earth, even so shall thy word be: it shall not return unto thee void."

Let not the word return void tonight; but now may thy servant in the most earnest manner, with the most fervent heart, burning with love to his Saviour, and with love to souls, preach once more the glorious gospel of the blessed God. Come, Holy Spirit, we can do nothing without thee. We solemnly invoke thee, great Spirit of God! thou who didst rest on Abraham, on Isaac and on Jacob; thou who in the night visions speaketh unto men. Spirit of the Prophets, Spirit of the Apostles, Spirit of the Church, be thou our Spirit this night, that the earth may tremble, that souls may be made to hear thy word, and that all flesh may rejoice together to praise thy name. Unto Father, Son and Holy Ghost, the dread Supreme, be everlasting praise. Amen.[2]

2. *The New Park Street Pulpit,* 1856, p. 43.

The essence of Spurgeon's theology is revealed in this prayer. He recognized that the human heart is set against God and that so severe is the nature of sin that unregenerate man "will not" and "cannot" come to God of himself. Man is lost in sin, and such is his condition that he can in no way help himself. Yet Spurgeon found assurance in knowing that Christ on the cross accomplished the full salvation of all whom God would call, and that God makes unwilling men willing "in the day of His power." He regarded himself as responsible to preach the gospel to them all—"to every creature"—and to do so as zealously as if the outcome depended entirely on himself. He knew that "salvation is of the Lord" and that as he went on with the mighty task he could be confident that the Word would "not return void," but that God would use it to bring about the salvation of souls.

His was a theology not limited by the response of man. It depended upon God, and it was to Spurgeon a theology of victory.

The earnestness manifested in his praying characterized also Spurgeon's preaching.

His first aim was that of bringing glory to Christ. In mentioning the strain he frequently experienced when he first began to preach in Exeter Hall, Mrs. Spurgeon wrote:

> I remember . . . the Sunday evening when he preached from the text, "His name shall endure forever." It was a subject in which he revelled, it was his chief delight to exalt his glorious Saviour, and he seemed in that discourse to be pouring out his very soul and life in homage and adoration before his gracious King.
>
> But I really thought he would have died there, in face of all those people! At the end of the sermon he made a mighty effort to recover his voice, but utterance well-nigh failed. and only in broken accents could the pathetic peroration be heard—"Let my name perish, but let Christ's name last forever! Jesus! *Jesus!* JESUS! Crown Him Lord of all! You will not hear me say anything else. These are my last words in Exeter Hall for this time. Jesus! *Jesus!* JESUS! Crown Him Lord of all!" and then he fell back, almost fainting, in the chair behind him.[3]

Together with his love for the Lord, Spurgeon's preaching manifested a great love for the souls of mankind. Christians were fed, and needy saints were comforted under his ministry, but above all

---

3. Iain Murray, ed., *The Early Years* (London: Banner of Truth, 1962), p. 294.

sinners were pleaded with to come to Christ. One of his early sermons closed with,

> "He that believeth and is baptized shall be saved, and he that believeth not shall be damned." Weary sinner, hellish sinner, thou who art the devil's castaway, reprobate, profligate, harlot, robber, thief, adulterer, fornicator, drunkard, swearer. Sabbath-breaker—list! I speak to thee as to the rest. I exempt no man. God hath said there is no exemption here. "*Whosoever* believeth in the name of Jesus Christ shall be saved." Sin is no barrier: thy guilt is no obstacle. Whosoever, though he were as black as Satan, though he were guilty as a fiend—whosoever this night believes, shall have every sin forgiven, shall have every crime effaced, shall have every iniquity blotted out; shall be saved in the Lord Jesus Christ, and shall stand in heaven safe and secure.
>
> That is the glorious Gospel. God apply it home to your hearts and give you faith in Jesus![4]

Almost every sermon contained, especially toward its close, an entreaty of this nature—warning, begging, pleading, urging the sinner to come to Christ.

Spurgeon took further steps in directing souls who had come to Christ and were therefore ready for baptism and membership in the church.

He did not ask people to walk to the front of the auditorium, raise a hand, sign a card, or perform any outward action. But throughout each sermon and especially as he drew it to its close, he pleaded with unsaved hearers to believe on Christ, and he expected them to do so then and there. At times he told them to go quietly to their homes, to go to a room alone, and to stay there seeking the Lord till He planted faith and repentance within their hearts.

During his first years in London he made himself available every Tuesday afternoon, that persons who were in trouble about their souls might seek his advice, or those who had recently come to know Christ might tell him of their experience. These were glorious occasions to him, and he rejoiced to point a seeking one to the Lord or to hear a testimony of the transformation of a life. In turn, on Tuesday evening, as the church gathered for prayer meeting, he presented the names of those he had reason to believe were truly born again, and often the person was there to tell of his experience before the large company. The church then voted to receive these

4. *The New Park Street Pulpit*, 1855, 1:40.

ones for baptism and church membership, and that happy task was almost the only business of the church.

Before long, however, the number of the persons who came to Spurgeon proved so large that he found it necessary to change his procedure. Names of persons who were known to be seekers or who claimed to have recently come to Christ were presented at the Tuesday evening meeting, and in each case a man whom the church called a "messenger" was appointed to visit the person in order, as far as possible, to ascertain the spiritual condition. The messenger wrote a report of his dealing with this person and entered it in a book entitled "Record of Enquirers," which was kept by the church.

The work done by the messengers reveals that they had developed a marvelous spiritual maturity. Undoubtedly, when Spurgeon first came to New Park Street the men of the church were little accustomed to dealing with inquiring souls. But under Spurgeon's instruction they learned to perform the sensitive task, and as one reads their reports it is impossible not to be struck by their wisdom.

In dealing with a person who testified he had come to know the Lord, the messenger looked for three marks of true conversion. *One,* had the person, knowing himself to be a sinner and unable to do anything toward saving himself, gone to God, begging for mercy, and had he entirely trusted his soul to Christ, believing in the saving merit of His death upon the cross? This individual experience of the soul with God was the unalterable and basic necessity, and without it there was no recognition of the person as truly converted. *Two,* had the person entered into newness of life, experiencing a change of affections, victory over sin, a love for the Word of God, and a desire to win others to Christ? *Three,* did he or she possess a basic understanding of the doctrines of grace, recognizing that salvation did not begin with himself or his own will, but with God's choice and God's action, and that God, who saved him, would keep him through time and through eternity?

The messengers dealt very tenderly and understandingly with these babes in Christ, and the reports of their visits possess a spiritual richness that is rare in Christian literature.

In cases in which the messenger was satisfied on these three matters, he expressed his rejoicing in the report and wrote at the bottom of the page "Gave him [or her] a card to see the Pastor." But when he was not satisfied, the report might read, in the case of a woman, "Recommend her to attend Mrs. Bartlett's Class. I will see her again in three months." A man would be directed to one of the

men's classes, and in some instances two and three dates on which
further visits were made were written in.

But there were several instances in which the messenger was not
satisfied that the person was truly saved, and each year a *List of
Refusals* containing perhaps sixty or seventy names was pasted into
the front of the book.

Spurgeon was still available each Tuesday afternoon to meet with
inquirers, but the work of the messengers had already done much
toward saving his time. On several occasions he remarked on the
joy he had in hearing the testimonies of these new Christians, and
he was often in tears as he heard them tell of the work of the Holy
Spirit in their hearts, of their struggles with sin and their victories
over it, and of their new life in Christ. Many mentioned the very
sermon under which their hearts had been smitten with a realization of their need, and some even spoke of a text he had used or a
single statement he had made that was used of the Lord to awaken
them and to draw them to Himself.

He gave encouragement and advice. In these interviews he came
to know the persons individually, and this acquaintance enabled
him, even when the membership rose to six thousand, to remember
almost every one of them by name. On various occasions he was so
lost in joy in hearing the accounts of conversion that he forgot all
about supper, and he was sorry when the hour for the prayer meeting arrived and he had to leave several individuals to be dealt with
the following week.

Those names were presented to the church that evening. The
people joined him in rejoicing as they heard the new converts, and
several each week were received for baptism and membership.
Sometimes the number was as low as twelve and often as high as
twenty and more.

In his extraordinary earnestness Spurgeon could not do less than
exercise this great care in dealing with souls. He truly believed in
hell, and he recognized the awful responsibility should he give
some person cause to believe he was saved if there was no evidence
that it was so.

Moreover, membership in the church was never allowed to become a mere formality. Members were given tickets, one of which
must be presented at each Communion service, and the names of
any who were absent four months without good cause were removed. Likewise the names of those who ceased to live in London—in those days many Englishmen emigrated to Australia, Can-

ada, and other lands—were deleted, and the principle that, except in the case of shut-ins, membership must be active was rigidly maintained.

The new members were very largely people who did not come from other churches. The vast majority were men and women who had never been in the habit of attending church, but they came, especially to the Music Hall, heard the gospel, and were converted. Many of these represented marvelous transformations—drunkards, harlots, and thieves with lives changed and homes made new—men and women who once did not know God, but now were happily living for the Lord and serving Him.

The blessing experienced under Spurgeon's ministry soon affected other churches. Although at first there had been the loud outcry against him, as time passed and as people read his sermons and saw his work, their opinions began to change. By the time he had been in London three years some of the papers wrote of him very favorably, and certain of the great literary and political figures of the nation frequently dropped into the services.

His fervor gradually had an influence on religious conditions in general. Several ministers who had been sorely lacking in zeal began to labor with diligence, special evangelistic efforts were conducted in many quarters, and some even followed Spurgeon in holding meetings in Exeter Hall. He spoke of his church as "the advance guard of the times."

> I cannot help observing that during the last four or five years a wonderful change has come over the Christian mind. The Church of England has been awakened. . . . Great services have been held. I cannot help remembering that God honoured us to let us stand in the front of this great movement. From our example the blessed fire has run along the ground and kindled a blaze. When I first heard that clergymen were to preach in Exeter Hall my soul leaped within me. . . . When I heard that Westminster Abbey was opened for the preaching of the Gospel, and then St. Paul's Cathedral, I was overwhelmed with gratitude, and prayed that only the truth as it is in Jesus might be preached in these places.[5]

A year later he asserted: "The times of refreshing from the presence of the Lord have at last dawned upon our land. Everywhere there are signs of aroused activity and increased earnestness. A spirit of prayer is visiting our churches. . . . The first breath of the rushing

5. Pike, 2:300.

mighty wind is already discerned, while on rising evangelists the tongues of fire have evidently descended."[6]

He spoke of the blessing God had bestowed upon his ministry as "a harvest which is not twenty, nor thirty-fold, but even seventy-fold." Yet he and his people were anticipating a still larger ingathering, for the days of their meeting in rented halls were almost ended. As 1861 dawned they were ready to enter their new church home, the great Metropolitan Tabernacle.

6. *The New Park Street Pulpit,* 1859, p. v.

Young
Charles Spurgeon,
age twenty.

Cottage where Spurgeon preached his first sermon.

The Metropolitan Tabernacle.

Main auditorium, Metropolitan Tabernacle.

The Pastors' College.

The Stockwell Orphanage.

Portrait produced from the last photograph
taken of Spurgeon,
January 8, 1892.

Spurgeon's funeral procession entering the cemetery.

THE
LONG PERIOD
OF
MATURE MINISTRY

1861—1886

Let God send the fire of His Spirit here, and the minister will be more and more lost in his Master. You will come to think less of the speaker and more of the truth spoken. . . .

Suppose the fire should come here, and the Master be seen more than the minister, what then? Why, this church will become two, three and four thousand strong. . . . We shall have the lecture hall beneath this platform crowded at each prayer meeting, and we shall see in this place young men devoting themselves to God; we shall find ministers raised up, and trained, and sent forth to carry the sacred fire to other parts of the globe. . . . If God shall bless us, He will make us a blessing to multitudes of others.

Let God but send down the fire, and the biggest sinners in the neighbourhood will be converted; those who live in dens of infamy will be changed; the drunkard will forsake his cups, the swearer will repent of his blasphemy, the debauched will leave their lusts—

Dry bones be raised, and clothed afresh,
And hearts of stone be turned to flesh.

Spurgeon, from his first sermon in the
Metropolitan Tabernacle, March 31, 1861.

9

The Metropolitan Tabernacle

Spurgeon had been in London merely two years when plans were begun to build a large new church.

Despite the enthusiasm in his ministry manifested by the deacons and the people, some questioned the wisdom of this action. Just thirty years earlier Edward Irving, the Presbyterian orator, had taken London by storm, and a magnificent church had been erected for him. But he had quickly faded from public attention, and there were those who said the same would be true of Spurgeon and that his people too would be left with a nearly empty building and a huge debt.

Nevertheless, the vast majority were strongly in favor of going forward with the project. An excellent piece of property was acquired at Newington Butts—an area south of the Thames at a busy junction of three roads—at the cost of £5,000. A design for a building to seat 3,600 and to have temporary seating and standing room for almost 2,000 more was accepted.

The new church was to be called "The Metropolitan Tabernacle." Spurgeon made much of the fact that the architecture was Grecian, a relationship, he said, that was dear to the evangelical heart, for the New Testament was written in Greek.

Much time was consumed in these preliminary arrangements, but meanwhile Spurgeon was, if possible, busier than ever.

Among other activities, he now addressed the largest gathering of his entire career. There had been a mutiny in India against Britain's rule over that land, and a service of national humiliation was planned. It was to be held in the Crystal Palace and was to be addressed by the one man with voice enough to reach the expected gigantic audience—C. H. Spurgeon.

The day before the service, he went to the Palace to weigh up the task he was facing. The building had not been planned with any thought of meetings, and in order to test the acoustics he repeated several times the Scripture, "Behold the Lamb of God which taketh away the sin of the world." His words were heard by a man who was working somewhere in the building. That man came to him some days later to say the message of the verse had reached his heart, and he had come to know the Lord Jesus Christ.

The people attending the service—counted at turnstiles as they entered—numbered 23,654. This was undoubtedly the largest indoor congregation ever reached with the human voice in all history until that time.

As he preached, Spurgeon was critical of England's actions in India. He called for national repentance and humiliation. "There were no words of commendation for the Government in that sermon. He impeached their treatment of India, and reminded them that only righteousness could exalt a nation."[1] An offering was received to help persons wounded in the mutiny, and it amounted to £675. Following the service—held on a Wednesday evening—Spurgeon was so exhausted that he slept two nights and a day. He did not wake up till Friday morning.

Spurgeon's chief project during that time was raising money for the new Tabernacle.

The estimated cost was £13,000, and he held to the principle that there must never be any debt in doing the Lord's work. This place must be entirely paid for before it was opened, and he was prepared to take upon himself the responsibility of providing a considerable portion of the costs.

To begin, he gave a series of weeknight lectures in Exeter Hall. His subjects were of general educational interest, and at each meeting an offering was received. He also accepted as many as possible of the numerous invitations he received to come and preach. When

---

1. Thomas Handford, *Spurgeon: Episodes and Anecdotes of His Busy Life* (Chicago: Morril, Higgins, 1892), p. 34.

the journey was short he traveled by horse and carriage, but for the longer trips he went by train, and that could be a grimy and exhausting experience. When being put up for the night in someone's home he asked for "a quiet place" and said, "It is the lionizing that tires me," and he sought escape from the pressure of the crowd. The story is told that when staying in a small hotel one night, he asked that he be awakened at five in the morning to catch a train. At three a youth knocked upon his door, and when Spurgeon finally answered, the lad said, "Just to let you know, sir, that you have only two more hours to sleep."

In accepting these invitations Spurgeon suggested to each pastor that half the amount received in the offering go to the work of that church and the other half be used toward the construction of his new Tabernacle. This was always an agreeable arrangement, but sometimes he saw some special need—for instance, a farmer who had suffered years of crop failure or a minister who was trying to bring up a family on £60 a year—and he devoted the whole to meet such a necessity.

This labor took Spurgeon to Ireland for some days of meetings. Many of the people at first considered him inferior to their own great evangelist, Grattan Guinness, but before long they forgot the human comparison and were much drawn to the gospel Spurgeon preached.

The heavy agenda of traveling and preaching he had set for himself soon proved too much for him to bear. After his return from Ireland he was too ill to continue and was laid aside for nearly a month. This was the first indication of the breaking down of his health and a sign that throughout the rest of his life his labors would often be conducted under severe physical difficulty.

Nevertheless, as soon as he was able, he became fully active again. On the afternoon of August 15, 1859, the foundation stone of the Tabernacle was laid. Although it was a weekday (Tuesday), some 3,000 persons were present; an esteemed Christian baronet, Sir Morton Peto, was in the chair. Spurgeon and his father each gave an address. A large ceramic jar containing a Bible, a copy of the Baptist confession of faith, Dr. Rippon's hymn book, and the program of the day's proceedings was placed beneath the stone. In the evening another meeting was held. That day the offering was well over £4,000.

Spurgeon was also devoting to the Tabernacle the income derived from the sale of his sermons. A sermon was published each week and was circulated among subscribers throughout the British Isles, in Canada, Australia, and New Zealand, and translations were being made into German, Dutch, French, Italian, and Swedish. There was also a very large circulation in America. Moreover, at the end of each year a volume containing fifty-two sermons was produced, and for that there was a similar international demand.

The Americans were not satisfied merely to read Spurgeon—they wanted to hear him, too. He received several invitations to visit the United States. The first offered him "£10,000 to preach four discourses in the splendid and spacious music hall of New York." Whether or not he decided to go we do not know, but a London paper said he did, and announced, "He will leave England in April, and will preach at Rochester, at Boston or Philadelphia as well as at New York." Another journal said he would not accept the £10,000, but would go on an independent basis.

The idea was soon dropped by both sides.

A young black man who had escaped from a slave owner in South Carolina was then in England, giving talks on his experiences. He was a true Christian, and Spurgeon had him come to an evening service and tell of his sufferings and his escape.

The matter of slavery was then sorely dividing America and leading toward civil war, and Spurgeon's action brought strong criticism upon him. Persons in both north and south demanded that he clearly declare his position on the matter, and in reply he wrote an article for an American publication.

> I do from my inmost soul detest slavery . . . and although I commune at the Lord's table with men of all creeds, yet with a slave-holder I have no fellowship or any sort or kind. Whenever one has called upon me, I have considered it my duty to express my detestation of his wickedness, and I would as soon think of receiving a murderer into my church . . . as a man-stealer.[2]

Of course, such statements drew a storm of protest, especially in the southern states. Effigies of Spurgeon were burned in several places, his American publishers suspended the printing of his sermons, and various papers urged readers to destroy any they might possess and to forgo all purchase of his publications in the future. Thus the income from America was largely cut off.

2. G. Holden Pike, *The Life and Work of Charles Haddon Spurgeon*, 6 vols. (London: Cassel, 1898), 2:331.

Spurgeon had recognized his statements would provoke severe opposition, so their reaction was no surprise. But being so strongly moved against slavery he could do nothing else, and he willingly suffered this financial loss.

Nevertheless, money came in steadily from other lands. In his task of preaching the gospel and raising support Spurgeon spent some days in Wales, was at Bristol and Birmingham, and took a trip to Scotland, ministering in various places in England on the way. He visited Europe, was warmly received in Paris where he preached by means of an interpreter, and in one of the great experiences of his life he preached in Calvin's pulpit in Geneva, Switzerland. And from all of these journeyings he came home with added funds toward the new building.

Providentially, one of the deacons of the church, William Higgs, was a successful contractor. He was a man of pronounced Christian character who also excelled at his profession, and he was awarded the contract for the construction of the Tabernacle. Between Higgs and Spurgeon there was the happiest relationship as stone by stone the great new structure took shape.

Construction lasted nearly two years, and the cost, which had been estimated at £13,000, became £31,000.

Just before the building was ready to be opened, since the entire costs had not yet been met, a great bazaar was held to raise the remaining amount. This action caused questioning in many evangelical minds then, and it will do the same today. But Spurgeon believed in the practice, and the receipts from the bazaar enabled him to open the building free from all debt.

The first Sunday service in the Metropolitan Tabernacle was held on Sunday, March 31, 1861.

Of course, this was a high day for Spurgeon. He was only twenty-six, yet under his leadership his congregation had grown from the eighty or so he first addressed in London to 6,000 or more and from the New Park Street Chapel to this great edifice—the largest Nonconformist church in the world. Yet his joy lay not especially in these accomplishments but in the fact that he would now have a church home, a building in which the activities of his people would center, in which they would be built up in the things of God, and to which outsiders would be drawn in great numbers to hear the gospel and to enter the Christian life.

The Tabernacle was admirably planned to meet the needs of Spurgeon's ministry. In addition to the floor level (referred to in those days as "the Area"), there were two galleries. The whole had seating for about 3,600. At the ends of the pews were flap seats, which, when lifted into position (held by iron rods) could seat another thousand. Besides this, there was standing room for well over a thousand more, and the reports of nearly 6,000 being packed into the building are probably true.

Behind the auditorium, at the level of the first gallery, were three vestries, the center one for the pastor, the others for the deacons and the elders. Above this level, parallel with the second gallery, were a ladies' parlor and rooms for storing Bibles and books, ready for distribution.

The auditorium had no actual pulpit. A curving platform projected out from the front of the first gallery. It had an open railing and contained a table and a settee for the pastor and behind them a row of chairs for the deacons. Beneath this preaching platform was another of equal size in which there was set a marble baptistry, which was, as Spurgeon desired, fully visible to all. A temporary floor was put over the baptistry for the celebration of the Lord's Supper, and on those occasions this area held the Communion table and chairs.

There was no organ and no choir. A precentor set the pitch of each hymn with a tuning fork and led the singing with his own voice. People who wished to attend regularly paid for a seat on a three-months' basis and were admitted by ticket. Others remained outside till five minutes before the beginning of the service, at which time the restriction was removed and the crowd rushed in and filled the rest of the building.

There were more than 3,000 seat holders, and the money thus received constituted the Tabernacle's chief income. There were no collection plates, and no offering was taken up during the services. Spurgeon accepted no salary after his books and sermons began to sell so widely, but there was a box near the entrance of the building in which gifts for the support of the college could be placed. There may have been other boxes for general contributions.

Since he was ever conscious of the Surrey Garden Music Hall tragedy, Spurgeon made sure the Tabernacle was very strongly constructed. Moreover, if ever the need should arise that the audience be removed from the building in a hurry, it could be done with speed and with safety, for each gallery had its own set of stairways. These were of adequate size and ran down all the way to their individual exit doors.

Beneath the auditorium was a full basement. It held a large lecture hall, extensive Sunday school facilities, and a well-furnished kitchen.

The meetings celebrating the opening of the Tabernacle lasted for two weeks. The first words Spurgeon spoke in the new building clearly declared his doctrinal position and his overall purpose.

> I would propose that the subject of the ministry in this house, as long as this platform shall stand, and as long as this house shall be frequented by worshippers, shall be the person of Jesus Christ.
>
> I am never ashamed to avow myself a Calvinist; I do not hesitate to take the name of Baptist; but if I am asked what is my creed, I reply, "It is Jesus Christ." . . . Jesus, who is the sum and substance of the Gospel, who is in Himself all theology, the incarnation of every precious truth, the all-glorious personal embodiment of the way, the truth and the life.[3]

Several other ministers joined Spurgeon and his people throughout those grand weeks. One day was given over to the exposition of "The Five Points of Calvinism," and Spurgeon had five visiting pastors share the speaking with him on this day of instruction and declaration. Spurgeon himself replied to objections often raised against Calvinism, asserting that most of the great men of God of previous centuries had held this form of doctrine and that this was the body of truth God had historically used in sending revival.[4]

As the church entered its long history of labor for the Lord in the new Tabernacle, one of the first features of its work was the baptism of large numbers of people and their reception into the membership. At one end of the baptistry were two built-in boxes, one at each side, and in those stood two deacons, ready to assist the candidates as they came into the pool. Other deacons guided the men to and from the baptistry, and Mrs. Spurgeon did the same for the ladies. Spurgeon conducted the ordinance with magnificent propriety, and the whole proved a beautiful picture of being "buried with Christ by baptism into death" and "raised with Him to walk in newness of life."

A month after the Tabernacle was opened 77 persons were received for baptism and church membership; the following month another 72 were thus received, and when another month had

3. Iain Murray, ed., *The Full Harvest* (London: Banner of Truth, 1973), p. 34.
4. The sermons delivered during the celebration of the opening of the Tabernacle can be found in *The Sword and the Trowel*, 1861, pp. 169-200 and 297-344.

passed a further 121 were added. If we bear in mind the evidence of true conversion that Spurgeon required—in contrast with the methods often used today—these figures become all the more noteworthy. The membership, which at the time of Spurgeon's coming to London had been 313 (less than 100 of whom were active), had become more than 2,000, and now that the church had its own home the prospect of growing still more rapidly lay immediately ahead.

The completion of the Tabernacle not only gave Spurgeon an adequate place in which to minister, but it also provided a statement of the solidness of his work. The New Park Street Chapel had always been sadly insufficient, and both Exeter Hall and Surrey Hall were someone else's property. The lack of a permanent meeting place of their own had given strength to the assertions that Spurgeon's ministry was not permanent and that he would soon fade away. But now all could not help but recognize that he was there to stay. In turn, the opposition, which for months had been gradually disappearing, became still less, and the tendency to accept and even to admire him was noticeably increased.

Spurgeon joyfully settled into his ministry at the Tabernacle. The building was to be the scene of his preaching, the center of his life, and the site of multiplied miracles of grace till thirty-one years later when, a tired warrior and a faithful servant, he heard the voice that called him home.

What was wanted was an institution where these rough-and-ready men could be drilled in the simple rudiments of education, and so fitted for the work of preaching and the discharge of plain pastoral duties.

From the commencement our main object was to help men who, through lack of funds, could not obtain an education for themselves. These have been supplied not only with tuition and books, gratis, but with board and lodging, and in some cases with clothes and pocket money. . . .

Scholarship for its own sake was never sought . . . but to help men to become efficient preachers has been, and ever will be, the sole aim of those concerned in its management. I shall not, in order to increase our prestige, refuse poor men, or zealous young Christians whose early education has been neglected. Pride would suggest that we take a "better class of men," but experience shows that . . . eminently successful men spring from all ranks, that diamonds may be found in the rough.

Spurgeon

10

Training Young Preachers

During Spurgeon's first year in London he came to know a young man named Thomas Medhurst. Medhurst had been brought up in James Wells's Church but had never been born again. He had recently done a little acting and hoped to earn a living on the stage.

But upon hearing Spurgeon he was converted and soon experienced a tremendous zeal to spread the gospel. He began to preach in the open air in some of London's roughest districts, and before long he brought two converts to Spurgeon asking that he baptize them. With great earnestness he expressed his certainty that God had called him to His work and declared his determination to spend his life preaching and winning souls.

Like numerous other young men in those days, Medhurst had little learning and was uncultured in his ways. Nevertheless, Spurgeon believed he was called of God, and recognizing he possessed both a true zeal and a native gift of utterance, he felt responsible to help him. He arranged for him to attend a boarding school operated by a minister at Bexley and undertook to defray all the costs. Once a week Medhurst was to visit Spurgeon for an afternoon of instruction in theology and in ministerial work in general.

In no time, other young men, moved by the spiritual fervor of Spurgeon's preaching, expressed their desire to have the same training. They too were zealous for God and were busy preaching in mission halls or Ragged Schools or on the street corners, but they also were sorely in need of education. In the face of this appeal Spurgeon realized God was placing upon him a heavy responsibility. He had not sought it, but it was now evident that he must found and maintain a ministerial training school, with all the burden and yet all the joy such as enterprise could bring.

With this prospect in mind he looked for a man capable of leading such an institution. The person selected must be sound in the faith and possess both theological knowledge and evangelical warmth, and he prayed God would raise up such a man. While he prayed, a man who possessed those qualities, George Rogers, was also praying for a means to begin the task to which he knew God had called him—that of training men for the work of the ministry.

Rogers was a Congregationalist and did not accept Spurgeon's position on believers' baptism. But the two men had all other doctrines in common, and an agreement was reached between them. Spurgeon formed an institution he called "the Pastors' College," and he made George Rogers its principal.

During its first years the classes were held in Rogers's home, and the eight students boarded there too. Spurgeon personally undertook the entire financial responsibility, depending largely on the income received from the sale of his sermons and books. But it was shortly after the college began that this income was greatly reduced by the lack of sale in America, and although he and Mrs. Spurgeon economized fully, they were often brought into difficulty. At one point Spurgeon spoke of selling his horse and carriage, but since he could not possibly get along without transportation Rogers talked him out of the idea. Then, at that very time, a note from a banker informed him that an anonymous donor had deposited £200 to the college's credit, and before long another £100 was similarly placed in the same bank. These events of miraculous supply steadily increased Spurgeon's faith and enabled him to believe the Lord would provide.

With the increase in the college attendance the classes were held in the New Park Street Chapel, and the students were boarded in the homes of members.

But with the opening of the Tabernacle the college was transferred to the lecture hall and its adjoining rooms in the lower level, thus giving it much improved facilities. Moreover, the deacons and the people of the Tabernacle realized this burden had become too large for their pastor to bear alone—there were now sixteen students, and several more had applied for admission—so they agreed to install a box in which offerings for the college might be placed.

Spurgeon had definite goals for the college. There were three other Baptist ministerial schools in England, but this one was to fill needs the others failed to meet.

Although some men who came to the college had been brought up in good homes and had received considerable schooling, the majority who applied came from poorer circumstances, and it was for those that Spurgeon had particular concern. He wanted men who (1) had been truly born again; (2) had experienced the call of God to the ministry; and (3) under the effect of those two experiences had begun to preach and had been active in this undertaking for some time—preferably two years. He made much of the fact that he was not trying "to make preachers," but to help some who were already engaged in that work "become better preachers."

It was not Spurgeon's purpose to produce men who were scholars and little or nothing else, as was the case with many schools. In his college, learning was a means to an end—to enable men to be powerful preachers and fervent soul-winners. The whole of the institution's life was patterned to fulfill this purpose.

The Pastors' College had also a clear doctrinal emphasis. "Calvinistic theology," said Spurgeon, "is dogmatically taught . . . not dogmatic in the offensive sense, but as the undoubted teaching of the Word of God."[1] The Regent's Park College also claimed to be Calvinistic in its theology, but Spurgeon doubted that those doctrinal concepts were taught there in a manner that aroused men to evangelistic zeal and gave powerfully convicting force to the message they proclaimed.

The course at the college lasted merely two years, and except in the case of a few who could afford to pay, the tuition and board were free, and clothing, books, and even pocket money were provided. There were no examinatons, no graduation exercises, and no degrees. The lack of such accepted accompaniments of college life, together with the shortness of the course, brought many criticisms from outsiders.

But this school had a benefit the others did not possess. The college was part of the life of the Tabernacle, and association with a great and active church provided a wealth of instruction and a power of inspiration to be found nowhere else.

Moreover, Spurgeon maintained a personal relationship with all

1. *The Sword and the Trowel,* 1866, p. 36.

his students. He interviewed the men who applied for admission, and although he refused many, those he accepted received his warm encouragement and immediately knew him to be their friend. This relationship continued throughout their days in the college, and men went to him freely for his advice and, if necessary, his reprimand. In his concern he was ever mindful of men's needs. For instance, noticing on one occasion that a certain student's clothes were badly worn, Spurgeon stopped him and asked that he go on an errand for him. He gave the man a note to deliver to a certain address and told him to wait for a reply. The address turned out to be that of a tailor's shop, and the reply was a new suit and coat with which the tailor provided him. Spurgeon's slightly playful action in this matter was typical of many such deeds he did on behalf of his students.

Shortly after the college was moved to the Tabernacle, Spurgeon began his Friday afternoon lectures. Some of those were later published and have long been widely known—*Lectures to My Students*. He said that the manner of teaching in the school was "not formal and dictatorial, but familiar and fraternal," and this was nowhere more true than in the Friday afternoon gatherings. The students had come to the end of a tiring week of study, and most were also preparing to preach on Sunday, and Spurgeon purposely mingled something of his native humor with his serious presentation concerning the work of the ministry. One of the students reported:

> In those days the President was in his prime. His step was firm, his eyes bright, his hair dark and abundant, his voice full of sweetest music and sacred merriment. Before him were gathered a hundred men from all parts of the United Kingdom, and not a few from beyond the seas. They had been brought together by the magic of his name and the attraction of his personal influence. . . . Many sitting before him were his own sons in the faith. Among his students he was at his ease, as a father in the midst of his own family. The brethren loved him and he loved them.
>
> Soon the floods of his pent-up wisdom poured forth, the flashes of his inimitable wit lit up every face, and his pathos brought tears to all eyes. It was an epoch in student life to hear him deliver his *Lectures to My Students*.
>
> What weighty and wise discourse he gave us on the subject of preaching! How gently he corrected faults and encouraged genuine diffidence! What withering sarcasm for all fops and pretenders!

Then came those wonderful imitations of the dear brethren's peculiar mannerisms; one with the hot dumpling in his mouth, trying to speak; another sweeping his hand up and down from nose to knee; a third with his hands under his coat-tails, making the figure of a water-wagtail. Then the one with his thumbs in the armholes of his waistcoat, showing the penguin style of oratory. By this means he held the mirror before us so that we could see our faults, yet all the while we were almost convulsed with laughter. He administered the medicine in effervescing draughts.

After this came the wise counsel, so kind, so grave, so gracious, so fatherly; then the prayer that lifted us to the mercy-seat, where we caught glimpses of glory, and talked face to face with the Master Himself.

Afterwards, the giving out of appointments for the next Lord's day took place; the class was dismissed for tea, and then came the men who wanted advice. Some were in trouble, others in joy, and the President listened patiently to all their tales; anon he would laugh, and then he would weep. At last, he is through, "weary in the work, but not weary of it." His cheery voice gradually dies away as he ascends the stairs to his "sanctum."[2]

Many of my readers will have read Spurgeon's *Lectures to My Students,* recalling with joy such subjects as "The Minister's Self Watch," "The Call to Ministry," "Sermons—Their Matter," and "The Faculty of Impromptu Speech." The lectures are evidence of the standards set in the college. At the time he gave them Spurgeon was only thirty-four.

The college now had three instructors beside Mr. Rogers. They were Alexander Ferguson, David Gracey, and W. R. Selway. The school majored on the study of theology, but the whole course was similar to that of many seminaries, and Rogers listed other chief subjects as "Mathematics, Logic, Hebrew, the Greek Testament, Homiletics, Pastoral Theology and English Composition."[3] Spurgeon mentions astronomy also as part of the course in physical science, and some of the men became, like himself, particularly interested in the stars and the laws governing the heavenly bodies.

To the work of the college throughout the day Spurgeon added that of evening classes, the regular pastoral course for those who could not be present in the daytime.

But there were also studies of a more primary nature. Since England had no national educational system at the time, the children of poorer families usually grew up with little or no schooling.

---

2. Iain Murray, ed., *The Full Harvest* (London: Banner of Truth, 1973), pp. 108-9.
3. *The Sword and the Trowel,* 1875, p. 6.

Many young men were unemployed, and several who had jobs were fixed in a condition of poverty, working long hours for small wages. Due to their lack of learning, they had virtually no prospect of improving their lot in life. For such men—particularly for those who were members of the Tabernacle—Spurgeon made the beginnings of an education available. The evening classes, like those of the day, were provided free of charge; the number in attendance was about two hundred each evening, and many young men who earnestly entered upon those studies found not only their mental powers disciplined and knowledge enlarged, but also their whole outlook elevated. Undoubtedly many rose to better conditions in life as a result of the evening classes, and we may be sure the social impact of this work was felt throughout the whole area of south London.

Though the college held no examinations, most students were motivated by a desire to earn Spurgeon's approval, and that motivated them still more when they went out into the work. The graduates of other colleges usually went into the ministry with little or no experience in actual preaching. But with Spurgeon's men things were different, for they had preached before entering the college, and during their student days most had been active nearly every Sunday. Thus, when they entered upon their full-time labors they did so with considerable preaching experience. Moreover, they possessed spiritual fervor and were determined to exercise a vigorous, sacrificial, and soul-winning ministry.

Several churches wanted Spurgeon men. Some were fairly large, some were smaller, and some were suffering difficulties. Knowing the situations, Spurgeon personally chose the men he believed would best meet them.

Many men went to places where there were no churches and built them. Some went to good residential areas, others to poor districts. Some went to the slums—and there they witnessed for the Lord, preached on the street corners, visited door to door, and gave out tracts. They then secured meeting places of some kind and gathered people in, won them to the Lord, baptized them, and organized them into a church.

By 1866, in London alone the Spurgeon men had formed eighteen new churches. For eight of those, new chapels had been erected, and the other ten were expecting soon to begin construction. Preaching was carried on at another seven stations, and the plans were that in each of those a church would shortly be organized.

Seven old and decaying churches had been revived, and among the other eighty former College men who were ministering in various parts of Britain blessings were being constantly manifested.[4]

One man went to a church that had been reduced to eighteen people. But within a few years he had baptized some eight hundred. Among college men, baptism was administered only after there was clear evidence of the new birth, and Spurgeon's students largely followed his own methods in leading souls to Christ and accepting them as believers.

The college added heavily to Spurgeon's already weighty load of responsibilities. Its operating expenses amounted to £100 a week. Money from sales in Australia, Canada, and several other lands, as well as from various parts of Britain, supplemented the giving of the Tabernacle people. Nevertheless, there were several occasions on which the treasury seemed almost depleted, and although he suffered under the burden, Spurgeon saw the hand of God move in the miraculous supplying of the need—often without his even knowing whence the money came.

During his first few months in London, Spurgeon taught his people to strive with God in prayer. And such true praying continued to characterize their lives. This was manifest especially during the Week of Prayer with which he usually opened the new year. The first week of 1856 was attended by a visiting minister, who told first of a time in which the failures of pastors were confessed.

> Sins of omission and commission, neglect and shortcomings were acknowledged. Solemn, simple, earnest appeal was made to the eye of the heart-searching God, that His servants might wish to hide nothing from His gaze. . . . And when the words, "Lord, is it I? is it I?" were uttered, many broke forth saying, "It is I! it is I!" The beloved pastor of the Tabernacle Church wept like a child, and sobbed aloud, while the brethren around could not restrain their weeping and groaning before God.[5]

Prayer then was made for the people in general, and "many felt that they had never before seen such real, awful, general grief as that which rolled over the spirits of that vast assembly. God the

4. These figures are given in G. Holden Pike, *The Life and Work of Charles Haddon Spurgeon*, 6 vols. (London: Cassel, 1898), 3:15.
5. *The Sword and the Trowel*, 1865, p. 68.

Holy Ghost was there, and His people had a sight of themselves, and of their ways, in the very light of His holiness. . . . Great, indeed, was the relief and calm, the peace which followed the sweet words uttered by Mr. Spurgeon: 'There is a fountain filled with blood.' "[6]

Then prayer was made for the unconverted. "The earnest work of supplication was ended by Pastors Scott and C. H. Spurgeon pleading with God for anxious and careless souls present. . . . a number of Christians retired into a room below with many anxious ones, several of whom received peace with God through faith in the precious Saviour. Many of these have since been seen by Mr. Spurgeon who tell us that he conversed personally with no less than seventy-five enquirers in one day subsequent to the meeting."[7]

This report, though much abbreviated from the magnificent account originally written, lets us see something of the intense fervor and reality of faith of Spurgeon's people, and it also reveals something more of the methods he used in leading souls to Christ.

Moreover, this praying opened the door to undertakings besides the Pastors' College—a monthly magazine, a home for aged women, and an orphanage for needy children.

6. Ibid.
7. Ibid.

In all probability every one of the great enter-prises which the Tabernacle has undertaken and ev-ery charity Mr. Spurgeon has espoused, either had its origin in some article in the Sword and Trowel *or was chiefly indebted to that publication for its con-tinued support. . . . The Orphanage was due to an article Mrs. Hillyard read in that magazine, and the first gift for the building of the Pastors' College and the first donation towards the Girls' Orphanage came directly in response to an editorial in the* Sword and Trowel.

Russell H. Conwell,
*The Life of Charles H. Spurgeon,*1892

11

The Growth of the Spurgeonic Enterprises

In 1865 Spurgeon took another historic step in his work—he began to publish a monthly magazine, *The Sword and the Trowel*. The title carried also a second line: "A Record of Combat With Sin, and Labour For the Lord."

In his first issue he declared its purposes.

> Our Magazine is intended to report the efforts of those Churches and Associations, which are more or less intimately connected with the Lord's work at the Metropolitan Tabernacle, and to advocate those views of doctrine and Church order which are most certainly received among us. . . .
>
> We feel the want of some organ of communication in which our many plans for God's glory may be brought before believers, and commended to their aid. Our friends are so numerous as to be able to maintain a Magazine, and so earnest as to require one. . . .
>
> We do not pretend to be unsectarian, if by this is meant the absence of all distinctive principles, and a desire to please parties of all shades of opinion. We believe and therefore speak. We speak in love, but not in soft words and trimming sentences. We shall not court controversy, but we shall not shun it when the cause of God demands it. . . .
>
> We shall supply interesting reading upon general topics, but our chief aim will be to arouse believers to action, and to suggest to them plans by

which the kingdom of Jesus may be extended. . . . We would sound the
trumpet, and lead our comrades to the fight. We would ply the Trowel with
untiring hand for the building up of Jerusalem's dilapidated walls, and
wield the Sword with vigour and valour against the enemies of the truth.[1]

The magazine showed something of the range and intensity of
Spurgeon's mind. Each month he published an article of some thorough spiritual and biblical substance; he frequently commented on
conditions in the religious world, providing facts and figures to
show the increase or loss experienced among various denominations. There was news of the Lord's work at home and in distant
lands, with reports of the going or return of missionaries. Each issue
carried book reviews, almost all of them written by Spurgeon himself. From time to time there could be a poetical composition from
his pen or an account of the life of some great Christian from
preceding centuries—one of the early Fathers, a Reformer, or perhaps some mighty figure from among the Puritans.

The magazine added heavily to Spurgeon's responsibilities. Already he published a sermon every week; in 1865 he produced his
Morning by Morning and a little later *Our Own Hymn Book.* Also
at this time he began working on the major literary production of
his career, *The Treasury of David,* the seven volumes of which
would appear one by one over the following twenty years.

By this time the Tabernacle had become a multifaceted organization with several activities that required his direction and care.

The Pastors' College in 1865 had 93 students, besides some 230
in the evening classes. The Sunday school had an attendance of
about 900 with 75 teachers, and Spurgeon's report stated that "other Sunday Schools and Ragged Schools are sustained and conducted
in other districts in connection with the Tabernacle." After mentioning "an Evangelists' Association which has numerous preaching
stations in neglected districts . . . sustained by the students at the
evening classes," the report goes on to state:

> There are numerous Bible classes in connection with the Tabernacle.
> One is held every Monday evening after the prayer meeting. . . . Bible
> Classses are conducted by Mr. Stiff, Mr. Hanks and Mr. John Olney. All are
> efficient and well attended. A ladies' class, conducted by Mrs. Bartlett, is
> both the most numerous and most remarkable in its immediate results: it
> numbers nearly 700, and 63 have joined the Church from it during the
> past year.

1. *The Sword and the Trowel,* 1865, pp. 1-2.

There is a Bible-society depot at the Tabernacle, at which Bibles are sold at cost price. There is a Tract Society in extensive operation. There is a Jews' Society which holds its meetings monthly. A Ladies' Benevolent Society, A Maternal Association, a Missionary Working Society and a Sunday School Working Society are also in full operation. A Ministers' Fraternal Association has lately been established. . . . Two City Missionaries are sustained by the Church and people; two other missionaries on the Continent, in Germany, and considerable aid is given to foreign missions.[2]

Spurgeon proved marvelously adept at choosing people to undertake various tasks. The activities operated without friction, and peacefulness was maintained not by the giving of orders on Spurgeon's part but by the people's desire to prosecute the work of the Lord. Nevertheless, the growing body of organizations was, in its final analysis, Spurgeon's burden, and from time to time he felt it was becoming too heavy for him.

The title *The Sword and the Trowel* provided a true picture of Spurgeon's ministry. He was ever in "Combat with Sin" and in "Labour for the Lord," fighting wrong belief and wrong action and striving mightily to build God's work.

In 1864 he engaged in one of the supreme conflicts of his life, the "Baptismal Regeneration Controversy." During the early 1830s the Tractarian Movement led by John Henry (later Cardinal) Newman had begun in Oxford. It asserted that since the clergy of the Church of England admitted that the authority for their ordination came through their church's descent from the Roman Catholic Church, they were really part of the Roman body and ought to return to it. On this basis Newman and several other clergy led numerous people to the Roman communion. In turn, a sentiment began to grow within the Church of England that favored the use of Roman practices and beliefs and accepted the idea that a total Anglican gravitation to Rome was highly probable.

Within the Church of England, however, there were a number of evangelical clergy who strongly opposed the Romanizing tendencies. Spurgeon held those men, especially their leader, Bishop J. C. Ryle, in high esteem. But he felt such men were working against the evangelical cause by their acceptance of "infant baptism," a rite, he said, believed by Anglicans to mean "regeneration." Spurgeon considered the practice to be teaching "salvation by works," which was

2. Ibid., pp. 174-75.

therefore a direct contradiction of "justification by faith" and of the Savior's declaration "Ye must be born again."

By 1864 Spurgeon felt he must declare his soul on this matter. He informed his publishers that the step he was about to take would severely lower the sale of his sermons and his books, but that he would not on that account refrain from preaching against a teaching that he believed was misguiding millions.

He preached a sermon entitled "Baptismal Regeneration." He spoke with conviction and force, declaring that the Prayer Book taught that the sprinkling of an infant made the little one regenerate, and he denounced the teaching as false. His words were directed especially against the evangelical clergymen, as he charged them with inconsistency in asserting that the babe was regenerate and then telling such a one when it grew up that it was unregenerate and must be converted. Something of his fervor is seen in his statement: "We want John Knox back again. Do not talk to me of mild and gentle men, of soft manners and squeamish words. We want the fiery Knox, and even though his vehemence should 'ding our pulpits into blads,' it were well if he did but rouse our hearts to action."[3]

News of this sermon spread quickly across Britain. But instead of reducing the sale of his sermons, it increased it. This one soon had a circulation of 180,000, and the figure rose shortly to 350,000. It provoked a tremendous number of replies, most against, but some for. He replied to some of the opposers and carried his battle further in three additional sermons, calling for all true believers to make the sacrifice of "going forth unto Him, without the camp, bearing His reproach."

Spurgeon's action cost him many friends. Lord Shaftesbury, who had stood with him in his charitable endeavors, now said, "You are a very saucy fellow!" Several clergymen had raised money toward the construction of the Tabernacle, and now they believed Spurgeon had betrayed their trust. Many of them were members of the Evangelical Alliance, of which he was a prominent figure. Believing he could no longer be linked with them in this way, he now withdrew his membership. There was strong feeling against him, yet almost all who entertained it recognized he spoke only from deep conviction, entirely without malice, and, as the future actions of many showed, they admired him still.

But though Spurgeon thus wielded the sword, he was much more

---

3. *The Metropolitan Tabernacle Pulpit,* 10 (1864):323.

active in using the trowel. All his enterprises were growing, and new ones also were being born.

A particularly useful new organization was the Colporteurs' Association.

The word *colporteur* was an old French term that meant "pedlar." In Reformation times it had been used of the men who went from place to place distributing tracts and selling Bibles, and in more recent years it had been applied to men who were doing a similar work in Scotland. Spurgeon had seen this labor and its fruits during his visits to that land, and despite the many activities for which he was already responsible he determined to launch into this undertaking in England too.

As soon as Spurgeon mentioned the idea a man offered a substantial sum of money with which to begin it—enough to purchase a stock of Bibles, books, and tracts. Spurgeon then drew up a statement of the purposes of the organization and appointed a committee to oversee it.

Men arose who were willing to serve as colporteurs. Spurgeon agreed to raise £40 per year for each man, but each was expected also to earn at least another £40 from the Bibles and books he sold.

The Association began with only two men. But their number rapidly rose, and within three years fifteen were employed. Each man was allotted a definite territory. Some of these were in the poor parts and even the slums of London and other cities, but most were placed in villages and rural areas. The plan was to carry the Bible's message into the parts of England that were unreached through other means.

The colporteur did much more than sell Bibles and books.

> He converses with the inmates about their souls, prays with the sick, and leaves a tract at each cottage. He is frequently able to hold prayer-meetings, open-air services and Bible-readings. He gets a room [a meeting place] if possible, and preaches; founds Bands of Hope, and makes himself generally useful in the cause of religion and temperance. He is, in fact, first of all a missionary, then a preacher, and by-and-by in the truest sense, a pastor. We have some noble men in this work.[4]

Despite the help of an excellent committee, this work was not conducted without difficulty. In time the number of colporteurs increased to nearly one hundred, and there were often occasions

4. G. Holden Pike, *The Life and Work of Charles Haddon Spurgeon*, 6 vols. (London: Cassel, 1898), 3:164.

when the treasury was short of sufficient funds to provide the initial £40 for each man. At such times and on occasions when decisions had to be made as to which man to place in a certain area or to tell a man he was not suited to the colportage work, the matter was left with Spurgeon. He gave heavily out of his own pocket to this enterprise and made earnest prayer for it. At one time, in an hour of depression he declared, "The Association is one child too many for me! I wish somebody would take it off my hands!" And yet, when someone offered to do so, he refused and continued to bear the burden himself.

Nevertheless, like his other organizations, this one also brought him much joy. He instituted a Colportage Association Annual Meeting for which all the men returned to London and after a hearty supper at the Tabernacle gave reports of their work. The men usually spoke in the dialects of their districts, thus adding to the color of the gathering, and Spurgeon was "especially cheered when they related instances of conversion through the reading of his sermons and other published works."

The following is an example of the accounts given by these men. Describing a fallen woman who had been brought to a sense of her sinfulness in the sight of God and who was afterward in a "despairing condition," the colporteur said:

> I drew her attention to many of the promises and invitations of the Gospel, sold her Mr. Spurgeon's "The Gentleness of Jesus," and asked the Lord to bless the reading of it to her soul.
>
> If I could find language sufficiently expressive, I would describe my visit to her on the following day. Holding the sermon in her hand, her voice tremulous with emotion and her face radiant with happiness, she read the following words:—"Hearts are won to Jesus by the silent conviction which irresistibly subdues the conscience to a sense of guilt, and by the love which is displayed in the Redeemer's becoming the great substitutionary sacrifice for us, that our sins might be removed. . . ."
>
> Then, still holding the sermon in her hand, she said to me, "Blessed be the Lord forever, I have found Him; or rather, He has found me! I am saved, pardoned, forgiven, accepted and blessed, for Christ's sake! Now I know what the poet means,
>
>> Nothing in my hands I bring,
>> Simply to Thy Cross I cling.
>
> Yes, yes! Jesus died for me, and I live through Him!"[5]

5. *C. H. Spurgeon's Autobiography*, comp. Susannah Spurgeon and J. W. Harrald, 4 vols. (London: Passmore and Alabaster, 1897), 3:164-65.

On one occasion, at the annual meeting, Spurgeon asked a colporteur to come to the platform with his pack upon his back and demonstrate his method of selling books. Reaching the platform the man immediately placed his pack on the table, took out a book, and began addressing Spurgeon, saying: "I have here a work that I can highly recommend you to buy. I can speak well of it, for I have read it and derived great benefit from it. The author is a particular friend of mine, he is always glad to hear that the colporteurs sell his books, for he knows that they are full of Gospel. The title of the volume is *Trumpet Calls to Christian Energy*, the author is C. H. Spurgeon and the price is 3 shillings, 6 pence. Will you buy it?"[6]

The audience was convulsed with laughter. Spurgeon joined as heartily as any, reached into his pocket, and bought the book.

It is impossible to estimate the value of the colporteurs' ministry. Those were days in which immoral and atheistic literature was becoming widely circulated, and shops that sold nothing else were opening. This material was filtering even to the backward rural districts—areas in which often the Christian voice was very weak. The colporteur counteracted that influence. He placed in home after home the Word of God and books that repeated its message, and in numerous instances the reader was won to Christ.

In 1878, one of the few years for which figures are available, there were 94 colporteurs, and they made the remarkable number of 926,290 visits. And this work grew even larger during the years that followed.

In January 1866 Spurgeon published in the *Sword and Trowel* a letter to all his members, announcing a special week of prayer.

Lord's Day. The Pastor will preach upon a subject having a direct tendency, by God's grace, to arouse the slumbering, whether saints or sinners. . . .

Monday. The Church Officers will meet at five to seek a blessing upon their own souls, that they may be prepared for the shower of mercy which they trust is coming.

At seven we shall hold a prayer-meeting. It would be a hopeful beginning if the house could be filled at this meeting by ourselves . . . As your friends may be more willing to come if assured of getting in, we shall issue tickets . . .

Tuesday. The Deacons and Elders invite the unconverted to meet them at seven. Whether you are under concern of soul or not, we pray you to come, and let us talk to you of the things which make for your peace.

6. Ibid.

Wednesday. The Pastor and Officers invite the young people of the congregation to tea at five o'clock, that they may afterwards hear a loving invitation to look to the Lord Jesus, that they may be saved. This is a meeting, not for young members, but for the unsaved.

Lord's Day. Deputations from the Church Officers desire to visit in the afternoon the class conducted by Mrs. Bartlett, and the classes conducted by Mr. Dransfield and Mr. Croker. The Lord has given prosperity to these works of love . . .

Monday. The Church will meet for thanksgiving, breaking of bread, and prayer, in the area [the main floor] of the Tabernacle at seven o'clock; and the congregation who are the objects of our anxious care are invited to fill the galleries. We desire as a Church to let our united and importunate cry go up to heaven.

Tuesday. The Deacons and Elders a second time invite the unconverted, that they may again uplift the Lord Jesus Christ before them. The Meeting will commence at seven o'clock.

Wednesday. The Pastor and Officers invite the Sunday School Teachers to tea, including all *Members of the Church* who are engaged in Sabbath school or Ragged School work. Meeting afterwards for fellowship in prayer and exhortation.

Friday. The Pastor and Officers will meet the Tutors and Students of the College for tea. Much prayer is requested that this important class of labourers may receive good from our visit.

Monday. Prayer meeting at seven, for the unconverted, with brief exhortations by the Pastor, Deacons and Elders.

Tuesday. Tea at half-past five, for the Tract Distributors, Evangelists, Missionaries, Bible women and other workers. . . .

Wednesday. Prayer Meetings at the various houses of the members, which will be open for the occasion at seven. . . . We pant for a great blessing on these household assemblies.

The series will close on [the following] Monday, with a meeting for praise for mercies which faith now anticipates, but which will then be actually received. O Lord, send now prosperity.[7]

The reports of the week of prayer are a further indication of the manner in which the work of seeking the salvation of the lost was conducted at the Tabernacle. These methods brought forth much fruit, not only at times of particular earnestness, but constantly the work of the Spirit was manifest in deep conviction and life-transforming conversion. Every week a number of persons came before the church to tell their experience of divine grace and to be received for baptism and church membership.

7. *The Sword and the Trowel*, 1866, pp. 91-92.

And while the Tabernacle grew under Spurgeon's ministry, so also did several other churches.

Mention has been made of the work of the College students in bringing new churches into being. In all those efforts Spurgeon took a vital interest, giving toward them himself, raising money for them at the Tabernacle, and obtaining helpers for the students among his people. In 1867 he reported the construction of a new chapel at each of the following: Ealing, Lyonshall, Red Hill, Southampton, Winslow, and Bermondsey, and at all of those and several other places he was asked to lay the first stone.

So often was he called upon to perform this duty that someone gave him a silver-plated trowel, and someone else donated a fine hardwood mallet. So proficient did he become with these tools that people "began to remark on the workman-like manner in which he used them."

So while he constantly used the trowel figuratively, building the work of the Lord by tongue and pen, he also used it literally as he led in the construction of new churches.

It was not long before the fabric of the Tabernacle needed attention. The interior was lighted by gas lamps, and that fuel did not burn cleanly but had a staining effect on walls and ceiling. The building was also subject to a great amount of use, for it was open every day of the week from seven in the morning till eleven at night, and by the time it had served six years it was beginning to look faded and worn. Spurgeon wanted everything in the Lord's work to be kept in first class condition, and therefore in 1867 a complete redecoration was undertaken.

The Tabernacle was under repair for nearly a month. During that time the services were held in a gargantuan structure, the Agricultural Hall. The place was not planned for meetings but for the display of farm and garden produce, and therefore it lacked the acoustic properties necessary for the carrying of the voice. A few persons had tried to use it for meetings but found they could not make themselves heard more than a few yards from the platform. But Spurgeon decided to use it and had seating installed enough to accommodate 15,000. There was standing room for two or three thousand more.

The hall was in the north of London, several miles from the Tabernacle, so many of Spurgeon's regular congregation could not attend. It was widely believed that this time he had attempted something that was too much for him.

But that anticipation proved false. At each of the services some 20,000 attended. Moreover, there was no complaint that any could not hear, and many persons who would never have gone all the way to the Tabernacle came and heard the gospel. In later years D. L. Moody was influenced to use this building for an evangelistic campaign because it had proved suitable for Spurgeon.

In addition to the duties of his ministry at the Tabernacle, with its more than 3,500 members and various organizations, Spurgeon constantly accepted invitations to preach at other churches. Almost every day except Sunday he hastened off to some other church in London. Often he traveled, either by carriage or train, to more distant places. He also journeyed to the Continent: in 1865 he visited Italy and established lasting friendships with the Baptists there; in 1866 he went again to Scotland and addressed the General Assembly of the Scottish National Church; in 1867 he traveled to Germany where he preached through an interpreter and raised money to pay off the debt on a church recently constructed at Hamburg. He became much taken with a Pastor Oncken, a man who, Spurgeon said, knew how to pray with extraordinary fervor.

As the years came and went Spurgeon witnessed the steady success of all the works of his hands. The Tabernacle was ever crowded, and conversions and baptisms were numerous. The attendance at the College was all the accommodation could handle, the readership of the published sermons spread to several lands, *The Sword and the Trowel* subscriptions constantly increased, and each year more colporteurs were added. Nothing failed or even suffered a temporary decline.

But matters were not so promising for Spurgeon himself. Up to this point he had experienced much of youthful health and vigor and had been able to enjoy almost unrestricted activity. But his physical strength began to wane. In October 1867, at the age of thirty-four, he was bed-ridden for a time, subjected as a result of overwork to nervous exhaustion. Upon recovering he thrust himself into his work again with full force but found he was beginning to suffer pain in his feet and legs. His grandfather had long been the victim of rheumatic gout, and now Charles learned that he was suffering from the same ailment. It was an affliction that he was to experience, sometimes amidst intense pain, throughout the rest of his days on earth.

In London alone, one hundred thousand children wander in destitution, preparing for our jails or for early graves. Children of the gutter, their food is scant, their lodging foul, their clothing ragged.

Mr. James Greenwood discovered a family of six living in one small room, among them three little children varying in age from three to eight, stark naked. They were so hideously dirty that every rib-bone of their little bodies showed plain, and they were in colour like mahogany. As soon as he put his head in the door they scattered to the "bed," an arrangement of evil smelling flock and old potato sacks.

Homeless children gather around a muck heap at Covent Garden Market, and gobble up discarded plums and oranges and apples—a sweltering mass of decay—with the avidity of ducks or pigs.

from Spurgeon's review of *The Seven Curses of London,* by James Greenwood

12

Almshouses and Orphanage

Dr. John Rippon, a former pastor of the New Park Street Chapel, had commenced a work to assist several needy widows. He erected a building called the Almshouses in which they lived free of charge, and he provided each with a weekly sum of money.

This work was in operation when Spurgeon came to London. He rejoiced to continue it, but after the Tabernacle was opened it became necessary to move these senior citizens to a location closer and more up-to-date. Therefore, he launched the construction of a new building for them.

The new structure consisted of seventeen small homes, which, in the manner of the times, were joined together in an unbroken row. The women who filled them—all of them elderly—were provided not only with this housing but also with food and clothing and other necessities.

To this structure another was added. Ever concerned to make education available among the host of children who were growing up with little or no means of obtaining it, Spurgeon had a school constructed adjoining the Almshouses. It was an institution accommodating nearly 400 students. At the other end of the Almshouses stood a house for the headmaster.

The Almshouses proved a considerable expense. Spurgeon hoped that some way might be found by which they could be endowed, but such money was not forthcoming, and for some years he paid for the heat, light, and other expenses from his own pocket. In later years, when the Tabernacle people gave him a large sum of money in commemoration of his quarter century of ministry among them, urging that he use it for himself, he gave it all to his charitable works, and the Almshouses had half of it.

At the very time in which he was building the Almshouses, Spurgeon was building also another and much larger institution: an orphanage.

The orphanage came about in the following manner. In addressing his prayer meeting in the summer of 1866 Spurgeon said, "Dear friends, we are a huge church, and should be doing more for the Lord in this great city. I want us, tonight, to ask Him to send us *some new work;* and if we need money to carry it on, let us pray that *the means also may be sent.*"[1]

A few days later Spurgeon received a letter from a Mrs. Hillyard, stating she had some £20,000 which she would like to devote to the training and educating of orphan boys.

From a human point of view this was an unlikely offer. Mrs. Hillyard, the widow of a Church of England clergyman, asked a friend (a man who was not a particular admirer of Spurgeon) to recommend some totally reliable public figure into whose hands she could place her money to have it used for orphan boys, and he immediately replied, "Spurgeon." She had never met the famous preacher, but upon hearing this recommendation she immediately wrote to him.

After further correspondence Spurgeon went, as Mrs. Hillyard requested, to visit her. He took with him his deacon William Higgs, and as they approached the given address they felt the very ordinary quality of the houses in the area hardly suggested an occupant possessing such a sum of money. So as the two men met with Mrs. Hillyard, Spurgeon said,

"We have called, Madam, about the two hundred pounds that you mentioned in your letter."

"Two hundred?" she replied, "I meant to write twenty thousand."

"Oh yes, you did put twenty thousand," said Spurgeon, "but I was not sure whether a nought or two may have slipped in by mistake, and I thought I would be on the safe side."

1. Iain Murray, ed., *The Full Harvest* (London: Banner of Truth, 1973), p. 162.

Spurgeon tried to avoid accepting the money. First he suggested there must be members of the family who ought to share in Mrs. Hillyard's charity, but she assured him no one was being over-looked. Spurgeon then suggested that perhaps the money ought to be given to George Müller, and he spoke of the great work Müller was doing at Bristol on behalf of orphans. But Mrs. Hillyard was firm in her decision that she wanted Spurgeon to have it and use it for fatherless boys, and she expressed the certainty that many other Christians would undoubtedly want to help too.

Spurgeon and William Higgs drove away from Mrs. Hillyard's home reflecting on the prayer meeting in which they had asked God to give the Tabernacle *some new work* and *the means* with which to perform it. He had answered their prayer and had given them both.

Within a month Spurgeon purchased a block of land for the project—two and a half acres situated at Stockwell—a district not far from the Tabernacle. Immediately further money began to come in. In speaking to his people later he reminded them:

> We met together one Monday night . . . for prayer concerning the Orphanage; and it was not a little remarkable that on the Saturday of that week the Lord should have moved some friend, who knew nothing of our prayers, to give five hundred pounds to that object. It astonished some of you that, on the following Monday, God should have influenced another to give six hundred pounds! When I told you of that, at the next prayer-meeting, you did not think perhaps that the Lord had something else in store, and that, the following Tuesday, another friend would come with five hundred pounds.[2]

Spurgeon went on to contrast the method of trusting the Lord and seeing Him supply in this way with the plan generally adopted in Christian circles. If he and his people followed Christian custom, they would, he said, "first look out for a regular income, and get our subscribers, and send round collectors and pay our percent-ages—that is, not trust God, but trust our subscribers."

He tells of a time when he and Dr. Brock, pastor of the Blooms-bury Baptist Church, were visiting a friend. Spurgeon declared his confidence that God would supply the needs of the orphanage. Dr. Brock warmly agreed, and as they talked a telegram arrived, an-nouncing that an unknown donor had just sent Spurgeon £1,000 for

2. Ibid., p. 165.

this project. Amazed, but filled with rejoicing, Dr. Brock began to pray, and Spurgeon later remarked, "The prayer and the praise that he then poured out, I shall never forget; he seemed a psalmist while, with full heart and grandeur both of words and sound . . . he addressed the ever faithful One."

The orphanage was planned according to certain concepts Spurgeon had developed. It was not to be like the average institution for needy children, with the youngsters quartered in a barracklike building, all dressed alike and made to feel they were objects of charity. It was to be several individual homes—the buildings joined together and forming a continuous row—each home to house fourteen boys and to be under the care of a matron who acted as a mother to the lads. There were to be discipline, education, and Christian instruction, with kindness and sport and individuality.

These homes were all sponsored by donors. One was "The Silver-wedding House," given by a woman whose husband had just given her £500 on the twenty-fifth anniversary of their wedding. Another, given by a businessman, was "The Merchant's House." William Higgs and his workmen donated another, "The Workmen's House." Another was "Unity House" given by William Olney and his sons, in memory of Unity Olney who had recently passed away. "The Testimonial Houses" were erected by funds donated by Baptist churches throughout Britain. The Tabernacle Sunday school provided "The Sunday School House," and the men of the Pastor's College donated "The College House."

A headmaster's house and a dining hall were also constructed, as well as a large play-hall (gymnasium). Before long a private hospital that they termed "The Infirmary" was added. In typical Spurgeonic fashion all were solidly constructed, and one cannot but be amazed that Spurgeon saw to it that there was a swimming pool. He was delighted to be able to state, "Every boy has learned to swim."

In the boardroom of the orphanage, Spurgeon erected a memorial window that pictured the meeting that he and William Higgs had with Mrs. Hillyard. It was a worthy tribute to the woman whose desire to assist the needy youngsters had led to the founding of this excellent organization.

A headmaster for the orphanage was also supplied in answer to prayer. For some months no suitable man seemed available. Finally Spurgeon's attention was drawn to Vernon J. Charlesworth, the assistant pastor of a Congregational church, and even though, like Rogers of the College, he was not a Baptist, Spurgeon engaged him for this task. Charlesworth proved to be the ideal person for the undertaking. Under his leadership the orphanage was operated with kindness and efficiency and also with discipline. After a few years he came into the strong conviction that he ought to be baptized, and Spurgeon was highly delighted to see him thus obey the Lord. The qualities of his character influenced the lives of the boys and girls under his care and also encouraged the prayer and the giving of the numerous friends of the institution.

Ten years after the boy's side of the orphanage was erected a similar building was constructed for girls. The two structures, together with the infirmary, formed a large quadrangle, and the area between was a grass-covered playing field, adorned at its edges and around the buildings with flowers and shrubs. What a difference many a child must have found in leaving some fatherless and poverty-stricken hovel and coming to this place, with food and warmth and loving care—a Christian home in these parklike surroundings!

Whenever Spurgeon visited the orphanage the children thronged around him. He knew virtually all of them by name, and he always had a penny—a coin of some value in those days—for each of them. He made it a particular point to call on any children who might be in the infirmary, to pray for them and show whatever special kindness he could.

The children came from all denominations. There were blacks as well as whites, Jews as well as Gentiles, and Anglicans, Presbyterians, Congregationalists, Catholics, Quakers, and Baptists. From time to time some of the youngsters were converted and asked for baptism, and there were boys who, upon growing up, experienced the call of God, attended the Pastors' College, and went on into a life in the ministry.

The orphanage was a lasting demonstration of the fact that Spurgeon's faith was not mere theory but that it produced good works. It was the kind of project that was widely regarded with strong good will, and many were moved both to pray for it and to give toward its support.

The Almshouses and the orphanage were, of course, the fruit of Christianity, and they stood out in sharp contrast to the lack of such institutions among the unbelievers. England had then its Free Thinkers' Societies and its Agnostic Associations, but those organizations did nothing to help the poor and the suffering. They labored to denounce Christianity, but they knew nothing of self-sacrifice for the sake of the needy. Like the Levite in the parable, they "passed by on the other side."

But evangelical Christians had long been associated with the building of homes for the aged and for orphaned children. Professor Francke had erected and maintained a great orphanage in Germany, and George Whitefield had molded his life around such a project in the American colony of Georgia. George Müller was conducting an orphanage that was home to more than two thousand youngsters in England. Dr. Barnardo gave up his medical practice to devote himself to aiding homeless children, and other less prominent Christians were now beginning to undertake similar efforts.

To an agnostic who one day accosted him and challenged his Christian beliefs, Spurgeon pointed out the failure of the unbelievers' organizations to take on any definite and sustained program of help to the thousands of needy around them. In contrast he pointed to the works that sprang from evangelical Christianity, and he closed the conversation by paraphrasing the triumphant cry of Elijah, vigorously asserting, as well he might, "The God who answereth by Orphanages, LET HIM BE GOD!"

People said to me years ago, "You will break your constitution down with preaching ten times a week," and the like.

Well, if I have done so, I am glad of it. I would do the same again. If I had fifty constitutions I would rejoice to break them down in the service of the Lord Jesus Christ.

You young men that are strong, overcome the wicked one and fight for the Lord while you can. You will never regret having done all that lies in you for our blessed Lord and Master.

Spurgeon, "For the Sick and Afflicted," 1876

13

Sunshine and Shadow

From the late 1860s onward, life for both Spurgeon and his wife became a mixture of the joy of the Lord and the suffering of sickness.

Spurgeon's ill health was very largely caused by the tremendous amount of work he tried to do and the burden of responsibility he constantly carried.

> No one living knows the toil and care I have to bear. . . . I have to look after the Orphanage, have charge of a church with four thousand members, sometimes there are marriages and burials to be undertaken, there is the weekly sermon to be revised, *The Sword and the Trowel* to be edited, and besides all that, a weekly average of five hundred letters to be answered.
>
> This, however, is only half my duty, for there are innumerable churches established by friends, with the affairs of which I am closely connected, to say nothing of the cases of difficulty which are constantly being referred to me.[1]

He could have listed also many other duties that formed part of his burden—the Almshouses, the school and the college, besides

---

1. Iain Murray, ed., *The Full Harvest* (London: Banner of Truth, 1973), p. 192.

his literary labors and his preaching some ten times a week at home and elsewhere.

Finally the deacons realized he could not continue to bear this tremendous load alone. They sought his wishes as to an assistant, and he mentioned his brother James. They quickly secured the agreement of the people, and James was asked to accept this office.

He was well-suited to the task. After graduating from Regent's College he had served in the pastorate for eight years. He and Charles were alike in doctrinal convictions and evangelistic practices, and he possessed sufficient preaching ability to supply the pulpit very acceptably should Charles be absent. Above all, James was a man of spiritual earnestness and soul-winning activity.

In view of the difficulties that so often arise between an assistant pastor and the pastor himself, Charles very wisely had the deacons write out the terms of James's association with the Tabernacle. He was to be the co-pastor but was to be responsible to his brother, and they pointed out that in event of Charles's death he would not necessarily assume the pastorate.

James was entirely in harmony with these terms, and at the beginning of 1868 he entered upon his new duties. He was an excellent businessman and became virtually comptroller of the entire Spurgeon enterprises. The numerous details and decisions in the operating of the Tabernacle and its various organizations were now left to him. Charles was delighted to be freed from these matters.

Charles had men begin to assist him also in other ways. For some time J. L. Keys had been his secretary, and now he engaged a second man, J. W. Harrald, to help in this work. A little later Spurgeon found he could no longer carry the full burden of *The Sword and The Trowel,* so he acquired the services of G. Holden Pike as assistant editor.

Spurgeon was greatly helped also by his deacons and elders. The deacons alone had originally been the chief officers, but as the church grew the office of elder was added, and by the late 1860s there were ten deacons and twenty elders.

The deacons looked after material matters—the finances and the physical aspects of the Tabernacle. The elders' responsibilities lay especially in spiritual affairs, and to each there was allotted a number of members whom he was to visit and in whom he was to take a steady spiritual interest. Spurgeon had visited diligently when the membership was small, but after it reached two and three thousand, the task was beyond him, and virtually all pastoral visitation was taken over by the elders.

Even during the periods of sickness that now began to occur much more often in Spurgeon's life, the work of the Tabernacle flowed smoothly. The co-pastor, deacons, and elders worked together in happy harmony. Spurgeon could always be at rest, knowing their personal love for him and their unfailing zeal for the Lord.

By the 1860s a warm attitude toward Spurgeon had returned throughout much of America. The opposition over his stand against slavery had largely died away, and numerous people from various states had come to hear him while visiting Britain. One of his chief American friends was H. J. Heinz, the pickle manufacturer. Mr. Heinz was an earnest Christian, and whenever he was in England he visited the Tabernacle. He enjoyed personal friendship with Spurgeon and spoke of him as "the most humble man I have ever known."

The people of America were still not satisfied merely to admire Spurgeon from a distance. Many wanted to hear him personally, and thus, in the late 1860s, he was again invited to visit the States. The invitation came from the Lyceum Bureau, a Boston organization that arranged lecture tours. It asked Spurgeon to come and lecture as often as he cared to at a fee of $1,000 a lecture, stipulating only that he lecture at least twenty-five times.[2] In those days $1,000 equalled £200. The American offer was exceedingly generous and manifests the desire there was to hear Spurgeon.

Undoubtedly, Spurgeon would have enjoyed going to America, but the form of invitation he had received did not suit him. For one thing the financial element in the offer was too strong—it implied he was moved chiefly by a desire for money—and it suggested a departure from his usual practice, for it did not ask him to preach, but rather to lecture. And there was also the matter of his own ill health. He was, however, intrigued by the offer, and he told his congregation, "I could have come home with . . . forty thousand pounds." Some people urged that he accept the invitation, but he wrote a gracious reply and turned it down.

It was well he did not leave for America at this time, for Mrs. Spurgeon now became extremely ill.

2. G. Holden Pike, *The Life and Work of Charles Haddon Spurgeon*, 6 vols. (London: Cassel, 1898), 5:66.

Dark days those were for both husband and wife, for a serious disease had invaded my frame, and little alleviation could be found from the constant, wearying pain it caused. My beloved husband, always so fully engaged about his Master's business, yet managed to secure many precious moments by my side, when he would tell me how the work of the Lord was prospering in his hands, and we would exchange sympathies, he comforting me in my suffering, and I cheering him on in his labour.[3]

The home in which the Spurgeons lived, Helensburgh House, was not beneficial to the health of either of them. It was becoming antiquated, so it lacked suitable conveniences. This moved several of their friends to provide the money for a new one. Deacon Higgs was to construct it, and Mr. Higgs's son, an architect, designed a fine home. Work was begun to remove the old Helensburgh House and where it had stood to build the new.

While the construction was in progress, Mrs. Spurgeon lived at Brighton. As often as possible Spurgeon went back and forth by train.

But during the weeks at Brighton Mrs. Spurgeon's condition grew steadily worse. Some time earlier, Sir James Simpson, an earnest Christian, a celebrated physician and the discoverer of chloroform, had offered his professional services without charge, and Spurgeon now accepted his offer. Sir James performed the necessary surgery, and it was considered fully successful, but, due perhaps to the lack of medical knowledge in those days, her recovery was very slow, and she remained in a semi-invalid state.

After several weeks she returned to Helensburgh House. To her delight and surprise not only was she in a totally new home, but her husband had planned many special things for her comfort as well. He mentions certain furniture he had bought for her, and she remarks that alongside his study there was a small room fitted up for her use. She particularly rejoiced in its cunningly-contrived corner cupboard, the doors of which, when opened, revealed a dainty washing apparatus with hot and cold water piped in. That kind of equipment was not at all common in those days, and it proved a happy convenience for the sick woman.

The new home was a boon for Spurgeon too. It gave him a study adequate for his multifaceted labor and also of sufficient size to provide room for his hundreds of books. The outside of the proper-

3. Murray, *The Full Harvest*, p. 177.

ty seems to have been all replanted, and Spurgeon's "man," George Lovejoy, was there to oversee it. A smooth area had been prepared for lawn bowling—a game Spurgeon greatly enjoyed, especially since it had been the favorite pastime of the Puritans.

Despite his wife's illness Spurgeon tried to maintain his own tremendous schedule.

But that was impossible, and he was soon forced to take to his bed, a very sick man. After being absent from his pulpit and being forced to leave his literary work undone, he wrote of his condition, saying in *The Sword and the Trowel* of October 1869:

> The Editor's painful indisposition compels him to forego his usual monthly notes, and also the Exposition of the Psalms. Too great pressure of work has produced a disorder whose root is more mental than physical. Wearisome pain, added to relative affliction and ever-increasing responsibility make up a burden under the weight of which unaided mortal strength must sink. An all-sufficient God is our joy and rejoicing.[4]

After several days of suffering Spurgeon recovered enough to be able to resume his work. But within two or three months he came down with smallpox, and while recuperating from that disease he suffered a very severe attack of the gout.

Of this attack he says nothing, but others followed it, and of one he endured in 1871 he wrote in a letter to his congregation a descriptive account. This provides an insight into the kind of suffering he experienced.

> Dear Friends,
>
> The furnace still glows around me. Since I last preached to you, I have been brought very low; my flesh has been tortured with pain and my spirit has been prostrate with depression. Yet, in all this I see and submit to my Father's hand. . . . With some difficulty, I write these lines in my bed, mingling them with the groans of pain and the songs of hope.
>
> It must, under the most favourable circumstances, be long before you see me again, for the highest medical authorities are agreed that only long rest can restore me. I wish it were otherwise. My heart is in my work and with you. . . . When I am able to move I must go away. I try to cast all my cares upon God, but sometimes I fear you may get scattered. O my dear brethren, do not wander, for this would break my heart! . . .

4. Ibid., p. 194.

The Orphanage funds are lower just now than they have been these two years. God will provide, but you know that you are His stewards.

You do pray for me, I know. . . . I am as a potter's vessel when it is utterly broken, useless and laid aside. Nights of watching and days of weeping have been mine, but I hope the cloud is passing. Alas! I can only say this for my own personal and light affliction; there is one who lies nearest to my heart whose sorrows are not relieved by such a hope.[5]

We notice his words "prostrate with depression." In some persons gout causes irritability, but in Spurgeon's case it was accompanied by depression of a very severe nature.

Spurgeon remained out of his pulpit for seven weeks. After he returned he reported something of what he had gone through. In an article in his magazine he said:

It is a mercy to be able to change sides when lying in bed. . . . Did you ever lie a week on one side? Did you ever try to turn and find yourself quite helpless? Did others lift you and by their kindness only reveal to you the miserable fact that they must lift you back again to the old position, for, bad as it was, it was preferable to any other. . . . Some of us know what it is, night after night, to long for slumber and find it not. . . . What a mercy have I felt it to have only one knee tortured at a time! What a blessing to be able to put the foot on the ground again, if only for a minute![6]

From his pulpit Spurgeon described how he pleaded with God when his agony was at its worst.

When . . . I was racked with pain to an extreme degree, so that I could no longer bear it without crying out, I asked all to go from the room and leave me alone; and then I had nothing I could say to God but this, "Thou art my Father, and I am Thy child; and Thou, as a Father, art tender and full or mercy. I could not bear to see my child suffer as thou makest me suffer; and if I saw him tormented as I am now, I would do what I could to help him. . . . Wilt Thou hide Thy face from me, my Father? Wilt Thou still lay on me Thy heavy hand, and not give me a smile from Thy countenance?" I . . . pleaded His Fatherhood in real earnest. "Like as a father pitieth his children, so the Lord pitieth them that fear Him." If He be a Father, let Him show Himself a Father—so I pleaded; and I ventured to say, when they came back who watched me, "I shall never have such agony again . . . for God has heard my prayer." I bless God that ease

5. Ibid., p. 195.
6. Ibid., p. 196.

came, and the racking pain never returned. Faith mastered it by laying hold upon God in His own revealed character—that character in which in our darkest hour, we are best able to appreciate Him. . . . We can still say "Our Father," and when it is very dark, and we are very weak, our childlike appeal can go up, "Father, help me! Father, rescue me!"[7]

Spurgeon was still very weak and needed a considerable period of rest. That was not possible as long as he remained in England, and therefore before the coming of winter (November 1871), he left for Italy. In that land, due to the language barrier, he could not often preach, and the damp and cold of Britain were exchanged for the sun and warmth of the south. After six weeks of vacation he could return home, ready to take up his work with improved health and new vigor.

Mrs. Spurgeon was too unwell to travel with him. "These separations," she wrote, "were very painful to hearts so tenderly united as were ours, but we each bore our share of the sorrow as heroically as we could, and softened it as far as possible by constant correspondence."[8] He wrote every day, and since he possessed a considerable gift in drawing he enclosed with many a letter a sketch of sights he saw—"of people, costumes, landscapes, trees, wells, or anything which particularly struck him."

Spurgeon was accompanied by his publisher, Joseph Passmore, and two other friends. They visited Rome, Naples, Pompeii, and the Isle of Capri, enjoying both the scenery and the weather. On the return journey they spent a few days at a place called Menton on the south coast of France, and Spurgeon liked it so well he declared, "It is calculated to make a sick man leap with health." He was so delighted with this sunny spot that he returned there almost every winter from that time on. It was there, in 1892, that he was to spend his last days on earth.

On the return journey to England he again suffered a severe attack of gout, and at Cannes he lay in bed for the better part of a week. He says that when he had improved sufficiently to move on, "A lady lent her Bath-chair [a hooded chair on wheels] to take me to the station, and porters lifted me into the carriage. There I had a nice sofa-bed and every convenience."[9] Sleep still proved difficult, but as the trip through France came to an end and as he prepared to

7. Ibid., p. 197.
8. Ibid., p. 198.
9. Ibid., p. 216.

cross the Channel, he said in a letter to Susannah, "I can now walk a little, and hope to be alright for Sunday. . . . I am indeed grateful to God for His goodness; still, 'there's no place like home.' This brings great loads of love all flaming. God bless thee ever!"[10]

In view of Spurgeon's own long sickness and that of his wife, it is difficult to believe that many people thought he possessed a "gift of healing." The best information available on the matter is to be found in Russell Conwell's *Life of Spurgeon,* particularly in his chapter "Wonderful Healing."

The idea began during the cholera epidemic. As we saw, Spurgeon visited numerous homes where the disease raged, and there he prayed that the sick one might be made well. In many instances, in someone who seemed near death the disease was stopped, and before long health returned. People were sure this was the result of prayer.

During further years Spurgeon prayed for persons in sicknesses of various kinds, and although in many a case there was no betterment, in others there was improvement that appeared miraculous. Dr. Conwell examined several of these experiences, and in 1892, the year of Spurgeon's death, he declared:

> There are now living and worshipping in the Metropolitan Tabernacle hundreds of people who ascribe the extension of their life to the effect of Mr. Spurgeon's personal prayers. They have been sick with disease and nigh unto death, he has appeared, kneeled by their beds, and prayed for their recovery. Immediately the tide of health returned, the fevered pulse became calm, the temperature was reduced, and all the activities of nature resumed their normal functions within a short and unexpected period. If a meeting were called of all those who attribute their recovery to the prayer of Mr. Spurgeon, it would furnish one of the most deserved tributes to his memory that could possibly be made.[11]

Conwell goes on to report seven specific instances of what was considered healing in response to Spurgeon's prayers. "The belief in Mr. Spurgeon's healing power became among some classes a positive superstition, and he was obliged to overcome the very false and extravagant impressions . . . by mentioning the matter from the pulpit, and rebuking the theories of the extremely enthusiastic. He

10. Ibid., p. 217.
11. Russell H. Conwell, *Life of Charles Haddon Spurgeon* (n.p.: Edgewood, 1892), p. 178.

felt it was becoming too much like the shrines of Catholic Europe."[12]

Spurgeon declared that the subject of divine healing was very much a mystery to him. He said he prayed about sickness just as he prayed about anything else, and that in some instances God answered with healing, whereas in others, for reasons beyond our understanding, He allowed the suffering to continue.

Although the Spurgeons suffered many trials during the 1870s, they also experienced much rejoicing.

One of the happiest events was the baptism of their sons. The date of the conversion of the two boys, Thomas and Charles, is not known, but in one of his sermons their father said, "Did not our hearts overflow, as parents, when we first discovered that our children had sought the Lord. That was . . . a time to be remembered, when we were called up to hear their tearful story, and to give them a word of comfort. We were not half so glad at their birth as we were when they were born again."[13]

On Sunday, September 21, 1874, Thomas and Charles were baptized. Due to his ill health their father had not performed any baptisms in some months, leaving this task to his brother. It was an event of special importance when he himself walked into the baptistry and immersed his two sons.

They were eighteen at the time, and within a month or two they began to preach on Sundays at Wandsworth Baptist Chapel, one taking the morning service and the other the evening. Two years later Thomas, since he possessed artistic talents, became apprenticed to an engraver. Charles was called to a church in Greenwich and in a service that recognized the beginning of his ministry there, his father preached, and the youth tells how "leaning over the pulpit rail, and looking down upon me, on the lower platform, he said in tender, yet thrilling tones, 'Preach up Christ, my boy! Preach HIM up!' "[14]

Both of the boys supplied the pulpit of the Tabernacle at times. They were able preachers, and each had something of their father's voice, but they lacked his exceptional gifts. Moreover, they were

12. Ibid., p. 184.
13. *C. H. Spurgeon's Autobiography*, comp. Susannah Spurgeon and J. W. Harrald, 4 vols. (London: Passmore and Alabaster, 1897), 3:291.
14. Ibid., p. 294.

never robust physically, and although their father had provided them with gymnastic equipment when they were boys, they seem not to have made any valuable use of it.

Another event that brought particular joy to Spurgeon during the mid 1870s was the opening of a new home for the Pastors' College. It was located on the street immediately at the rear of the Tabernacle and was large enough to meet the needs of at least 150 students. It contained several classrooms. On the opening day the president led a prayer meeting in each room, solemnly dedicating it to the Lord.

The building did not contain any dormitories, however. The men still boarded among the families of the Tabernacle. Spurgeon believed that if they all lived together there would be too much joking and lightness, as was generally the case in other colleges. "Levity of conduct in my brethren," he stated, "brings heaviness of heart to me. . . . Oh, how can ministers be . . . talking lightness and wantonness, when sinners are perishing? It must not be so among us."

The College building cost £15,000, much of which was either given by Spurgeon or was brought in by him from his preaching at other churches. The building became the headquarters of the Colportage Association, and it was the meeting place of the Annual Conferences of most of Spurgeon's organizations.

Although the construction of the college fulfilled one of the great ambitions of Spurgeon's life, it also added to his burdens. Had he been in excellent health he could more capably have carried the load, but subject as he was to the periodic attacks of gout with all their pain and depression, he felt the weight of the institutions was becoming too much for him to bear. "I feel," he wrote on one of his days of dejection, "as though I had created a great machine and it is ever grinding, grinding, and that I may yet be its victim." But most of his time he lived in the joy of the Lord and was an attractive example of Christian happiness.

It is one of the delights of my life that my beloved wife has made ministers' libraries her great concern. The dear soul gives herself wholly to it.

You should see her stores, her book-room, her busy helpers on the parcel-day, and the waggon load of books each fortnight. The Book Fund at certain hours is the ruling idea of our house. Every day it occupies the head and heart of its manager.

The reader has scant idea of the book-keeping involved in the book-giving; but this may be said,—the loving manager has more than 6000 names on her lists, and yet she knows every volume that each man has received from the first day till now. The work is not muddled, but done as if by clockwork, yet it is performed with a hearty desire to give pleasure to all receivers and to trouble no applicant with needless inquiries.

Spurgeon, 1882

14

Mrs. Spurgeon and Her Work

Throughout much of her married life Mrs. Spurgeon was a semi-invalid. For long periods of time she was confined to her home and was not well enough even to attend the Tabernacle. But she bore up nobly under those conditions. She encouraged her husband under his frequent sufferings and did not complain about her own.

Nevertheless, she longed to be busy for the Lord. Every sentence from her pen that has come down to us and every mention of her that has been left by others reveals a very gracious and spiritually-minded woman.

In 1875 a door of rich usefulness was opened before her. Her husband's *Lectures to My Students* had recently been published, and upon reading the book she told him, "I wish I could send a copy to every minister in England!"

"Then why not do it?" he responded. "How much will you give?"

She began to do some mental figuring, deciding what she could save from her housekeeping expenditures. Then she remembered that for some time she had been putting aside every five-shilling coin she received. She found she had just enough to purchase 100 copies of the *Lectures*.

Soon she sent a copy to each of one hundred needy ministers. She thought that was the end of the matter, but although she did not allow her husband to mention what she had done, news of her action spread, and friends began sending her money so she could send out more books. Several of the pastors who had been given the copies sent letters that expressed their thanks and made it evident that books were sorely needed.

Moved by a strong recognition of the need and feeling God wanted her to continue the endeavor, she ordered a number of sets of *The Treasury of David.* (Spurgeon had written four volumes of that work at the time.) Those also went to needy pastors, and again there came the letters of thanks and further evidence of need. Many men were trying to maintain homes and bring up families on meager incomes.

Although there was still no public mention of what Mrs. Spurgeon had done, money continued to arrive and with it urgent requests that she continue the good work. For instance, one man sent £50, asking that she send a copy of the *Lectures* to the nearly 500 pastors of the Calvinistic Methodist Churches of North Wales. Then another £50 came to help defray the costs of that undertaking. That was followed by £100 to send the book to the ministers of the same denomination in South Wales.

News of the gifts spread still further, and ministers of various denominations wrote, stating that a copy of the *Lectures,* the *Treasury,* or Spurgeon's other writings would be of great help, but that they were too poor to purchase them. And as those letters reached Mrs. Spurgeon, more money arrived. She could see she had a lasting work to do, an undertaking given by God.

By the time she had been performing the task for five months she wrote:

> The number of books given up to this moment is 3,058, and the persons receiving them have been pastors of all denominations. But, ah! dear friends, when I look at the list of names, I see the only shadow of sadness that ever rests upon my Book-Fund. It is the grief of knowing that there exists a terrible necessity for this service of love; that without this help . . . the poor pastors to whom it has been sent must have gone on famishing for mental food, their incomes being so wretchedly small that they scarcely know how to "provide things honest" for themselves and their families, while the money for the purchase of books is absolutely unobtainable.
>
> It is most touching to hear some tell with eloquence the effect the gift produced upon them. One is "not ashamed to say" he received the parcel with "tears of joy," wife and children standing around and rejoic-

ing with him. Another, as soon as the wrappings fall from the precious volumes, praises God aloud and sings the Doxology with all his might; while a third, when his eyes light on the long-coveted "Treasury of David," "rushes from the room" that he may go alone and "pour out his full heart before his God."[1]

To emphasize how thankful they were for the books, many pastors or pastors' wives told of the financial difficulties they constantly faced. Some lived on a salary of £80, others on £60, and some on as little as £40. Several had large families. Some spoke of sick wives and heavy doctors' bills. Almost all faced the burden of educating their children. Many families were in need of better and warmer clothing or more bedding or personal items.

Mrs. Spurgeon determined to do everything in her power to meet those needs. To the Book Fund she added another work, the Pastors' Aid Fund. *The Sword and the Trowel* reported the needs that existed among numerous pastors, and she appealed for gifts of money, clothing, and blankets. The appeal brought a tremendous response, and she had the goods sent to the Tabernacle. From there a company of volunteers sent them along to those in need. The books were packaged at the Spurgeon home. Every two weeks a full cartload of precious volumes left for the railroad station.

Mrs. Spurgeon kept very accurate account of the money that came in and of its expenditure. She spoke of herself as "corresponding secretary, as well as treasurer, general manager, etc.," of the two funds. There were times she performed her duties in weakness and pain, and other times she was so ill that her labors were entirely prevented.

Nevertheless, over and above the value of the books and the goods to the various recipients, the enterprise was especially valuable to Mrs. Spurgeon herself. It gave her reason to feel that despite her condition she was able to serve. Spurgeon spoke of the endeavor as divinely ordered, and he reported the change it had made in Susannah, saying:

> I gratefully adore the goodness of our Heavenly Father, in directing my beloved wife to a work which has been to her fruitful in unutterable happiness. That it has cost her more pain than it would be fitting to reveal, is most true; but that it has brought her boundless joy is equally

1. Russell H. Conwell, *Life of Charles Haddon Spurgeon* (n.p.: Edgewood, 1892), pp. 251-52.

certain. Our gracious Lord ministered to His suffering child in the most effectual manner, when He graciously led her to minister to the necessities of His service.

By this means He called her away from her personal grief, gave tone and concentration to her life, led her to continual dealings with Himself, and raised her nearer the centre of that region where other than earthly joys and sorrows reigned supreme. Let every believer accept this as the inference of experience, that for most human maladies the best relief and antidote will be found in self-sacrificing work for the Lord Jesus.[2]

And Mrs. Spurgeon testified:

> I am personally indebted to the dear friends who have furnished me with the means of making others happy. For me there has been a *double* blessing. I have been both recipient and donor. . . . My days have been made indescribably bright and happy by the delightful duties connected with the work and its little arrangements . . . that I seem to be living in an atmosphere of blessing and love, and can truly say with the Psalmist, "My cup runneth over."[3]

As the months came and went Mrs. Spurgeon increased the books she made available. She frequently sent copies of her husband's sermons, sometimes six volumes at a time. She added several of his other writings and frequently added works from other men. "Solid, old-fashioned, Scriptural, Puritanic theology goes forth."

The area of ministry soon extended far beyond the shores of Britain. She spoke of sending books to missionaries in Patna, Bengal, Ceylon, Transvaal, Samoa, China, Oregon, Jamaica, Kir Moab, India, Trinidad, Equatorial Africa, Russia, Natal, Canada, the Congo, Buenos Aires, Cayman, Damascus, Madrid, Lagos, and Timbuctoo. Letters came in from all those places and from many more. She personally replied to them all.

> The Book Fund has been nourished and fed from the King's Treasury, and I must "make my boast in the Lord" that all needful supplies for the carrying on of the work have plainly borne the stamp of heaven's own mint. I say this because I have never asked help of anyone but *Him*, never solicited a donation from any creature, yet money has always been forthcoming, and the supplies have constantly been in proportion to the needs.[4]

2. Ibid., pp. 241-42.
3. Ibid., p. 249.
4. *The Sword and the Trowel*, 1878, p. 77.

In 1885 Mrs. Spurgeon put the story of this ministry into print—
Ten Years of My Life in the Service of the Book Fund. She reported
the income, year by year, with the number of volumes sent forth
and the denominations of the men to whom they were given. Interspersed were expressions of praise.

The book earned her a nice little sum in royalties, and that
provided further joy for she put it into the fund to purchase more
books for others. She quoted extensively letters from pastors and
pastors' wives, without revealing their identity, of course, but telling of their struggles. She had deep compassion for these needy
ones, and her heart was moved to do everything possible to help
them.

In 1895 she wrote another book, *Ten Years After.* It continued
the report of the Book Fund and the Pastors' Aid Fund. Although
here and there, between the lines, we can see she was a sick woman
and often did her work in pain, the project increased in its scope.
For instance, in her summary for 1889, she wrote: "Books Distributed:—6,916 Volumes. Also 13,565 single sermons. The recipients
comprised 148 Baptists, 81 Independents, 118 Methodists, 152
Church of England, 48 Missionaries, 6 Presbyterians, 2 Walden-
sians, 3 Plymouth Brethren, 1 Moravian, 1 Morrisonian.—Total
560."

Four years before this latter book appeared, Charles Spurgeon
had passed from this life. Mrs. Spurgeon's sorrow and loneliness are
often evident in her words, but she also wrote with the sense of
triumph that only a Christian knows:

> I have travelled far now on life's journey, and having climbed one of
> the few remaining hills between earth and heaven, I stand awhile on this
> vantage ground and look back across the country through which the
> Lord had led me. . . .
> I can see two pilgrims treading the highway of life together, hand in
> hand—heart linked to heart. True, they have had rivers to ford, moun-
> tains to cross, fierce enemies to fight and many dangers to go through.
> But their Guide was watchful, their Deliverer unfailing, and of them it
> might truly be said, "In all their affliction He was afflicted, and the Angel
> of His presence saved them; in His love and in His pity He redeemed
> them; and He bare them and carried them all the days of old."
> Mostly they went on their way singing; and for one of them at least,
> there was no greater joy than to tell others of the grace and glory of the
> blessed King to whose land he was hasting. And while he thus spoke, the
> power of the Lord was seen and the angels rejoiced over repenting
> sinners.

But at last they came to a place on the road where two ways met. And here, amidst the terrors of a storm such as they had never before encountered, they parted company—the one being caught up to the invisible glory, and the other, battered and bruised by the awful tempest, henceforth toiling along the road—alone!

But the "goodness and mercy" which for so many years had followed the two travellers, did not leave the solitary one. Rather did the tenderness of the Lord "lead on softly," and choose green pastures for the tired feet, and still waters for the solace and refreshment of His trembling child.

He gave, moreover, into her hands a solemn charge—to help fellow pilgrims along the road, therewith filling her life with blessed interest, and healing her own deep sorrow by giving her power to relieve and comfort others.[5]

5. Susannah Spurgeon, *Ten Years After* (London: Passmore and Alabaster, 1895), pp. vi-vii.

How pleased and blest was I
To hear the people cry,
"Come, let us seek our God to-day!"
Yes, with a cheerful zeal
We haste to Zion's hill,
And there our vows and homage pay.

Zion, thrice happy place,
Adorned with wondrous grace,
And walls of strength embrace thee round;
In thee our tribes appear,
To pray and praise and hear
The sacred Gospel's joyful sound.

There David's greater Son
Hath fixed His royal throne,
He sits for grace and judgment there:
He bids the saints be glad,
He makes the sinner sad,
And humble souls rejoice with fear.

My tongue repeats her vows
Peace to this sacred house!
For there my friends and kindred dwell;
And since my glorious God
Makes thee His blest abode,
My soul shall ever love thee well.

Isaac Watts, 1674-1748

15

Daily Life in the Great Church

The Metropolitan Tabernacle was not, as some have assumed, merely a highly popular preaching center. It was not a church whose people largely came in from some miles around and, after listening to a marvelous exercise in Christian oratory, returned to their homes and seldom thought about the place again till the following Sunday morning.

The Tabernacle was a great, working church. The vast majority of the members lived in the heavily populated area of London south of the Thames, and many were so near they could walk to the services. A very large number of young men—apprentices and young businessmen—had been converted under Spurgeon's ministry. Now they attended regularly and brought their wives and children with them. Apart from the sick and infirm, there were very few who came only on Sundays. There were activity and work that brought great numbers to the Tabernacle on many occasions during the week.

Besides the Tabernacle itself, there were a number of other organizations which, speaking in the human sense, had sprung up under Spurgeon's ministry. The most important of those were, of course, the Pastors' College, the Almshouses, the Orphanage, and the Colporteurs' Association.

But there were also several less prominent institutions: the Evangelists' Association, the Country Mission, the Home and Foreign Working Society, the Loan Tract Society, the Sermon Loan Society, the Maternal Society, the Police Mission, the Coffee House Mission, the Loan Building Fund, the Christian Brothers' Benefit Society, the Flower Mission, the Gospel Temperance Society, the Female Servants' Home Society, the Blind Society, the Ladies' Benevolent Society, the Tabernacle Evangelistic Society, and the Spurgeon's Sermons Tract Society.

That is an amazing list, but it is not complete. In fact, on the occasion of Spurgeon's Jubilee—the celebration of his twenty-five years in London—his secretary, J. W. Harrald, read the names of his institutions, and they then amounted to the amazing number of sixty-six.

Besides those organizations, Spurgeon had had part in forming some forty missions in various parts of London, and his people were conducting several Sunday schools and Ragged Schools. There was also copious use of the printed page: the weekly sermon, the monthly *Sword and Trowel,* and Spurgeon's books (forty-four titles had been published by 1875), which were circulating by thousands throughout much of the world.

The Tabernacle was busy in foreign missions as well. Several of the men from the College had gone out to distant lands, and we read especially of their working in India, China, Ceylon, and various African countries. The Tabernacle was very largely the source of the support of those missionaries.

This entire enterprise depended on Spurgeon for leadership. As we noticed, he had placed its general management into the hands of his brother, but the basic responsibility for its vigorous continuance and its financial sustenance remained with him. The students called him "the Gov'nor," and some of the people used this term in its Old Testament form, "the Tirshatha." The nickname well indicated his place. With the exception of the Almshouses each institution had originated under his influence, he had planned its form of organization and had overseen its growth, and his word was supreme in all its affairs.

Nevertheless, throughout the whole movement the matter of authority was not even considered. There was a spontaneous recognition of Spurgeon, and the relationship was one of his love for the people and the people's love for him. Under his example they prosecuted the work with affection and fervor. He never exerted his authority—he never needed to—but the entire organization moved steadily forward in harmony under his strong generalship.

The Tabernacle was a place of almost constant activity. On each of the seven days of the week the doors were opened at 7:00 in the morning and did not close till 11:00 at night, and there were persons coming and going all of the time.

For twelve years the College had held its classes in the lecture hall and the adjoining basement rooms, and even after the new building was constructed the students were still in and out of the Tabernacle with much frequency. The College also held evening classes twice a week with some 200 in attendance, and after shorthand was added to the curriculum the figure increased to 300.

The Tabernacle was the center for the various institutions' annual meetings—so many of them that one was held almost every week. The Ladies' Benevolent Society met there in a sewing circle to make clothes for the children of the orphanage, for poor people of the congregation, and for other needy ones of the area. The Maternal Society ladies gathered to prepare gifts for expectant women, and from the Tabernacle they went forth to assist them when they became mothers. Flowers were gathered at the Tabernacle by the Flower Society, and after being made into attractive baskets and bouquets they were taken to the homes of the sick and to hospitals. Mrs. Spurgeon maintained a Bible nurse at her own expense, and other such nurses also functioned from the Tabernacle.

Outside organizations likewise made use of the Tabernacle from time to time. The Bible Society, the Baptist Union, several missionary societies, and other such groups often were allowed the great building for some special occasion.

A large number of meals were served at the Tabernacle. Until the opening of its own building the College had dinner for its men there, and during the pastors' conferences and the annual meetings of various organizations meals were served—sometimes three a day. Thus there was the frequent arrival of carts carrying food, and a large amount of work was done in preparing and serving it and in setting and waiting on tables and washing dishes. Once a year the sixteen hundred members of the Christian Butchers' Association held their annual meeting at the Tabernacle. When we read of them eating a supper of roast beef we wonder whether they brought this immense supply of meat with them, already cooked, or whether it had to be cooked on the premises. At any rate they held a rousing meeting of testimonies and preaching after they had eaten their meal.

When in 1898 the building was destroyed by fire, the blaze began in a kitchen chimney that had become overheated during the cooking of a meal for a conference.

Although the Tabernacle records make no mention of it, the task of keeping the building clean and tidy must also have demanded much labor. Spurgeon required that everything in the Lord's work be done well, and he allowed nothing to be let go in a careless manner. Since he found part-time employment for students whenever possible, it is possible that a group of them was given this large janitorial duty.

But the chief labor in connection with the Tabernacle was spiritual. A number of members, after attending the morning service, filled the rest of the day with work for the Lord.

The Sunday school met in the afternoon. It was a fervent institution with well over a thousand boys and girls in attendance and something like a hundred teachers. Many of those who taught must have been truly devoted to their task, but we notice especially the work of one of them.

Back in the days when Spurgeon first came to London, Mrs. Lavinia Bartlett took over a class of three girls at New Park Street. Under her leadership it made steady growth, till inside of ten years it regularly numbered 500, and at times the attendance rose to 700 and more. When the deacons or elders (the "messengers") interviewed a woman who was not clear as to the way of salvation they advised her to "attend Mrs. Bartlett's Class," and by the time she was called home in 1875 between 900 and 1,000 members of her class had come to know the Lord. Spurgeon said of her:

> She aimed at soul-winning every time she met the class. . . . In pursuing this object she was very down-right, and treated things in a matter-of-fact style. The follies, weaknesses and temptations of her sex were dealt with very pointedly, and the griefs, trials and sins of her class were on her heart. . . . Her talk never degenerated into story-telling, or quotations of poetry . . . but she went right at her hearers in the name of the Lord, and claimed their submission to him.[1]

---

1. Iain Murray, ed., *The Full Harvest* (London: Banner of Truth, 1962), p. 81.

Other classes at the Sunday school did not become as large as that of Mrs. Bartlett, but the same purpose largely characterized them all.

On Sunday afternoons and evenings large numbers of the Tabernacle people were busy for the Lord at other places. Several assisted the College students, some of whom were in well-to-do areas, while others labored in more ordinary districts. Still others were working in the slums, and in those locations conditions were usually deplorable. For instance, the student, together with his helpers from the Tabernacle, regularly visited the inhabitants of lodging houses—sites of terrible poverty, iniquity, and sorrow—or held a meeting in a room where the air was foul and vermin abounded. From such scenes they came away with their clothes carrying the noxious odor, but their hearts rejoicing in the privilege of witnessing for Christ to such needy souls.

Spurgeon encouraged his people to be out carrying the gospel on Sundays. During his career he frequently arranged to have a group of members leave the Tabernacle to start a new church, and often one of the prominent men of the Tabernacle went with them to provide leadership.

One man who led in the founding of such a mission work was J. T. Dunn. For a time Mr. Dunn had served as Spurgeon's assistant, doing pastoral visitation and secretarial duties. But in 1869, with Spurgeon's blessing, he launched out upon an effort in a poor district.

> The building was an old shed and he began with four boys whom he invited in off the street, sitting them on two scrubbed wooden benches. A candle stuck into a teapot spout served as a source of illumination. . . ; The neighbourhood was populated with a great many fish curers, the children helping in the business. The building was of such a low pitch that the room used was frequently named the Black Hole of Calcutta by Spurgeon. Many of the children were far from clean and the atmosphere often resulted in women teachers being taken out into the street to revive them from a fainting fit.[2]

But Mr. Dunn continued his effort. He moved the mission to another building, but here "rain came through the roof and rats ran

---

2. Eric W. Hayden, *A History of Spurgeon's Tabernacle* (Pasadena, Tex.: Pilgrim Press, n.d.), p. 29.

across the floor." Nevertheless, he saw "some of the scholars converted and baptized at the Metropolitan Tabernacle, and then become Sunday school teachers themselves. Others learned to preach
in the open air, and some were trained in Spurgeon's College for the
regular ministry. . . . In 1874 there were five hundred children and
young people in regular attendance on Sundays, with fifty teachers."[3]

J. T. Dunn remained an elder of the Tabernacle during all the
years he led this mission work. He undoubtedly was present at the
Tabernacle for its Tuesday and Thursday evening meetings and also
on Sunday morning. But on at least one or two weeknights and on
Sunday afternoon and evening he was engaged in the activities of
the mission. Those duties, besides his work at making a living, must
surely have given him a very busy life.

This pattern was that in general of the deacons and elders of the
Tabernacle. Several of them were engaged in activities of this nature. William Olney, whom Spurgeon termed "Father Olney," had
been Spurgeon's chief assistant until his death in 1870, but his four
sons carried on his labors. William, Jr., began a meeting in a men's
club room in Bermondsey, an area much better than that of Mr.
Dunn, and he used the men of his Tabernacle Bible class as his
helpers. He preached each Sunday evening, did open air work,
engaged in tract distribution, and conducted a weekly prayer meeting. After ten years the work had grown to such an extent that a fine
new building was erected, and, in reference to Spurgeon's middle
name, it was called Haddon Hall. Like Dunn, while doing this
excellent work, Olney remained a deacon of the Tabernacle and
well fulfilled his office there.

It seems that nearly every officer of the Tabernacle had also a
second labor. Each instructor at the College was also the pastor of a
church and found time to perform both duties. James Spurgeon
carried a constant load as co-pastor of the Tabernacle, yet he also
started a work in the London suburb of Croydon, and under his
ministry it became a church of hundreds.

Much more might be said about the duties and double duties
performed by members of the Tabernacle. As Spurgeon remarked,
the Tabernacle was "like a hive of bees," and for the vast majority of
its people to be a member meant to live a very busy life.

In all this endeavor Spurgeon was the motivating figure. His own

3. Ibid.

days were so full that it is difficult to credit the amount of work he
accomplished. Something of the orderliness and abundant activity
that characterized his organization is manifest in the following report made by an American journalist. Speaking of his visit to the
Pastor's College he wrote:

> Dropping in quite unexpectedly we found everybody at his post, and
> the whole complicated machinery working without a hitch. In one room
> we opened the door on some thirty or forty young men celebrating the
> Lord's Supper. In another we found an aged lady, with some twenty
> grown-up girls around her, conducting a Bible Class.
>
> In the spacious rooms below, tables were being laid for about one
> thousand six hundred for tea, as the Annual Church Meeting was to be
> held in the evening. A secretary, with two clerks under him, form the
> staff required for conducting the correspondence.
>
> In another room was a man up to his eyes in books, whose business it
> was to manage the "Colportage," while in yet another was a sort of local
> Mudie's, where boxes of books are packed and sent to former students,
> now pastors in outlying chapels . . .
>
> Over this labyrinth I was conducted in the most cheery way by the
> *Atlas* who bears on his single pair of shoulders the whole mass; and this
> is the man whom we are too apt to regard as merely the preacher on
> Sundays! "Mr. Spurgeon," I could not help saying, "you are a regular
> Pope!" "Yes," he replied, "though without claiming infallibility. This is
> indeed a democracy, with a very large infusion of constitutional monar-
> chy in it."[4]

Deacon Olney, in speaking at Spurgeon's Jubilee in 1884, made
the statement that on Sunday evenings the number of Tabernacle
people who were out conducting meetings amounted to at least a
thousand. This is an amazing fact, but even more amazing is it that
commencing with 1870 Spurgeon began, every three months, to
ask all members to remain away from the evening service on the
following Sunday, since by filling the Tabernacle they were prevent-
ing the unconverted from getting in and from hearing the gospel.
His people cooperated, and on the Sundays they were absent the
building was more crowded than ever, as thousands who did not
know the Lord, feeling that this time they would probably get in,
came with much enthusiasm. Nothing delighted Spurgeon more
than to have a great host of the spiritually needy to preach to, and

4. G. Holden Pike, *The Life and Work of Charles Haddon Spurgeon*, 6 vols.
(London: Cassel, 1898), 4:342.

those occasions—rare, indeed, in Christian history—were times when many believed on Christ and were later baptized.

Many of the Tabernacle people seldom went out of the section of London south of the Thames. The homes of a vast majority of them lay in that general district, and so did their places of employment. For instance, several worked for Sir Henry Doulton, whose factory, manufacturing the famous Royal Doulton chinaware and figurines, was in that area. Sir Henry was an earnest Christian who regularly attended Spurgeon's ministry, and he employed a large number of Tabernacle people.

The affections of the members were entwined around the Tabernacle and its activities. The services of many a church may prove boring, but not so those of this great church. With grand delight people went up from what was often the drudgery of daily life to the house of the Lord on Sunday mornings and Sunday evenings and at least two evenings of the week, and there their hearts were lifted, their minds informed, and their souls inspired. Many of the women were there again at various hours of the day, preparing meals or sewing garments for the orphans, and many of the young men were at the Tabernacle in the evenings, gaining an education or learning something more about doing the Lord's work.

For hundreds of persons the Tabernacle was the center of their existence. The message they heard there had been the means of transforming their lives, remaking their homes, saving them from sin, and giving them new affections and new joys, and they loved the place and especially loved the man whom God had used in bringing it all about.

In Spurgeon's time London's streetlights burned gas but still had to be lit individually. It is to this practice that Spurgeon is referring in the following note:

Coming one Thursday in the late autumn from an engagement beyond Dulwich, my way led up to the top of the Herne Hill ridge. I came along the level out of which rises the steep hill I had to ascend.

While I was on the lower ground, riding in a hansom cab, I saw a light before me, and when I came near the hill, I marked that light gradually go up the hill, leaving a train of stars behind it. This line of new-born stars remained in the form of one lamp, and then another and another. It reached from the foot of the hill to its summit.

I did not see the lamplighter. I do not know his name, nor his age, nor his residence; but I saw the lights which he had kindled, and these remained when he himself had gone his way.

As I rode along I thought to myself, "How earnestly do I wish that my life may be spent in lighting one soul after another with the sacred flame of eternal life! I would myself be as much as possible unseen while at my work, and would vanish into eternal brilliance above when my work is done.

Spurgeon in *The Early Years*

16

Ten Years of
Mighty Ministry

Between 1875 and 1885 Spurgeon's ministry reached heights it had never attained before. Although the seed sown in London had already brought forth a great harvest, during these years the fruit proved still more abundant, and it came with a richness and a steadiness that was new even to a work so blessed of God as his had been.

By this time Spurgeon's preaching had changed to some extent. During his first few years in London he had been full of physical as well as spiritual vitality, and that had been reflected in his speaking. He had moved about on the platform with unbounded vigor, had frequently dramatized what he was saying, and had given an oratorical flourish to many an element in his discourse. His manner was very natural, and the whole was characterized by his tremendous earnestness.

With the passing of the years his style had altered. As he had matured personally, there had come upon him a still greater determination to be able to say with Paul, "We preach not ourselves, but Christ Jesus the Lord." He had become still more concerned lest by some oratorical gesture or some particularly striking statement he should draw attention to himself and should thereby cause his hearers to fail to see Christ. By 1875, in an effort to subdue the people's tendency to be conscious of him as he preached, he had taken on a more conversational style of utterance, moved around very little during the sermon, and attempted to avoid anything that could look like mere human oratory. He prayed that as he preached he might be hidden behind the cross and longed that sinners should not be concerned with him but should look upon the Savior.

Nevertheless, his message was still the same, and his earnestness was perhaps greater than ever. No matter what text he chose, he always declared the great fundamental principles of the faith. With a burning heart he pleaded with men and women to be reconciled to God.

In turn, a stronger sense of the reality of divine truth gripped men's hearts. A still larger number came to him on the Tuesday to inquire the way to Christ or to say they had recently found Him. Most of these people also told of their experience before the church on Tuesday or Thursday evening and were baptized on the Sunday. These constant additions gave the Tabernacle a membership of more than 5,000 and made it by far the largest Baptist church in the world.

Throughout this period, however, both Spurgeon and his wife were unwell much of the time. Mrs. Spurgeon's spirit was uplifted and her health somewhat improved by her undertaking the work of the Book Fund. But there were times when for days or weeks she was too sick to perform her task and was reduced again to the condition of a semi-invalid.

Spurgeon also was often laid low by illness. Throughout the years that are now before us he frequently suffered attacks of gout, with their terrible pain and their attendant depression. In 1879 he experienced a physical breakdown, the result of his excessive labor and responsibility. For five months he was absent from the Tabernacle.

He was more careful of his health now than he had been formerly. Each summer he tried to get away to Scotland for two weeks, where he was the guest of a well-to-do and very earnest Christian, James Duncan of Benmore Castle. And almost every winter he was able to spend a month or six weeks at Menton in southern France, and those periods of release from the damp and chill of England did much toward providing the health he needed to carry on with some measure of vigor during the rest of the year.

Accordingly, as we think of Spurgeon throughout this period—in fact, throughout the remaining years of his life—we must recognize that only infrequently was he in normal health, that his work was often hindered by sickness, and he knew many hours of pain. During those ten years Spurgeon witnessed several special events. The first was the visit to London of American evangelist D. L. Moody. In the early days of his Christian activity Moody had been greatly inspired by Spurgeon's success and had come to England to hear him. At a later date, 1873, accompanied by his song leader, Ira D. Sankey, Moody had returned to Britain and had launched a series of evangelistic campaigns in Scotland and England. While he was at Glasgow Spurgeon wrote, asking that when he came to London he would preach for him, and Moody's letter of reply closed with the statement:

> In regard to coming to your Tabernacle, I consider it a great honour to be invited; and, in fact, I should consider it an honour to black your boots; but to preach to your people would be out of the question. If they will not turn to God under your preaching, "neither will they be persuaded, though one rose from the dead."
>
> Yours with much love
>
> D. L. Moody.[1]

In 1875 Moody held an extended campaign in London. He and Sankey faced strong criticism, especially the charge of fanaticism, and Spurgeon came to their defense. In addressing a meeting of the Bible society at which the Archbishop of Canterbury was present, he strongly denied there was anything fanatical about the ministry of the two evangelists. And in speaking to another meeting he stated:

> We are happy to have our friends here [in London] because somehow or other they manage to get the popular ear. Our brethren have got a grip on the masses, and they preach the Gospel. We do not have it very distinct from a great many voices. But I know what Mr. Moody means when he speaks and what Mr. Sankey means when he sings. I have never seen men carry their meaning more fully upon their lips.[2]

Moody was burdened with labor in London, and after Spurgeon had preached at one of his meetings, Moody wrote:

1. *C. H. Spurgeon's Autobiography,* comp. Susannah Spurgeon and J. W. Harrald (London: Passmore and Alabaster, 1897), 4:169.
2. G. Holden Pike, *The Life and Work of Charles Haddon Spurgeon,* 6 vols. (London: Cassel, 1898), 5:155.

Dear Spurgeon:

   Ten thousand thanks for your help last night. You gave us a great lift. I
wish you would give us every night you can for the next sixty days.
There are so few men who can draw on a week night, and I want to keep
up the meetings in the East End and the West at the same time. It is hard
on me to have to speak twice the same evening. . . . Do all you can for
the work and we shall see blessed results.

Yours in haste,

D. L. Moody.[3]

   In 1881 Moody returned to England, and Spurgeon, who was in
Menton at the time, wrote asking him to take a Sunday at the
Tabernacle. Moody replied:

Dear Mr. Spurgeon:

   Yours of the 9th is to hand, and in reply let me say that I am thankful
for your very kind note. It quite touched my heart. I have for years
thought more of you than of any other man preaching the Gospel on this
earth; and to tell you the truth, I shrink from standing in your place. I do
not know of a church in all the land that I shrink from as I do from
yours:—not but what your people are in sympathy with the Gospel that
I try to preach, but you can do it so much better than I can.

   I thank you for inviting me, and (D. V.) I will be with your good
people Nov. 20. Will you want Mr Sankey, or will your own precentor
have charge. Either will suit me. Remember me to your good wife, and
accept my thanks for your letter of cheer.

Yours truly,

D. L. Moody[4]

   There were certain points of belief on which Moody and Spurgeon were not in full agreement. But they were united on the great
principles of the Christian faith, they admired one another, and
each encouraged and assisted the other in every way possible.

   In 1878 Spurgeon received an invitation to visit Canada. But as in
the case of his invitations to America—he had received at least five
of them—he had neither the time or the health to do so and thus
wrote a gracious refusal. It is to be wished that he might have been
able to go to the American continent, and one can imagine him

3. Spurgeon, *Autobiography,* 4:169-170.
4. Ibid.

spending some days with Mr. Moody in Chicago, ministering to his congregation, and probably repeating some of his *Lectures to My Students* at the Bible Institute.

But although Spurgeon did not visit America, during the following year (1879) his brother James spent nearly two months in the United States and Canada. He and his wife visited New York and Buffalo and "were deeply impressed with the great industrial enterprise of the people." Crossing into Canada, they paused to view Niagara Falls, and then went on to Toronto and Montreal and several smaller cities. James preached frequently in each country, and his ministry was everywhere highly regarded.

The second special event of these years took place in 1879: the twenty-fifth anniversary of Spurgeon's ministry in London.

He would have let the event pass unnoticed, but his people saw it as an opportunity to recognize his accomplishments and to express their gratitude. Under the arrangement of the deacons, two evenings were devoted to a commemoration of his labors and to praising God for his ministry. The congregation manifested their rejoicing by giving him a large sum of money, £6,476, stressing they intended he should use it for himself. But he immediately put it into the support of his institutions, and in thanking the people he said:

> Some churches have one crown, some another; our crown, under God, has been this,—the poor have the Gospel preached unto them, souls are saved, and Christ is glorified. O my beloved church, hold fast that which thou hast. . . . As for me, by God's help, the first and last thing I long for is to bring men to Christ. I care nothing about fine language, or about the pretty speculations of prophecy, or a hundred dainty things; but to break the heart and bind it up, to lay hold on a sheep of Christ and bring it back to the fold, is the one thing I would live for.
>
> Well, we have had this crowning blessing that, as nearly as I can estimate, since I came amongst you, more than nine thousand persons have joined this church. If they were all alive now, or all with us now, what a company they would be! . . .
>
> What I have done, I shall do still: namely, love you with all my heart, and love my Lord as His grace enables me. I mean to go on preaching Jesus, and His Gospel, and you may be sure I shall not preach anything else, for with me it is Christ or nothing. I am sold up, and my stock-in-trade is gone if Jesus Christ is gone. He is the sum of my ministry, my All-in-all.[5]

5. Ibid., 4:19, 22.

The words about having nothing if he had not Christ were un-doubtedly prompted by the unbelief that was then finding its way into numerous pulpits. Before many years had passed Spurgeon was to find it necessary to take a stand, defending the great truths of the Scripture. His attitude in contending was that those who did not believe in the deity of Christ had abandoned Christianity and had nothing whatsoever of it left.

The following year (1880) saw a major change in the daily life of the Spurgeons: they moved to another house. People had long told Spurgeon that because of his rheumatic condition and his wife's ill health he ought to live outside the city and on higher ground to escape the damp and fogs of London. Moreover, the Nightingale Lane area in which they had lived for twenty-three years had be-come largely commercial in nature. Although that lessened the pleasure of living there, it also increased the value of the property.

As he considered the advisability of relocating, Spurgeon found himself attracted by a For Sale sign on a suburban estate south of London and situated on a height of land called Beulah Hill. When a friend suggested it would be an ideal home for him and Mrs. Spur-geon he immediately replied it was too grand a place for him even to think of. But at that very time a developer expressed a desire to buy the Nightingale Lane property and offered an excellent price. The amount was almost sufficient to cover the entire cost of the Beulah Hill estate and, believing the Lord had opened the way, Spurgeon purchased it.

The new property, which was nine acres in extent, bore the name *Westwood*. It had several mature trees and an abundance of flowers and shrubs, together with a garden, stables, and pasture. The house was a typical Victorian gentleman's home. Spurgeon immediately used the drawing room as his library and the billiard room, with its large window, as his study. The surrounding area was quiet and peaceful, with a fine view to the south over the fields of Thornton Heath, and the place afforded the weary man, during whatever hours he was able to spend there, a sense of pleasant relaxation.

Of course, some people made loud complaint. Exaggerated de-scriptions of the house and the grounds were circulated, and it was said Spurgeon lived in a home fit for a prince. There was a small scenic pond on the property, but it was spoken of as a fine lake, and an American minister, after visiting London, likened the estate to that of Buckingham Palace.

Under the Spurgeons' ownership, however, Westwood was not

only a home: it also became a place of much business. Each morning two secretaries arrived, and the one, J. L. Keys, began opening the mail, a great pile of which awaited him every day. Some letters he answered himself, but many he set aside for Spurgeon's personal attention. The other secretary, J. W. Harrald, performed numerous duties in connection with Spurgeon's literary endeavors, made arrangements regarding his travels, and decided whether persons who called, wanting to see Spurgeon, should be allowed to take up his time.

Here, every Monday the work of preparing the sermon for the printer was done—always an exacting task. And here too *The Sword and the Trowel* was edited each month, a duty which meant that the assistant editor, G. Holden Pike, spent many a day in the study at Westwood. The Book Fund also operated from Westwood, and Mrs. Spurgeon had a room that overflowed with books, and there was much activity on her part in answering letters while her helpers worked at parceling and mailing bundles to needy pastors.

And above all, this was the scene of Spurgeon's manifold labors. His library contained 12,000 volumes, and every month he reviewed ten or twelve new ones for his paper. Besides the numerous books that he wrote, he penned around 500 letters every week. When we remember those were written by hand, and with a pen that had to be constantly dipped into an ink bottle, we can understand something of the labor involved. Undoubtedly, had the telephone been available in that day he would have made abundant use of it. It would have spared him the labor of many of the little notes he wrote in making arrangements for his visits to other churches, for the work of his institutions, and the printing of his writings. But it would have necessitated a full-time switchboard operator, who would have had the responsibility of dealing with the innumerable callers and of deciding whether or not to put them through to him.

Westwood was truly a fine place, but it also served a grand use. It was Spurgeon's home throughout the rest of his earthly journey, it made his burdens a little less heavy to bear, and it allowed him to perform many tasks that otherwise would not have been possible.

The fourth special event that marked the lives of Spurgeon and his wife during these years was the celebration of their silver wedding anniversary. It actually fell on January 8, 1881. Spurgeon was too ill at the time to go to the Tabernacle as the deacons hoped, and therefore the planning for this event, which was to have been held there on a Monday evening, was dropped. But the deacons and a few close friends spent the evening in happy fellowship with the Spurgeons at Westwood.

The other event we must notice took place three years later. This was Spurgeon's fiftieth birthday, which fell on June 19, 1884, and which the people called his Jubilee.

At the time the year opened Spurgeon was in Mentone. He was too ill to return to England at the date he had intended, and on January 10 he wrote to his people saying:

> Dear Friends,
>   I am altogether stranded. I am not able to leave my bed, or to find much rest upon it. The pains of rheumatism, lumbago and sciatica, mingled together, are exceedingly sharp. If I happen to turn a little to the right hand or to the left, I am soon aware that I am dwelling in a body capable of the most acute suffering.[6]

In another two weeks he came home, took a Sunday's services at the Tabernacle, and then was prostrated once more. This time he wrote, "Literally, my trouble is to get on my feet again. I am a poor creature. Evidently I am in the extreme of physical weakness. Nevertheless, the Lord can cause His spiritual power to be shown in me, and I believe He will. Your great love will bear with me, and I shall be in the front again, bearing witness to the faithfulness of the Lord."[7]

He gradually recuperated and was able to return to his ministry. By June he was ready to take part in the Jubilee celebration. Throughout the afternoon of the nineteenth he sat in his vestry and greeted the numerous people who called. In the evening the Tabernacle was filled for a meeting at which, on behalf of the church, the deacons expressed their thanks to God for Spurgeon and his ministry. Brief greetings were brought by a number of ministers, among them Spurgeon's father, his brother James, and his son Charles. A particular joy arose from the fact that Mrs. Spurgeon was present; after being absent for some years she was now sufficiently improved in health to attend this historic gathering, to the great delight of her husband and of the people.

Mr. Moody also spoke that evening, and we notice his address in part:

6. Iain Murray, ed., *The Full Harvest* (London: Banner of Truth, 1973), p. 385.
7. Ibid., p. 386.

Mr. Spurgeon has said to-night that he had felt like weeping. I have tried to keep back the tears, but I have not succeeded very well. . . .

Twenty-five years ago, after I was converted, I began to read of a young man preaching in London with great power, and a desire seized me to hear him, never expecting that, some day, I myself should be a preacher. Everything I could get hold of in print that he ever said, I read. . . .

In 1867 I made my way across the sea; and if ever there was a sea-sick man for fourteen days, I was that one. The first place to which I came was this building. I was told I could not get in without a ticket, but I made up my mind to get in somehow, and I succeeded. I well remember seating myself in this gallery. I recollect the very seat, and I should like to take it back to America with me. As your dear Pastor walked down to the platform, my eyes just feasted upon him. . . .

It happened to be the year he preached in the Agricultural Hall. I followed him up there, and he sent me back to America a better man. . . . While I was here I followed Mr. Spurgeon everywhere; and when, at home, people asked if I had gone to this and that cathedral, I had to say "No," and confess I was ignorant of them; but I could tell them something about the meetings addressed by Mr. Spurgeon.

In 1872 I thought I would come over again to learn a little more, and I found my way back to this gallery. I have been here a great many times since, and I never come into this building without getting a blessing to my soul.

I think I have had as great a one here to-night as at any other time. . . . When I look down on these orphan boys, when I think of the 600 servants of God who have gone out from the College, of the 1500 or 2000 sermons from this pulpit which are in print, and of the multitude of books that have come from the Pastor's pen . . . I would fain enlarge upon these good works. . . .

But let me just say this, if God can use Mr. Spurgeon, why should He not use the rest of us, and why should we not all just lay ourselves at the Master's feet, and say to Him, "Send me, use me"?

. . . Mr. Spurgeon, God bless you! I know that you love me, but I assure you that I love you a thousand times more than you can ever love me, because you have been such a blessing to me. . . . We may never meet again in the flesh, but by the blessing of God, I will meet you up yonder.[8]

Spurgeon's regular work went on with steady pace and everywhere met with still greater success.

"Everything grows and demands more and more attention,"[9] he

8. Ibid., pp. 396-98.
9. Pike, 6:216.

declared in reference to the Tabernacle and its institutions. One biographer tells us, "The spiritual work of the church was never more prosperous . . . in the last month of 1880 over a hundred persons were received into church fellowship."[10] And of one occasion during this time Spurgeon reported, "I sat from two till seven seeing enquirers desirous of entering the church, and I saw thirty-three of them without resting. I never had a more joyous time."[11] At his suggestion two hundred and fifty members left the Tabernacle to begin a new church at Peckham. Several other instances of this starting of new causes by Tabernacle people took place. "The Pastor was always pleased when such a battalion left the main army to carry on operations elsewhere."[12]

Despite his rheumatic condition Spurgeon did a great deal of preaching besides at the Tabernacle. One time in Leeds, well to the north in England, it was reported that "hundreds were unable to obtain admission. The announcement of Mr. Spurgeon's intention to preach . . . evinced his continued popularity by attracting hundreds from many miles distant." Of a meeting he addressed at Bristol we read, "The admission was, of course, by ticket, but the crowd at one time rushed past the police at the entrance and gained admittance. The desire to procure tickets was scarcely comprehensible to those who did not understand the preacher's unique popularity. . . it was even said that £10 had been offered for a seat."[13]

Those are but two of numerous reports of Spurgeon's itinerant ministry during these years. Judged by today's standards, travel by either train or horse and carriage was slow and uncomfortable, and as one reads G. Holden Pike's reports of Spurgeon's very frequent visits to other cities it is impossible not to wonder at so widespread a ministry on the part of a rheumatic man. Even when he went on his summer vacation to Scotland he could not refrain from preaching, and it was not unusual for him to preach to 10,000 and 15,000 in the open air on a Scottish hillside.

As we have seen, Spurgeon had received five invitations to visit America and one to visit Canada. Another reached him from Australia and, as in the former instances, he had to refuse. "How I wish I could glide over and return in a month,"[14] he wrote, and his words

10. Ibid.
11. Ibid., 6:257.
12. Ibid., 6:228.
13. Ibid., 6:206.
14. Ibid., 6:215.

seem to anticipate the liberty men have achieved today in the privilege of flight.

By November of each year Spurgeon was worn out and had no choice but to get away to Mentone. One year, before leaving he became so weak in the midst of his sermon that he had to pause and ask the congregation to sing a hymn while he recovered. He then continued the preaching, but he did so with difficulty, and on the morrow the rumor spread around London that he was dying. It was false, but he was terribly unwell, and in another day's time he set out on his trip to the south.

The work of the men from the College also experienced unusual blessing during these years. The men very largely followed Spurgeon's method of making sure, as far as was humanly possible, that anyone they baptized had truly been born again. Yet in the twelve years preceding 1880 the number of persons they had baptized amounted to some 39,000. Thus churches were built and increased everywhere throughout the land. Two of the College men, Clarke and Smith, were evangelists, and Spurgeon reported that in one year they conducted 1,100 services. Another year this team undertook the work of the Tabernacle during Spurgeon's six weeks at Mentone, and when he returned there were nearly four hundred persons who had professed conversion during his absence, waiting to be baptized.

Lord Shaftesbury was the chairman of the meeting that commemorated Spurgeon's fiftieth birthday, and after listening to the list of the sixty-six organizations that Spurgeon conducted he remarked:

> He has not been puffed up by success, but humbled, and animated the more to go on in his noble career of good . . . for the benefit of mankind.
> . . .
> I want to tell you what we *outsiders* think. What a tale of his agencies [was] read to you just now! How it showed what a powerful administrative mind our friend has. That list of associations, instituted by his genius, and superintended by his care, were more than enough to occupy the minds and hearts of fifty ordinary men. It seems to me to be the whole world in a nutshell. He carries on his Orphanage and various other institutions, and I would impress upon you that in which I think he shines the brightest—in the foundation and government of the Pastors' College. My worthy friend has produced a large number of men, useful in their generation, to preach the Word of God in all its simplicity and force . . . no man has produced such a body, capable and willing to

carry on the noble work as our friend whose jubilee was celebrated to-day.[15]

And a London newspaper, conscious of the constantly increasing nature of Spurgeon's work, remarked:

> Other men have had vicissitudes, reverses, disasters. Mr. Spurgeon's only vicissitudes have arisen from his continually increasing influence. He has had anxiety, no doubt, as other men; but it has only been the anxiety of growth, never of decline.[16]

Despite the health of the Tabernacle and its institutions, Spurgeon's illness was keeping him out of the pulpit many Sundays of the year. When he expressed his regret to the deacons and spoke disparagingly of his long absence in Mentone each winter, they declared their deep gratitude for whatever portion of the year he was able to give them. "We would rather have you for merely six months than anyone else for the entire twelve!" It was a good testimony to his ability, their appreciation, and the prosperity of the work.

15. Ibid., 6:275.
16. Ibid., 6:274.

Charles Haddon Spurgeon was in no respect ordinary. He was great as a man; great as a theologian; great as a preacher; great in private with God; and great in public with his fellow men. He was well versed in the three things which, according to Luther, make a minister: temptation, meditation and prayer. The school of suffering was one in which he was deeply taught."

James Douglas, *The Prince of Preachers*, 1894

17

Personal Characteristics

So pronounced a personality as C. H. Spurgeon could not but be marked by several features of thought and action that distinguished him from other men. We must look at those features, for by knowing them we shall have a better understanding of our great subject.

The chief element of Spurgeon's entire career was his walk with God. Among evangelicals such Christians as David Brainerd, Henry Martyn, John Fletcher, and Robert Murray McCheyne are remembered for the holiness of their lives. Spurgeon fully merits a place among such holy men.

We recall, for instance, the declaration of his dedication to the Lord, which he wrote shortly after his conversion. It asserted his glad yielding of himself to God, and in the diary that followed he recorded the manner in which he carried out that purpose. It is impossible to read his words without seeing the beauty of that young life in its purity and its selfless devotion.

The same principles motivated him when he came to London. Amidst a success so great that it would have driven many a man to unbounded pride, he remained humble and was often utterly broken before the Lord. He taught his people to pray, doing so far more by his own example than by any preaching he did on the subject. People heard him pray with such reality that they became ashamed of their own mere repetition of words, and, gradually overcoming the practice, they began to wrestle with God in fervent fellowship, as he did.

Spurgeon was ever a man of prayer. Not that he spent any long periods of time in prayer, but he lived in the spirit of communion with God. An American, Dr. Wayland Hoyt, provides an example of his practice.

> I was walking with him in the woods one day just outside London and, as we strolled under the shadow of the summer foliage, we came upon a log lying athwart the path. "Come," he said, as naturally as one would say it if he were hungry and bread was put before him, "Come, let us pray." Kneeling beside the log he lifted his soul to God in the most loving and yet reverent prayer.
>
> Then, rising from his knees he went strolling on, talking about this and that. The prayer was no parenthesis interjected. It was something that belonged as much to the habit of his mind as breathing did to the habit of his body.[1]

Another American, Dr. Theodore Cuyler, tells of a similar incident. As he and Spurgeon walked one day in the woods, "conversing in high spirits," suddenly Spurgeon stopped and said, "Come, Theodore, let us thank God for laughter." That was how he lived. "From a jest to a prayer meant with him the breadth of a straw."[2]

William Williams, who after his course at the Pastors' College became a successful minister, was often in Spurgeon's company. He says:

> One of the most helpful hours of my visits to Westwood was the hour of family prayer. At six o'clock all the household gathered into the study for worship. Usually Mr. Spurgeon would himself lead the devotions. The portion read was invariably accompanied with exposition. How amazingly helpful those homely and gracious comments were. I remember, especially, his reading of the twenty-fourth of Luke: "Jesus Himself drew near and went with them." How sweetly he talked upon having Jesus with us wherever we go. Not only to have Him draw near at special seasons, but to go with us whatever labour we undertake. . . .
>
> Then, how full of tender pleading, of serene confidence in God, of world-embracing sympathy were his prayers. With what gracious familiarity he could talk with his Divine Master! Yet what reverence ever

1. W. Y. Fullerton, *Charles H. Spurgeon* (Chicago: Moody, 1966), p. 150.
2. Ibid.

marked his address to his Lord. His public prayers were an inspiration and benediction, but his prayers with the family were to me more wonderful still. The beauty of them was ever striking: figures, symbols, citations of choice Scriptural emblems, all given with a spontaneity and naturalness that charmed the mind and moved the heart.

Mr. Spurgeon, when bowed before God in family prayer, appeared a grander man even than when holding thousands spellbound by his oratory.[3]

Such words make us realize what a magnificent experience it must have been to hear Spurgeon pray.

The man who lived in this constant fellowship with God manifested in his daily life all the fruits of the Spirit. Here love, joy, peace, patience, kindness, goodness, faithfulness, gentleness, and self-control were ever present, and with them there was a hatred of their opposites—a loathing of every form of sin.

This picture of Spurgeon as a man of unusual holiness is entirely true. Accordingly the statement we must now make will to many seem inconsistent. Nevertheless, it also is true, and we must make it. It is that Spurgeon both smoked cigars and drank alcoholic beverages.

When his smoking began is not known, but in Spurgeon's time the practice was believed to be beneficial to one's health. Robert Hall, the famous preacher of the St. Andrew's Street Baptist Church, Cambridge, had been ordered by his physician to become a smoker, and since Spurgeon lived at Cambridge and attended that church in his teens, he was undoubtedly familiar with this event. Moreover, there were no qualms whatsoever about the practice in the minds of many ministers in the Church of England and the Church of Scotland and in the churches of France and Holland.

Of course, Spurgeon made not the slightest attempt to hide his practice. One press reporter described him as he drove to the Tabernacle each morning, and his account closed with the words "enjoying his morning cigar." While out on a jaunt with his students one morning, when several of them had lighted pipes or cigars Spurgeon said, "Aren't you ashamed to be smoking so early!" and they immediately put out their fire. Then he produced a cigar and lit it, and both he and they laughed at his little joke, but his point was that he was in no way ashamed of the practice. It must be

3. William Williams, *Personal Reminiscences of Charles Haddon Spurgeon* (1895), p. 83-85.

emphasized he saw nothing wrong in his smoking and that he did it
openly.

But he received a sudden shock.

In 1874, Dr. George F. Pentecost, a Baptist pastor from America,
visited the Tabernacle, and Spurgeon had him sit on the platform for
the evening service. Spurgeon preached "strongly and plainly upon
the necessity of giving up sin, in order to success in prayer," and he
spoke against the seemingly unimportant little habits many Christians practice that keep them from true fellowship with God.

After concluding his sermon he asked Dr. Pentecost to speak,
suggesting especially that he apply the principle he himself had
declared.

It is probable Dr. Pentecost did not know that Spurgeon smoked.
At any rate, he applied Spurgeon's principle by telling of his own
experience in giving up cigars. He said, "One thing I liked exceedingly—the best cigar that could be bought,"[4] yet he felt the habit
was wrong in the life of a Christian, and he strove to overcome it.
The habit, however, proved so strong that he found himself enslaved, till after much struggling he took his cigar box before the
Lord, cried desperately for help, and was given a complete victory.
He told, with much praise to God, how he had been enabled to
defeat the habit. Throughout his words ran the idea that smoking
was not only an enslaving habit, but that the Christian must look on
it as a sin.

We must assume that if ever in his lifetime Spurgeon was embar-
rassed it was now! He arose and stated:

> Well, dear friends, you know that some men can do to the glory of God
> what to other men would be a sin. And, notwithstanding what Brother
> Pentecost has said, I intend to smoke a good cigar to the glory of God
> before I go to bed to-night.
>
> If anybody can show me in the Bible the command, "Thou shalt not
> smoke," I am ready to keep it, but I haven't found it yet. I find ten
> commandments, and it is as much as I can do to keep them; and I've no
> desire to make them eleven or twelve. The fact is, I have been speaking
> to you about real sin, and not about listening to mere quibbles and
> scruples. . . . "Whatsoever is not of faith is sin," and that is the real
> point of what my Brother Pentecost has been saying. Why, a man may
> think it is a sin to have his boots blacked. Well then, let him give it up
> and have them whitewashed. I wish to say I am not ashamed of anything

4. J. D. Fulton, *Spurgeon, Our Ally* (Chicago: H. J. Smith, 1892), p. 344.

whatever that I do, and I don't feel that smoking makes me ashamed, and therefore I mean to smoke to the glory of God.[5]

In no time the statement "a cigar to the glory of God" spread across England. The press carried the news and received a host of letters, some condoning Spurgeon's practice, but most condemning it. He had no choice but to attempt to defend himself, and in a letter to the *Daily Telegraph* he declared:

> Together with hundreds of thousands of my fellow-Christians, I have smoked, and with them I am under the condemnation of living in habitual sin, if certain accusers are to be believed. As I would not knowingly live even in the smallest violation of the law of God, and sin is the transgression of the law, I will not own to sin when I am not conscious of it. . . . When I have found intense pain relieved, a weary brain soothed, and calm, refreshing sleep obtained by a cigar, I have felt grateful to God, and have blessed His name: that is what I meant.[6]

Among the several pronouncements on the subject the most important was a lengthy open letter addressed to Spurgeon and published in pamphlet form. Its manner was calm, and its reasoning strong; it told him he was doing himself not physical good but physical harm by smoking. It reminded him of the example he was setting and mentioned the effort of Christian parents to keep their youths from the practice, only to be told, "Spurgeon smokes!"

William Williams tells us that in later years Spurgeon partially desisted from his smoking, sometimes going for months without a cigar. It is possible that this was an effort to prove to himself and others that he was not enslaved by the habit. About two years before his death he appears to have given up smoking completely, perhaps having by then realized it was not the help to his health that he had expected. Nevertheless, many of us today cannot but wish he had never undertaken the practice.

During a considerable portion of his life Spurgeon also used alcoholic drinks as a beverage.

In his day pure drinking water was difficult to obtain, and in order to avoid contamination most people used beer and ale at their meals. This had been human custom since time immemorial, and there can be little doubt that Spurgeon had been introduced to it as

5. Ibid., p. 345.
6. Ibid., pp. 346-47.

a boy in the homes of his grandfather and his father and that he had grown up accustomed to the practice. In turn, he had not long been in London when we find him using such drinks as beer, wine, and brandy, though in very moderate amounts. And this practice, like that of smoking, he did not in any way attempt to deny or to hide.

In 1863 the American Temperance orator John B. Gough was in England, and he published some strong statements against Spurgeon's use of alcohol. It appears that he exaggerated the extent of Spurgeon's practice, and Spurgeon asserted in an article in an American magazine, "I had always honoured Mr. Gough as a great and good man. . . . I had supposed, also, that he was a gentleman, and better still a Christian who esteemed the cause of religion even more highly than that of teetotalism."[7]

In 1871 Gough was in England again, and now he learned much better things about Spurgeon. He learned he no longer used alcohol, and after calling on him in his home Gough wrote: "I am glad to be able to say that I know he is at present, and has been for some time, a total abstainer, and that when he took stimulants it was by his physician's prescription. When he took it he made no secret of his course, but freely spoke of it wherever he might be."[8]

It is possible that Gough was somewhat mistaken as to the date of Spurgeon's change of habit, but several of the students of the College were strong opponents of all use of alcohol. Spurgeon's two sons were also abstainers, and it is probable their stand was influential upon their father. During the 1870s Spurgeon dropped the practice, and in later years he had Mr. Gough lecture at the Tabernacle against alcohol and in favor of abstinence.

In these two practices we see that Spurgeon was very human—a man of his times. Moreover, he was not alone in the indulgence. For instance, though John Wesley totally opposed the drinking of tea, hence the term "tee-totaler," he was something of an authority on the taste of ale. Charles Wesley also indulged, and the picture seems rather incongruous when we see the grand old Methodist warrior during the last years of his life listing his expenditures for drinks for the guests attending his son's musical concerts. Whitefield's practice was similar; we find him writing, "Give my thanks to that friendly brewer for the keg of rum he sent us."

I reported these matters regarding Spurgeon with much reluc-

7. G. Holden Pike, *The Life and Work of Charles Haddon Spurgeon*, 6 vols. (London: Cassel, 1898), 3:49.
8. Ibid., 5:11.

tance. They seem sadly regrettable in the life of so righteous a man, yet in the name of either Christian honesty or scholarly accuracy they could not be omitted.

There are, however, many further items of a very different and very worthy nature to be reported about Spurgeon, and we continue to consider them.

We notice first his physical person. He had nothing of the tall stately elegance of Edward Irving, which many Londoners then remembered, but was of medium height and not of an attractive build. His body was short in the upper leg, but he possessed an orator's powerful chest, his head was large, and it was said, "There were no angles about him." In his early thirties he began to grow a beard, which basically improved his appearance. It also protected him from the dampness and chill of England's winters, and, above all, it saved him the time formerly spent in shaving.

His face was highly expressive. The features were of themselves somewhat heavy but were ever lightened by the eyes, around which, even in his times of pain, a smile seemed unfailingly to glow. An artist once undertook to paint his portrait, but after four sittings he gave it up, saying, "I can't paint you. Your face is different every day. You are never the same."

A description of Spurgeon was made by one who knew him well, James Douglas.

> Could any face more fully express geniality, friendliness, warmth of affection, and overflowing hospitality? We know of none in whom these traits so shone forth. His greeting was warm as sunshine. . . . it mattered not what might be the shadow on the spirit or the trouble of the heart— it all vanished away at the voice of his welcome. There was light on his countenance that instantly dispersed all gloom. I have never known one whose presence had such charm, or whose conversation was such a rich and varied feast. . . .
>
> His voice stamped him as pre-eminent, being an organ in itself of amazing compass and sweetness of modulation. His speech was music. He was a born speaker, both as to the quality of note and the ease of utterance. He needed no training in elocution, for he had it in him. . . .
>
> Nor was his discourse ever verbiage, or a mere melodious sound in the ear. The born orator—as in Edward Irving's case—often lays himself open to this charge. Mr. Spurgeon's diction was never high-sounding or bombastic. . . . With the grandeur of his theme he soared; the transcendant never became small in his hands. If the thought was sublime he would give it sublime expression; if homely, he bedecked it accordingly.
> . . .
>
> His intellect [was] an equal associate of his great heart. The brain of

this truly great man was of a giant order. . . . He did with ease, and
spontaneously, mental feats which men of name and inordinate vanity,
struggle in vain, even by elaboration, to accomplish. . . . He could grasp
the bearings of a subject, hold his theme well in hand, and deploy his
thoughts like troops in tactical movements. He was never "at sea." . . . All
was orderly arrangement.[9]

Spurgeon always had a love for animals. Though during his first
years in London he used a one-horse carriage, after he moved to
Westwood, having farther to drive to the Tabernacle, he changed to
a two-horse conveyance. The horses were kept in excellent condition, and he jokingly spoke of them as "under the law"—they rested
each Saturday. Some of the strongest statements one will find anywhere in all his works are in an article he wrote against cruelty to
animals, as with fierce vehemence he cited one instance after another of terrible treatment of horses and dogs that had come to his
attention.

He kept a hive of bees at Westwood and took delight in caring for
them himself when he had the time. He was fascinated with the
system of life the bees used in the hive. On one occasion a great
number lighted on him, but he ran into the house and removed the
outer clothes without receiving a single sting.

After a thief broke into his house and stole a gold-headed walking
cane that John B. Gough had given him, Spurgeon obtained a dog.
But it was not a watchdog—merely a little one of the Pug variety,
and it had the affection of Mrs. Spurgeon and himself. There were
goldfish in the pond at Westwood, and it was said they would swim
to him and wait to be stroked when he came to the edge of the
water. Nevertheless, we may be sure he brought something they
liked to eat and that that was their special attraction.

During the last twenty or so years of his life Spurgeon tried to use
Wednesday as his day of freedom from work. And there were times
he took a holiday that lasted half the week. On those occasions,
whether the one day or four, he would take as his companion one of
the young pastors who had been a student of his college, or perhaps
a fellow minister—sometimes one of the American pastors who was
visiting London. Dressed in some carefree togs he would drive his
horse and carriage and set out on quiet country roads to the south

9. James Douglas, *The Prince of Preachers* (London: Morgan and Scott, n.d.), pp.
85-87.

of London, stopping at some picturesque inn for lunch or for over-
night accommodation. At times they left the horse in the stable at
the inn and walked in the woods or found some secluded spot in
which to sit and behold the divine handiwork in nature all around
them.

On these jaunts Spurgeon put away the thoughts of his burden of
responsibility and was the soul of merriment. He talked about the
history of villages or buildings in the area, he knew plants and
flowers by their names in both English and Latin and, indeed, could
converse on all manner of subjects with accuracy and enjoyment.
The Archbishop of Canterbury had a large estate in this part of
England, and he asked Spurgeon to make use of it just as if it were
his own. And when the outing was over, his companions usually
regarded the event as one of the grand occasions of their lives and
spoke of him as the most charming and fascinating host.

We cannot adequately know Spurgeon unless we recognize also
his strong sensitivity.

Although he was a rugged and distinctively masculine individual,
he was also very tender and was easily moved to tears. His whole
person was alive to the various experiences of life, and he felt
things deeply. For instance, we are told that there were two occasions on which he was so disturbed in his spirit that he prayed all
night; one of those was so sacred that it was not further mentioned,
but the other was the time when his son Tom was about to sail to
Australia and take up a new life in that warmer climate. Spurgeon
had hoped that as he aged he would increasingly have the help of
his two sons, but now Tom was leaving and was going so far away,
and he felt he would never see him again. He preached that Sunday
evening on "Hannah, a Woman of Sorrowful Spirit," and during the
hours that followed he wrestled with God, and before the morning
dawned he had calmly submitted to his son's departure.[10]

Another element of his sensitivity lay in his fear of crossing a road
when the traffic was heavy. In that day the streets of London were
full of horses and carts and carriages, some drivers urging their
steeds onward as speedily as possible and with no rules of the road
to control them. On one occasion, amidst this hustle and bustle,
Spurgeon stood on a corner near the Bank of England and could not
summon enough courage to cross the road. But a blind man approached and asked that he help him make his way through the

10. Fullerton, p. 151.

stream of moving traffic, and in view of the blind man's need Spurgeon responded, and the two of them crossed in safety.

Spurgeon experienced severe depressions, and although those were to some extent the result of the gout, there probably was also another reason.

All manner of persons came to him to pour into his ear the tale of their trials and to seek his advice. This was true of hundreds of the Tabernacle people but was especially true of the men of the College who had gone out into the ministry. There were problems in their churches to be met and decisions to be made, and they came, first to unburden themselves to him, and then to have him pray for them and assist them with his wise counsel. One of the best of the College men, James Douglas, said that he saw Mr. Spurgeon so often bearing other men's burdens in this way that he determined never to bring him any trial of his own, but that when he came to him it would be with some account of blessing that would raise his spirits.

But although he thus heard the troubles of numerous others, Spurgeon had no one to whom he could tell his own. In view of Mrs. Spurgeon's frequent sickness he undoubtedly did not tell her the full tale of the load he bore. There was the great machine he had created—the Tabernacle and its associated organizations—to be maintained, all at tremendous cost. The deacons and elders shouldered their measure of responsibility, yet so much depended on him that in many senses he bore the great load alone. Truly he trusted the Lord, yet he also felt the strain of his burdens and having no one to whom he could fully unburden himself, he built up a sense of trial within his breast, and it gradually bore him down into severe depression.

What he suffered in these times of darkness we may not know. They usually accompanied his days and nights of physical agony under the strength of a gout attack, and even his desperate calling upon God often brought him no relief. "There are dungeons," he said, "beneath the Castle of Despair," and he had often been in them.

Those terrible experiences had their good effect upon his ministry, however. In his audiences each Sunday sat hundreds of persons who had come from a week of trial and who needed kindness and encouragement, and here was the man who could give it. His voice was often broken with his feeling for the sorrowing. Many a time he was in excruciating pain as he preached. He knew what suffering was, and his words were full of sympathy that lifted spirits and sent tried men and women forth to face their circumstances with new strength.

In spite of the depression, Spurgeon was basically a very happy man. William Williams was often in his company, and he wrote:

> What a bubbling fountain of humour Mr. Spurgeon had! I have laughed more, I verily believe, when in his company than during all the rest of my life besides. He had the most fascinating gift of laughter . . . and he had also the greatest ability for making all who heard him laugh with him. When someone blamed him for saying humorous things in his sermons, he said, "He would not blame me if he only knew how many of them I keep back."[11]

The following passage from his lectures gives us insight into Spurgeon's behavior when under depression.

> Gentlemen, there are many passages of Scripture which you will never understand thoroughly until some trying or singular experience shall interpret them to you.
>
> The other evening I was riding home after a heavy day's work. I felt wearied and sore depressed, when swiftly and suddenly that text came to me, "My grace is sufficient for thee." I reached home and looked it up in the original, and at last it came to me in this way, "My grace is sufficient for THEE," and I said, "I should think it is, Lord," and I burst out laughing. I never understood what the holy laughter of Abraham was till then. It seemed to make unbelief so absurd. . . . Oh, brethren, be great believers! Little faith will bring your souls to heaven, but great faith will bring heaven to your souls.[12]

11. Williams, p. 17, 18.
12. Ibid., p. 19.

How many souls may be converted by what some men are privileged to write and print!

There is, for instance, Dr. Doddridge's Rise and Progress of Religion in the Soul. *I could wish that everybody had read that book, so many have been the conversions it has produced. I think it more honour to have composed Watts's* Psalms and Hymns *than Milton's* Paradise Lost; *and more glory to have written old Thomas Wilcock's book* A Choice Drop of Honey From the Rock, Christ, *or the booklet God has used so much,* The Sinner's Friend, *than all the works of Homer.*

I value books for the good they may do. Much as I respect the genius of Pope, or Dryden, or Burns, give me the simple lines of Cowper that God has owned in bringing souls to Him. Oh, to think, that I may write and print books which shall reach poor sinners' hearts!

Spurgeon, 1855

18

Spurgeon as an Author

From the time of his boyhood Spurgeon manifested a desire to put his thoughts on paper and have others read them. When he was only twelve he produced what he called *The Juvenile Magazine*— a few small hand-written sheets that he circulated among his sisters and his brother. It contained news of a weekly prayer meeting that he conducted, and it offered advertising space at the rate of three lines for half a penny. Though it was but a childish endeavor it showed the attraction he felt toward the work of publishing.[1]

At the age of fifteen he wrote an essay, 295 pages in length, entitled *Popery Unmasked*.[2] He submitted it in a contest, and although it did not win the prize, in recognition of its high quality one of the sponsors awarded him a gift of £1.

When he reached the age of seventeen and had become a pastor, his writing broke into print for the first time. He produced a few brief articles to present the way of salvation, and those were published as the *Waterbeach Tracts*. Then some further short items from his pen were accepted by the *Baptist Reporter*.

1. Iain Murray, ed., *The Early Years* (London: Banner of Truth, 1962), p. 46.
2. *C. H. Spurgeon's Autobiography*, comp. Susannah Spurgeon and J. W. Harrald, 4 vols. (London: Passmore and Alabaster, 1897), 1:57.

Those early endeavors, however, were but a foretaste of the great work of publishing that lay before him.

Spurgeon had been in London only six months when one of his sermons was published in the *Penny Pulpit*. This was so well received that the *Baptist Messenger* published one also, and the *Penny Pulpit* published three or four more. The response made it evident that there was a large possible readership for the discourses of the rising young preacher.

One of the deacons of the New Park Street Chapel was especially interested in this development. This was Joseph Passmore, who, with a partner, James Alabaster, had recently opened a printing business. Mr. Passmore was an earnest Christian and an enterprising businessman, and he suggested that Spurgeon allow him to publish one of his sermons every week. Spurgeon was then in the midst of his great burst of fame, and he dreaded the thought of being projected still further into prominence. Nevertheless, he recognized the published sermon might well be used of God in the salvation of souls, and therefore he consented.

Moreover, besides this weekly production, each January the fifty-two sermons published during the preceding year were reprinted. They were bound together as a single volume, *The New Park Street Pulpit*.

By the time this first volume appeared (January 1855), Spurgeon had already published his first two books, *The Saint and His Saviour* and *Smooth Stones Taken from Ancient Brooks*. And he intended to continue the weekly and yearly publication of the sermons and also to produce further books.

He was warned against doing so by a very worthy friend, Dr. John Campbell. Dr. Campbell had retired from the pastorate of the Whitefield Tabernacle and had become the editor of a religious paper, the *British Banner*. He was a warm-hearted evangelical and a capable writer, and he had used his magazine in Spurgeon's favour, commending his actions and defending him from his attackers. But Campbell was convinced that no one was likely to succeed at both preaching and writing, and that Spurgeon had better stick solely to the former and drop the latter.

"We think it will be wise in Mr. Spurgeon," he wrote, ". . . to moderate his expectations in this quarter. The number of those, either in past or present times, who have attained to eminence both with tongue and pen is small. The Greeks produced none, the

Romans only one, and Great Britain has hardly been more successful."[3]

Dr. Campbell went on to urge Spurgeon not to try to be an author, and since Spurgeon thought so highly of him he could not but have felt the force of his warning.

Moreover, the task of writing did not come as easily to Spurgeon as did that of preaching.

> Writing is to me the work of a slave. It is a delight . . . to talk out my thoughts in words that flash upon the mind at the instant when they are required, but it is poor drudgery to sit still, and groan for thoughts and words without . . . obtaining them. Well may a man's books be called his "works," for if every mind were constituted as mine is, it would be work indeed to produce a quarto volume.[4]

But despite Campbell's warning and the "drudgery" he experienced in writing, Spurgeon had strong reason to use the printed page. His sermons, when preached, had been remarkably blessed of God, and the same had proved true when they were published. The weekly issue and the yearly volumes had brought letters in abundance telling of the conversion of sinners and the comforting of saints, and in view of the results he had no thought but to continue to present his message in print.

Spurgeon became as successful as an author as he was as a preacher.

In 1855 he began editing a sermon every Monday and having it come forth from the press every Thursday. He continued that week by week, without fail, till his death in 1892.

This was in itself a remarkable achievement. It is recognized that, in general, few people bother to read printed sermons. Scores of the great men of God have published a volume of their sermons, and after being read, usually no more than once and in general by other preachers, these books have been forgotten. But Spurgeon's sermons were read, not only by numerous ministers but also by a host of people in all walks of life, and the demand was so sustained that it increased steadily throughout his whole lifetime.

Indeed, thousands of people in various countries looked forward

3. Early years, 1:405.
4. Early years, 1:404-5.

excitedly each week to the arrival of the new sermon. These discourses were sold on the streets of London and other English cities, they went forth in the mail throughout Britain and to other lands, and they were carried by the colporteurs in their visits to villages and to rural homes. The circulation in Scotland was especially large, and in America, after the opposition to Spurgeon's declamation against slavery had died down, they were bought in larger numbers than even in Britain.

Several foreign translations appeared. The first was in Welsh, and a new sermon was published in that land each month. Spurgeon was loved in Holland, and his sermons were translated regularly; the queen was one of the readers, and when Spurgeon was in her country she requested that he call on her.

> In Germany a score or more of publishers issued versions. . . . The sermons in Swedish circulated largely among the upper classes and the translator informed Spurgeon that there had been cases of conversion among some of noble and even of royal birth. . . .
> Other languages into which the sermons have been translated include Arabic, Armenian, Bengali, Bulgarian, Castilian, Chinese, Congo, Czech, Esthonian, French, Gaelic, Hindi, Hungarian, Italian, Japanese, Kaffir, Karen, Lettish, Maori, Norwegian, Polish, Russian, Servian, Spanish, Syriac, Tamil, Telugu and Urdu. Some sermons were also prepared in Moon and Braille type for the use of the blind.[5]

Several persons lent their aid to the distribution of the sermons. One man gave away no fewer than a quarter of a million copies—some of them were made into volumes of forty-two discourses and expensively bound, and those he sent to all the crowned heads of Europe. Another man submitted several sermons translated into Russian to the Orthodox church and was granted permission to circulate them with that church's seal of approval stamped upon the cover. Bearing this mark, a million sermons went forth in that land.

In many countries where people lived at a distance from a church, groups of people gathered each Lord's Day to hear the reading of one of Spurgeon's sermons. He tells, for instance, of hearing from such a company in some remote district of England. The letter stated that approximately two hundred persons had been

---

5. Charles Ray, *A Marvellous Ministry: The Story of Spurgeon's Sermons* (London: Passmore and Alabaster, 1905), pp. 27-28.

converted in such a gathering, and they wanted a minister to come and form them into a church. Likewise there were out-of-the-way areas in Scotland where people had no idea who was the Prime Minister of Great Britain, but they all knew about Spurgeon through the reading of his sermons.

A Quaker advertised the sermons in several papers, stating they could be obtained from his place of business. Not only did he sell thousands, but he also brought the sermons in general to the attention of the public of his area. An Australian regularly printed the sermons as advertisements in several newspapers, and Spurgeon says that cost the man "week by week a sum which I scarcely dare to mention, lest it should not be believed."

There is no possible means of estimating the number of copies of Spurgeon's sermons that have been issued. But an English author writing in 1903 declared "The total number of Spurgeon's sermons issued in print during half a century must be between two and three hundred millions!"[6]

A vast number have been produced since that date. The yearly volumes containing sermons he had prepared for the press but had not published were printed after his death in 1892, and that continued till it was brought to a stop in 1917, not by any lack of further sermons but because of a wartime paper shortage. A total of sixty-two volumes, each containing some 480 pages, were thus produced. The collection constitutes an immense theological and homiletical library.

Numerous sermons in volume form have since been reprinted by several publishers in both Britain and America.[7] Single sermons have been published on numerous occasions in magazines and papers, and how many have thus been produced cannot be known.

Of late years, however, a still greater work of republishing Spurgeon has been accomplished. During the early 1970s the Banner of Truth Trust of Edinburgh reprinted several of the yearly volumes of sermons, and they were readily received. At the same time Pilgrim Publications of Pasadena, Texas, undertook the same heavy task and photocopied the entire sixty-two volumes, together with a complete set of *The Sword and the Trowel*. With those Pilgrim pro-

6. Charles Ray, *The Life of Charles Haddon Spurgeon* (London: Passmore and Alabaster, 1903), p. 449.
7. In certain reprinted volumes and magazine reproductions some of Spurgeon's doctrinal emphases, particularly his Calvinism, have been deleted without mention of the change.

duced also some five or six smaller works about Spurgeon and the Tabernacle. The whole keeps Spurgeon in prominence before the Christian public and makes a knowledge of his preaching, his doctrine, and his general activities readily available.

Of course the question arises as to what there is about these sermons that has caused this extraordinary interest.

First is the reality of Spurgeon's preaching. Most people who heard him were struck by his earnestness—the realization that the things of God were vitally real to him. As one reads his sermons it is evident the great matters with which he dealt were not mere theories, as with many preachers, but they were to him assured truths, and he delivered them as being directly commissioned of God to do so.

Their simplicity is also appealing. Spurgeon dealt with some of the grandest and deepest matters known to the human mind—God, man, sin, atonement, judgment, eternity—but in his discourses, he gave those vast truths a simplification that rendered them grippingly understandable to the common man. The years of his ministry in the Surrey Gardens Music Hall were particularly notable in this regard, for his congregation there was composed to a large extent of persons with little education, and though he still preached on the great doctrines of the Scriptures he more than ever spoke in a manner that would not be above the grasp of the very unlearned. And the simplification that marked the sermons when preached is equally evident in them in their printed form. Spurgeon possessed a rare combination of gifts, but his ability to make himself understood by ordinary mankind is one of the rarest and most important of all.

Nevertheless, Spurgeon's sermons appeal also to persons of learning. Members of Parliament, judges, university personnel, important figures in the literary world, and industrial magnates frequently had their place in his congregation. And numerous persons of similar standing have long enjoyed and profited from the reading of his sermons. As Sir William Robertson Nicoll stated in 1903, "Spurgeon was a great and trained theologian, master in every part of his own system."[8] And furthermore, Charles Ray notes, "The sermons preached fifty years ago are a living message to-day, and one dares to

8. William Robertson Nicoll, *An Introduction to Spurgeon's Sermons* (London: Nelson, n.d.), p. 8.

prophesy they will not be out of date when this twentieth century is drawing to its close."[9]

While the sermons came out singly each week and in volume form each year, Spurgeon also produced his magazine, *The Sword and the Trowel,* each month. It contained news of the religious world in general, with his comments upon it, but especially of the Tabernacle and its associated organizations. There were also biblical expositions and warm spiritual articles and exhortations to Christian zeal. One of its most remarkable features was the series of book reviews. These were virtually all written by Spurgeon himself, and they manifest something of the vast extent of his reading and of his ability to express an all-covering opinion in a few words.

Besides the sermons and the monthly *Sword and the Trowel* Spurgeon produced also a large number of books—more than one hundred and forty separate titles.

The chief of these was a seven-volume work, a commentary on the Psalms, entitled *The Treasury of David.* It contained "an original exposition of the book, a collection of illustrative extracts from the whole range of literature, a series of homiletical hints upon almost every verse and a list of writers upon each Psalm." A secretary, J. L. Keys, assisted in the research for these volumes, but the writing was done by Spurgeon himself, and more than twenty years elapsed from the date he started till the time he finished. Nearly 148,000 volumes sold during his lifetime, and the set has since been reprinted several times. It is regarded as one of the greatest works on the Psalms ever written.

Another work that deserves particular mention is Spurgeon's *Commenting and Commentaries.* He says that in writing this work "I have toiled, and read much, and passed under review some three or four thousand volumes," and of this large number of books he chose 1,437 on which he expressed his opinion. His treatment of these works reveals something of his extraordinary ability, for not only was he able to weigh each of them, extolling their merits or pointing out their faults, but he did so in a remarkable manner. In other hands this subject could have been dry and boring, but in his it becomes alive and attractive and is even marked by much humor.

But from those writings that manifest a vast extent of learning, Spurgeon could go to the opposite extreme and write of the sim-

---

9. Ray, *A Marvellous Ministry,* p. 71.

plest things of everyday life. His *John Ploughman's Talk* and *John Ploughman's Pictures,* in the most down-to-earth manner, presented a series of brief parables or proverbs and applied them to everyday life. By 1900 the *Talk* had sold 410,000 copies and the *Pictures* more than 150,000, and those figures have since greatly increased.

Mention must also be made of his *Morning by Morning* and *Evening by Evening,* devotional readings with which to begin and close the day. These two little volumes are characterized by Spurgeon's rare ability to put deep truths into simple language and to do so in a rich, warm, spiritual tone. Both books have been reprinted several times, and since by the time of his death some 230,000 had been sold we must assume that the circulation by now is at least a half a million.

Much more might be said about the other productions of Spurgeon's pen. Of the total 140, 21 are listed in the Bibliography of this book, and those are sufficient to indicate something of the extent of his thinking and the versatility of his mind. So great was the output of his books that it kept the Passmore and Alabaster firm constantly busy, and in order to meet these requirements they moved to new and much larger premises. He once jokingly said to Mr. Passmore, "Do I work for you, or do you work for me?" and between the two men there was a warm and lasting friendship. The business arrangement was considerably profitable for each. It thoroughly established the publishers and likewise provided an excellent income for Spurgeon, allowing him to live without accepting any salary from his church and enabling him to contribute extensively to his various enterprises.

Spurgeon had also a measure of poetic ability. We have seen some verses[1] that he wrote to his wife, and there were several occasions when he thus addressed her in rhythmic sentences. When he compiled *Our Own Hymnbook* he included metrical versions that he had written of certain of the psalms. Some of his hymns, particularly "Sweetly the holy hymn, Breaks o'er the morning air" and "The Holy Ghost is here, Where saints in prayer agree," are widely known and frequently used. But his most popular production is his communion hymn.

> Amidst us our Beloved stands,
> And bids us view His piercéd hands;

1. pp. 60-61.

Points to His wounded feet and side,
Blest emblems of the crucified.

What food luxurious loads the board,
When at His table sits the Lord!
The wine how rich, the bread how sweet,
When Jesus deigns His guests to meet!

If now with eyes defiled and dim,
We see the signs, but see not Him,
Oh may His love the scales displace
And bid us view Him face to face.

Our former transports we recount,
When with Him in the holy mount;
These cause our souls to thirst anew,
His marr'd but lovely face to view.

Thou glorious bridegroom of our hearts,
Thy present smile a heaven imparts
Oh lift the veil, if veil there be,
Let every saint Thy glory see.

Spurgeon placed great emphasis on the Communion service. He made it a time of remembering Christ, especially Christ in His death, and as he spoke of His suffering and endeavored to understand something more of His atonement, he was often so moved that he could barely speak, his voice was rich with emotion, and his eyes flowed plentifully with tears. We can imagine the great congregation at such an hour singing Montgomery's "According to thy gracious word," Watts's "How sweet and awful is this place," or this hymn from his own pen, undoubtedly with many in the audience as overcome as he was himself with a love for the Lord Jesus and with fresh desires to go forth to serve Him.

It has been mentioned that Spurgeon wrote about five hundred letters every week. They were not dictated to a secretary but were the product of his own hand and were written with a pen that had to be dipped every few seconds into an ink bottle. Moreover, his hand was often so swollen from his arthritic condition that he could scarcely hold a pen, and then the writing which was normally so well formed and readable became irregular and rough. Most of his letters were written either to comfort a saint or to plead with some sinner to receive Christ, and the pain of moving the hand could not be allowed to hinder so important a responsibility.

Spurgeon proved as capable as an author as he was as a preacher. He constantly received letters from almost every country on earth, telling of blessing that he had been brought through his printed works. He learned of miracles of grace, of men and women being converted and turned from the bondage of sin to the glories of the Christian life. For instance, a condemned murderer about to be executed in South America wrote to say a copy of one of the sermons had been given to him some months earlier; he had read it repeatedly, and now had believed on Christ and was facing his approaching death in peace. Spurgeon mentions a bedridden woman in England who wrote to say, "Nine years I was dark, and blind and unthinking; but my husband brought me one of your sermons. I read it and God blessed it to the opening of my eyes. He converted my soul by it, and now, all glory to Him, I love His name. Each Sabbath morning I wait for your sermon. I live on it all the week, it is marrow and fatness to my spirit."[10]

Toward the end of his life Spurgeon stated, "For many years, seldom has a day passed, and certainly never a week, without letters reaching me from all sorts of places, even at the utmost ends of the earth, telling me of the salvation of souls by means of one or other of the sermons."[11]

Professor James Stalker summed up what he called Spurgeon's power to express himself in writing. He said:

> We have scores of ministers who are ambitious of writing for the world of the cultivated; but a book frankly and successfully addressing the average man, in language which he can understand, is one of the rarest products of the press. It really requires very exceptional power. It requires knowledge of human nature, and knowledge of life. It requires common sense; it requires wit and humour; and it requires command of simple and powerful Saxon.
>
> Whatever the requirements may be, Mr. Spurgeon had them in an unexampled degree.[12]

10. Murray, *The Early Years*, p. 392.
11. Ibid., p. 399.
12. Iain Murray, ed., *The Full Harvest* (London: Banner of Truth, 1973), p. 418.

THE FINAL YEARS

1887—1892

I marvel that ye are so soon removed from him that called you into the grace of Christ unto another gospel:

Which is not another; but there be some that trouble you, and would pervert the gospel of Christ.

But though we or an angel from heaven, preach any other gospel unto you than that which we have preached unto you, let him be accursed.

As we said before, so say I now again, If any man preach any other gospel unto you than that ye have received, let him be accursed.

Galatians 1:6-9

19

Earnestly Contending
for the Faith

The Metropolitan Tabernacle was a member of the Baptist Union of England. As is normal in Baptist practice, the Union had no authority over the churches, and it served only as a means of fellowship, information, and missionary cooperation. But, as is *not* normal in Baptist practice, it had no doctrinal statement and required simply the belief that the immersion of the believer is the only Christian baptism. The presumption was that all such churches were thoroughly evangelical, and for years that had been almost entirely true.

Spurgeon had proved a strong help to the Union. From the time of his coming to London the public recognition of the fact that he was a Baptist had gradually brought the denomination into a prominence greater than it had ever known. Under his influence huge attendances were drawn to the Union's annual meetings, and the Union's financial receipts were much increased. He also founded the London Baptist Association and did much to assist in the construction of new Baptist churches, especially those under the ministry of his students.

During the early 1860s Spurgeon foresaw a large future prosperity for the Baptists of England. He stated that in view of their zeal and the exceptional blessing they were experiencing, their numbers would undoubtedly double within the next ten years, and he even went so far as to suggest they might one day become the country's major denomination.

At that time, not only were the Baptists especially active, but there was much zeal among other Christians too. The revival taking place in 1859 was marked by considerable evangelism in other denominations, and all gave evidence of a new fervor and witnessed many professions of faith.

The prospects were especially bright and well would it have been if they had stayed that way. But at the same time forces of an entirely opposite nature were working against Christianity and were doing so with strong effect.

This opposition to evangelical truth sprang first from the publication in 1859 of Darwin's *Origin of Species.* Teaching that life had originated not by divine creation but by blind chance, it directly contradicted the Scriptures and obviated the very idea of the existence of God.

Second, the Christian foundations were undermined by what was called Higher Criticism. This was an attempt to reconsider the sources of the books of the Bible, and it brought new ideas as to the identities and the dates of the writers. It led to attempts to explain away the miracles of the Bible and to reduce the inspired Word to the level of a merely human book.

This new concept of the Bible was taught in many university classrooms. Moreover, during the 1860s it was given a friendly ear in certain ministerial training schools, and in the 1870s it could be heard from several pulpits. Certain men felt themselves courageous in denying the truths their fathers had believed and in contradicting ideas they considered to be no more than ancient myths. They called their teaching the *New Theology* or *New Thought* and declared they were leading the people out of bondage and into liberty.

By 1880 much of England was stirred by the change that was thus being made in Christian beliefs. The new ideas were reported in both the secular and the religious press, and several books appeared propounding them. The evolutionary theory was propagated by a number of very able men. Several ministers likewise supported it and also endorsed the claims of the higher critics. This departure from the fundamentals of Christianity was evident in every denomination and to some extent was to be found in various men of the Baptist Union.

Spurgeon's attitude toward this situation was immediately one of militant opposition. From the beginning of his ministry he had met instances of unbelief and had raised his voice against it. But now matters were much worse and, although he was so often in ill health, he nevertheless determined to take a clear stand in favor of the Scriptures and to do everything in his power to contradict the teachings of the new theology.

Several people throughout Britain wrote to Spurgeon, telling him of instances of departure from the faith among Baptist ministers in their part of the country. Moreover, Dr. S. H. Booth, the secretary of the Baptist Union, both met with him and corresponded with him, giving him the names and statements of certain men in the Union who no longer believed the fundamentals of the faith. Booth asked his advice as to how best such a situation could be handled.

In replying to Booth, and in his dealings with the officials of the Union, Spurgeon declared the Union must make its position clearly known. He urged that it adopt a statement of faith—one that plainly enunciated the evangelical position—and that acceptance of it be the basis on which membership of a church or a person in the Union would be continued.

The earnestness of Spurgeon's efforts to get the Union to take action is evident in many of his statements. For instance, he spoke of "my private remonstrances to officials and my repeated appeals to the whole body." "I have repeatedly spoken," he wrote, "to the secretary upon the subject, as he will willingly admit." He said he had also taken the matter up with Booth's assistant, Mr. Baynes, asserting, "On each occasion one or other has heard my complaints till they must, I fear, have been wearied. . . . With Mr. Williams and Dr. [Alexander] Maclaren I have had considerable correspondence."[1]

But Spurgeon's request that the Union adopt a statement of faith was rejected. When the Union met it was voted down on the argument that Baptists had always believed in the liberty of every man to state his beliefs in his own way and that so long as a person held to the doctrine of baptism by immersion, no more was necessary.

Realizing in ever increasing measure the fact that unbelief was spreading rapidly and knowing he could expect no action to be taken by the Union, Spurgeon took action himself. He published an article entitled "The Down-Grade" in his magazine, and it opened with the statement:

---

1. G. Holden Pike, *The Life and Work of Charles Haddon Spurgeon,* 6 vols. (London: Cassel, 1898), 6:292.

No lover of the gospel can conceal from himself the fact that the days are evil . . . yet our solemn conviction is that things are much worse in many churches than they seem to be, and are rapidly tending downward. Read those papers which represent the Broad School of Dissent, and ask yourself, How much further could they go? What doctrine remains to be abandoned? What other truth is to be the object of contempt? A new religion has been originated which is no more Christianity than chalk is cheese; and this religion, being destitute of moral honesty, palms itself off as the old faith with slight improvements, and on this plea usurps pulpits which were erected for gospel preaching. The Atonement is scouted, the inspiration of Scripture is derided, the Holy Ghost is degraded into an influence, the punishment of sin is turned into a fiction, and the Resurrection into a myth, and yet these enemies of our faith expect us to call them brethren and maintain a confederacy with them!

At the back of the doctrinal falsehood comes a natural decline of spiritual life, evidenced by a taste for questionable amusements, and a weariness of devotional meetings. . . . Are churches in a right condition when they have only one meeting for prayer in a week, and that a mere skeleton? . . . The fact is, that many would like to unite the church and the stage, cards and prayer, dancing and sacraments. . . . When the old faith is gone, and enthusiasm for the gospel is extinct, it is no wonder that people seek something else in the way of delight.[2]

Spurgeon continued at some length, describing in words of this nature the apostasy of the times and the spiritual deadness it was causing in numerous churches. He expressed his deep sorrow over such a situation and then went on to deal with the question of a Christian's remaining in association with men who deny the Word of God. His statement is of importance for our day as much as for his.

It now becomes a serious question how far those who abide by the faith once delivered to the saints should fraternize with those who have turned aside to another gospel. Christian love has its claims, and divisions are to be shunned as grievous evils; but how far are we justified in being in confederacy with those who are departing from the truth? It is a difficult question to answer so as to keep the balance of the duties. For the present it behoves believers to be cautious lest they lend their support and countenance to the betrayers of the Lord.

It is one thing to overleap all boundaries of denominational restriction for the truth's sake; this we hope all godly men will do more and more. It

---

2. *The Sword and the Trowel*, August 1887.

is quite another policy which would urge us to subordinate the mainte-nance of truth to denominational prosperity and unity. Numbers of easy-minded people wink at error so long as it is committed by a clever man and a good-natured brother, who has so many fine points about him.

Let each believer judge for himself; but for our part we have put on a few fresh bolts to our door, and we have given orders to keep the chain up; for under colour of begging the friendship of the servant, there are those about who aim at robbing THE MASTER.[3]

This article caused a severe commotion throughout the Baptists of Britain. A large number of persons entirely agreed with Spurgeon and let him know of their warm allegiance. But numerous others just as heartily disagreed, and in homes and churches everywhere in the land his statements were vigorously discussed and debated. Likewise the press, both secular and religious, took up the matter, some declaring their favor of his stand and others voicing their firm opposition.

Spurgeon's article appeared in the August 1887 issue of *The Sword and the Trowel,* and in the next three issues he published further articles. First came his "Reply to Sundry Critics," then "The Case Proved," and finally "A Fragment on the Down-Grade Contro-versy." In these he carried his case further, giving strong proof that he was not, as his opposers declared, merely spreading unfounded suspicions. He wrote not with the least joy in that he had shown his accusers to be wrong but with deep sorrow that such apostasy had come about in the land.

Moreover, during the weeks in which he wrote these later articles Spurgeon answered in his own mind the question as to whether he was giving aid to those who denied the Lord by remaining in associ-ation with them. He reasoned out the whole matter, and as he came to the concluding paragraph of his third article he stated:

One thing is clear to us: we cannot be expected to meet in any union which comprehends those whose teaching upon fundamental points is exactly the reverse of that which we hold dear. . . . With deep regret we abstain from assembling with those whom we dearly love and heartily respect, since it would involve us in a confederacy with those with whom we can have no fellowship in the Lord.[4]

3. Ibid.
4. Ibid., October 1887.

At the same time he wrote to Dr. Booth, stating:

> Dear Friend, I beg to intimate to you, as the Secretary of the Baptist Union, that I must withdraw from the society. I do this with the utmost regret; but I have no choice. The reasons are set forth in *The Sword and the Trowel* for November, and I trust you will excuse my repeating them here. I beg you not to send anyone to me to ask for reconsideration. I fear I have considered too long already; certainly every hour of the day impresses upon me the conviction that I am moving none too soon.
>
> I wish also to add that no personal pique or ill-will has in the least degree operated upon me. . . . It is on the highest ground alone that I take this step, and you know that I have long delayed it, because I hoped for better things. Yours always heartily,
>
> C. H. Spurgeon.[5]

Thus Spurgeon took the historic step. The date was October 1887, and he was fifty-three years old.

He did not try to lead others out of the Union with him, and he did not do as many hoped he would—form a new association of Baptists. Rather, he wanted to see men and women come to a clear decision in their own minds, and he believed he had given enough information in his articles to enable them to know the course they should take.

The Tabernacle membership immediately expressed its decided support of what the pastor had done, and it too withdrew from the Union. Likewise numerous letters arrived declaring the same strong stand and heartily commending what Spurgeon had done.

But there was much opinion of a directly opposite nature. One man who had been probably the largest financial supporter of the orphanage, the Almshouses, and the College wrote expressing his strong opposition and stating that his giving was finished. A few lesser givers did the same thing. The editor of *The Christian World* exulted in his abandonment of the old beliefs. "Modern thought," he wrote, "is in Spurgeon's eyes 'a deadly cobra'; in ours it is the glory of the century. It discards many of the doctrines dear to Mr. Spurgeon . . . not only as untrue and unscriptural, but as in the strictest sense immoral. . . . It is not so irrational as to pin its faith to verbal inspiration, nor so idolatrous as to make its acceptance of a true Trinity cover polytheism."

Spurgeon faced criticism also from one of the major figures

5. Pike, 6:287.

among the Baptists of England, Dr. John Clifford, the president of
the Union. Dr. Clifford was a man of strong intellectual powers and
high principles, but he had surrendered his belief in the inerrancy
of the Scriptures and had accepted many of the views of the higher
critics. He was a most honest man, yet he had somewhat deceived
himself, for he assumed that the New Theology was actually the old
evangelicalism—merely that it wore new clothes.

On the basis of this assumption he could see no grounds whatsoever for Spurgeon's action. In an article published in a widely
circulated paper he declared it was Spurgeon's responsibility to
produce evidence of his accusations that not all Baptist pastors
remained true to the faith, and he asserted that Spurgeon could
better spend his time and talents in encouraging the people, rather
than in causing division and grief.

> Is it too late to ask Mr. Spurgeon to pause and consider whether this is
> the best work to which the Baptists of Great Britain and Ireland can be
> put? Is not the fateful crop of disturbing suspicions, broken promises,
> imperilled churches, and wounded but faithful workers, already in sight,
> enough?
>
> Oh! it pains me unspeakably to see this eminent "winner of souls"
> rousing the energies of thousands of Christians to engage in personal
> wrangling and strife, instead of inspiring them, as he might, to sustained
> and heroic effort to carry the good news of God's Gospel to our fellow-
> countrymen![6]

Despite Clifford's effort to place the responsibility for the distur-
bance of the Baptist work on Spurgeon, the officials knew that when
the Union met for its general assembly his charges of apostasy
would have to be handled. Accordingly, they decided upon a course
of action—they determined that when the matter was introduced
they would reply that since Spurgeon had failed to mention the
names of the men whom he assumed had departed from the faith,
his assertions were too flimsy to be considered by the assembly.
They would state that until he provided such evidence there was
nothing they could do in the matter.

But in several letters he had received from the Union's secretary,
Dr. Booth, Spurgeon had been given various names and statements
of men in the Union who preached the New Theology. Highly
aroused by the charge that he had spoken carelessly and without

6. Ibid., 6:297

foundation, Spurgeon wrote to Booth saying, "I will give the information you have given to me." But Booth, who was not a man of
courage or high principles replied, "My letters to you were not
official, but in confidence. As a matter of honour you cannot use
them."[7]

Accordingly, Spurgeon remained silent as to the information
Booth had given him. But when the matter of the correspondence
was mentioned to the meeting, Booth began to hedge and implied
he had never brought the subject of the New Theology and the
holders of it to Spurgeon's attention and that Spurgeon had never
complained about the unbelief.

When Spurgeon learned of Booth's evasions he said, "For Dr.
Booth to say I never complained is amazing. God knows all about it
and He will see me righted."[8] Some of the New Theology men were
very bitter toward Spurgeon and the gospel he preached, and they
propagated the charge that he had created groundless suspicion
concerning the ministers and had also placed a stigma upon all the
Baptist people. This idea began to be believed by many, and one of
Spurgeon's biographers, writing in 1933, stated:

> Spurgeon was never righted. The impression in many quarters still
> remains that he made charges which could not be substantiated, and
> when properly called upon to produce his evidence he resigned and ran
> away. Nothing is further from the truth. Spurgeon might have produced
> Dr. Booth's letters. I think he should have done so.[9]

The assembly was held in April 1888. In order to accommodate
the crowd that was expected, a large building—Dr. Joseph Parker's
Congregational Church—was used. An attempt was made toward
restoring harmony by the introduction of a resolution that it was
thought would please both sides of the controversy. It could be
regarded as evangelical in nature and yet could also be interpreted
as not hostile to the New Theology. It was moved by a Charles
Williams, who in making his motion spoke strongly against the
evangelical doctrines, and it was seconded by James Spurgeon, who
felt the resolution would further the evangelical cause.

7. J. C. Carlile, *C. H. Spurgeon—An Interpretative Biography* (London: Religious
Tract Society, 1933), p. 247.
8 *C. H. Spurgeon's Autobiography*, comp. Susannah Spurgeon and J. W. Harrald, 4
vols. (London: Passmore and Alabaster, 1897), 4:120.
9. Carlile, pp. 248-49.

The result was that the difference between the doctrinal position of the two parties was blurred still further. Dr. Clifford had done his work well, and the resolution served to convince many that the New Theology was indeed the old evangelicalism and that no one should be concerned over the new clothes that it wore.

In turn, when the vote was called for, two thousand replied in the affirmative and merely a paltry seven in the negative. And of the two thousand, a considerable proportion assumed they were voting for evangelicalism and were defending the action Spurgeon had taken. Yet the result was thereafter trumpeted abroad as "a vote of censure" against Spurgeon and as an evidence that the vast majority of the Baptists of England had rejected him.

During later months, although Spurgeon had taken his decided stand and had withdrawn, other men steadily continued the controversy. Some declared their opposition to the New Theology, but others were bitter in their attitude toward Spurgeon and published distorted accounts of his actions.

Dr. Booth wrote to him while he was at Menton to say that he, together with Drs. Maclaren, Culross, and Clifford wished to visit him there, and their hope was that they might influence him to reconsider his withdrawal. But Spurgeon replied there was nothing to be gained by their coming, that unbelief existed in the Union, and that they had done nothing about it, but he added that he would meet with them upon his return to England.

In the midst of the controversy Spurgeon wrote,

> The Lord knoweth the way that I take, and to his divine arbitration I leave the matter. . . . I have borne my protest and suffered the loss of friendships and reputation, and the infliction of pecuniary withdrawments and bitter reproach; I can do no more. My way is henceforth far removed from their way.
>
> But the pain it has cost me none can measure. I can never compromise the truth of God. . . . It is not a matter of personalities, but of principles. And where two sets of men are diametrically opposite in their opinions upon vital points, no form of words can make them one.[10]

Numerous persons in America, upon learning of the conflict in England, were likewise divided in their attitude. Some asserted that Spurgeon's withdrawal from the Union was entirely unnecessary,

10. H. L. Wayland, *Charles H. Spurgeon, His Faith and Works* (Philadelphia: Amer. Baptist Publication Soc., 1892), p. 223.

but many others agreed with what he had done. Replying on June
18, 1888, to a letter from the States that had enclosed a sum of
money for his work, he said:

> I am so glad to forget all this when writing to you. . . . I send hearty
> thanks [for the money that had been sent]. I am cheered when I need
> cheering. See how I have been in storms:
>   1. These Union troubles.
>   2. Then wife very ill these seven weeks and ill still.
>   3. Next, my dear mother died.
>   4. On the day of the funeral I was smitten by my old enemy [the gout]
> very fiercely, and have undergone a baptism of pain. Cannot walk yet,
> and barely stand. Still I rejoice in God. Lots of Americans here; choice
> specimens. Hearty love.[11]

The growth being made by the New Theology concepts emphasized the need for all true Christians to know them and to stand
together against them. In view of this situation a great rally of the
Evangelical Alliance was held not long after Spurgeon withdrew
from the Baptist Union. The Alliance was composed of people of all
denominations, and the enthusiasm with which Spurgeon was
greeted at this gathering reveals something of the esteem in which
he was still held by a vast number of the people. One of his most
faithful helpers, Robert Shindler, wrote:

> Never shall we forget the first meeting called by the Alliance for
> testimony to the fundamental truths of the Gospel, which was held in
> Exeter Hall. The reception given by the audience to Mr. Spurgeon when
> he rose to speak was overpowering in its fervour and heartiness. We
> occupied a seat on the platform near enough to witness the powerful
> emotions that agitated him, and the tears that streamed down his cheeks
> as he listened to the previous speakers; and though only a very few of his
> Baptist brethren were present, there was not wanting such a display of
> sympathy as must have cheered and comforted his heart.[12]

The controversy proved very hard on Spurgeon physically. He was
sick before it began, and he had frequent attacks of gout while it
went on. Moreover, at this stage in his life he was suffering from the
beginnings of a disease of the kidneys which sometimes made him

11. Ibid.
12. E. J. Poole-Connor, *Evangelicalism in England* (London: Fellowship of Inde-
     pendent Evangelical Churches, 1951), p. 248.

exceedingly weak. And, as we have seen from his statement, Mrs. Spurgeon was still very unwell.

The experience proved all the more difficult for him because he did not like to fight. He was utterly unflinching in his stand for what he believed to be God's truth, but his affections for his fellow-men were very large, and it was with deep sorrow that he parted from many dear friends in the Union. His battle was waged with boldness and decision, yet he labored to avoid anything that would cause the least unnecessary strife. "I am anxious to have nothing said," he wrote, "which can trouble our friends or cause discord. A few heedless persons would be glad to see strife; but I can differ and not quarrel."[13]

There was difficulty even among the Pastors' College men. "Over a hundred ministers trained at the College signed 'a mild protest' against Spurgeon's intended procedure of inviting only such as made a certain declaration to the Conference." The protest was addressed to Spurgeon, and his reply reads, in part: "I could not endure to give up our Conference to one long wrangle. . . . The expense, not merely of money, but of my life would be too great for a purposeless conflict. The strain has nearly broken my heart already, and I have had all I can bear of bitterness."[14]

Exerting his authority as president, he disbanded the existing College Conference and then formed a new one—this one based on a clear declaration of the evangelical doctrines, which was now written into its statement of faith. Four hundred thirty-two men voted in favor of the disbanding step taken by Spurgeon, and sixty-four voted against it. Some of this latter number were bitter in their attitude, terming him "the New Pope," and thereafter had no more fellowship with him. Thus were his sorrows multiplied.[15]

Part of the difficulty in the Union lay in the fact that although nearly all the ministers recognized the presence of unbelief in their midst, many told themselves it would probably do no harm. It was on this matter that Spurgeon was in direct disagreement, for he could see a future course leading to lifeless and fruitless churches. At the beginning of 1888 he gave a report that compared the work of the men of his college with that of all the other pastors of the Union. The 370 College men had, during the preceding year, bap-

13. R. B. Cook, *The Wit and Wisdom of Spurgeon* (New York: E. B. Treat, 1892), p. 257.

14. Pike, 6:298.

15. Ibid.

tized 4,770 persons, and the increase in their membership had amounted to 3,856. But the rest of the Union, with 1,860 pastors and 2,764 churches, reported an increase of only 1,770 members for the year. And Spurgeon viewed the success of his men as an evidence of the blessing that accompanies the gospel, whereas the bringing in of unbelief robs the church of its power and places it on what he called the downgrade.

Many thought Spurgeon's concept of the harmful effects of the New Theology was quite wrong, but with the passing of the years he has been proven entirely correct. As he foretold, with the denial of the Scriptures church attendances began to fall off, prayer meetings became places of a mere few till they were dropped altogether, and the miracle of a life transformed by the grace of God was witnessed less and less, if at all. Church after church, in city, town, and hamlet, gradually died out. Throughout England one could see what had once been a church now used as a shop or a garage, or could see where one had formerly stood, but it had since been torn down.

All manner of reasons were given for this sad condition, but the prime cause was the lack of the gospel in the pulpit. All the attempted substitutes failed to attract the people. Where there is no acceptance of the Bible as inerrant and a belief in the great fundamentals of the faith, there is no true Christianity, the preaching is powerless, and what Spurgeon declared to his generation a hundred years ago is the outcome.

The failure of the New Theology, or modernism—call it what we will—is forcefully brought out by E. J. Poole-Connor in his *Evangelicalism in England*. He tells of a conversation between the editor of an agnostic magazine and a modernist minister. The editor told the minister that despite their different vocations they had much in common. "I don't believe the Bible," said the agnostic, "but neither do you. I don't believe the story about creation, but you don't either. I don't believe in the deity of Christ, nor in His resurrection or ascension—I don't believe any of these things, but neither do you. I am as much a Christian as you, and you are as much an infidel as I!"

Such a condition, infidels in the ministry, was the direct outcome of the *New Theology* and a clear proof of the rightness of Spurgeon's action in withdrawing from all confederacy with it.

During the 1880s a group of American ministers visited England, prompted especially by a desire to hear some of the celebrated preachers of that land.

On a Sunday morning they attended the City Temple where Dr. Joseph Parker was the pastor. Some two thousand people filled the building, and Parker's forceful personality dominated the service. His voice was commanding, his language descriptive, his imagination lively, and his manner animated. The sermon was scriptural, the congregation hung upon his words, and the Americans came away saying, "What a wonderful preacher is Joseph Parker!"

In the evening they went to hear Spurgeon at the Metropolitan Tabernacle. The building was much larger than the City Temple, and the congregation was more than twice the size. Spurgeon's voice was much more expressive and moving and his oratory noticably superior. But they soon forgot all about the great building, the immense congregation, and the magnificent voice. They even overlooked their intention to compare the various features of the two preachers, and when the service was over they found themselves saying, "What a wonderful Savior is Jesus Christ!"

20

Last Labors

Spurgeon's action in the controversy was not taken without much suffering on his part.

After he had withdrawn from the Baptist Union, as he went on to dissolve the old College Conference and to form a new, he found himself almost crushed under the burden. In a letter to his brother, written March 31, 1888, he said:

> My Dear Brother,—I was taken ill while trying to preach on Thursday. An awful depression and a choking sensation made my preaching a great misery. I have taken medicine twice but feel half dead.
>
> Will you come prepared with a sermon on Sunday night for I may not be able to preach? My teeth made me nervous, my liver made me giddy, and my heart made me sorrowful. I hope I may get through the Conference, but yesterday I was very far from hoping it. The strain is terrible.
>
> I want to get the College Report done, and time is running close. . . . Hearty love,
>
> Your grateful brother,
Charles.[1]

He met criticism also from certain religious papers. We notice especially two American magazines, both of which were evangeli-

---

1. G. Holden Pike, *James Archer Spurgeon* (London: Alexander & Shepherd, 1894), p. 164.

cal but held that there was no reason for Spurgeon's act of separating from the Union. One declared:

> As to the charges he brought, not against the Union, but against some few nameless members of it, all that can be said is "Non proven." . . . To assail the Union because, out of its hundreds of members, some half a dozen men are not in full accord with what Mr. Spurgeon holds (and what we hold also) to be the Gospel of our Lord is to set to work to burn down a house because a dozen rats are hidden in the cellar.[2]

Spurgeon had spoken, of course, with much graciousness of Alexander Maclaren and other evangelicals in the Union, but he had dealt severely with unbelief itself. A New York paper, however, confused the two attitudes, and stated:

> His language regarding the Council of the Union . . . is pervaded by extreme bitterness. Their expressions of kindness and brotherly love for him he terms the velvet pad covering the claw. This is hardly becoming language to use concerning men like Maclaren and Angus, and Underhill and Landels, leaders in the church of God.[3]

Others, however, made statements of a very opposite nature. They charged that Spurgeon had been too gracious in the controversy and that his actions ought to have been more militant. They asserted that he ought to have published the names of the men who had departed from the faith and should also have reproved those who failed to oppose apostasy.

The reasons for his attitude he declared in reply to a letter that commended his withdrawal from the Union.

October 5, 1888.

To the Ministers and Delegates forming the Baptist Convention of the Maritime Provinces of Canada.

Dear Brethren in Christ, I heartily thank you for all the words of cheer which you have sent me. Such a resolution, from such brethren, at such a time, gladdened me greatly. . . .

I am grateful that you have not misjudged my action in reference to the English Baptist Union, from which I have felt bound to separate

2. G. Holden Pike, *The Life and Work of Charles Haddon Spurgeon,* 6 vols. (London: Cassel, 1898), 6:299.
3. Ibid., 6:300.

myself. I have not acted from sudden impulse, much less from any personal grievance; but I have been long protesting quietly, and have been at last compelled to make a stand in public. I saw the testimony of the churches becoming obscure, and I observed that in some instances the testimony of the pulpit was very wide of the Word of God, and I grieved over the state of things which is sure to follow upon defection from the Gospel. I hoped that the many faithful brethren would be aroused to the peril of the situation and would earnestly endeavour to cleanse their Union of the most flagrant offenders. Instead of this, I am regarded as a troubler in Israel by many, and others feel that, important as truth may be, the preservation of the Union must be the first object of consideration. . . .

The pain I have felt in this conflict I would not wish any other man to share; but I would bear ten thousand times as much with eagerness, if I could see the faith once for all delivered to the saints placed in honour among the Baptist churches of Great Britain.

I resolved to avoid personalities from the very beginning; and though sorely tempted to publish all that I know, I have held my peace as to individuals, and thus have weakened my own hands in the conflict. Yet this also I had rather bear than allow contention for the faith to degenerate into a complication of personal quarrels. I am no man's enemy, but I am the enemy of all teaching which is contrary to the Word of the Lord, and I will be in no fellowship with it. . . .

Unable to write all that I feel, I turn to prayer, and beseech our God in Christ Jesus to bless you exceeding abundantly above all that we ask or even think. Yours most gratefully and lovingly,

C. H. Spurgeon.

Weary and worn and ill—my motto is "Faint, yet pursuing." . . . The inspiration of the Scriptures is the point assailed, and with it all true religion stands or falls. May you be kept from this dread tidal wave which is rolling over our country.[4]

The particular value of this letter lies in the fact that not only does it help us to understand Spurgeon's stand in the controversy, but it also reveals something of his physical and mental condition. He says little concerning these things in his *Autobiography* and seldom mentions them in his sermons, but in this letter we have his expression "Weary and worn and ill" and his reference to "the pain I have felt in this conflict." Other letters contain similar expressions. He was hurt by the bitter treatment received from some of

---

4. Ibid., 6:306-7.

the New Theology men, but he was wounded still more by the increasing spread of their views.

He found relief from the sorrows of the controversy in hard work. More than ever people invited him to come and minister to them in churches in London and elsewhere, and he responded to as many requests as he possibly could. Although he never made the controversy the subject of his preaching, he often warned against the inroads being made by unbelief and urged a strong stand for the faith.

He was busy also, as always, in the weekly editing of a sermon, in the monthly preparation of his magazine, and in his other writing. Sermon number 2,000 came from the press at this time, and the Tabernacle people made the event something of a celebration, commemorating this milestone in his work with much joy. Likewise, a reunion at the orphanage drew a large company, and both children and grown-ups rallied around him and manifested their love. New supporters arose to take the places of those who had stopped giving, and though he was sometimes anxious, the £300 that was necessary every week to maintain the different enterprises never failed to be provided. This activity and labor proved a tonic for Spurgeon.

Nevertheless, his burdens proved too much for him. In July of 1888 he was laid aside in sickness and found himself too weak even to hold a pen. After two weeks he recuperated to some extent and returned vigorously to his work but in November was prostrated again. Subdued by his condition, he wanted to set out for Menton right away, but he was too weak to travel. He stated, "I cannot get better till I am in another climate, and I cannot reach that other climate till I get better." In December he became sufficiently well to attempt the journey and therefore set out for the southern sunshine.

This time, however, his days at Menton were marred by a severe fall on a stone stairway. At this period of his life he was a fairly heavy man. His feet and legs were almost always somewhat swollen, and he found it necessary to lean upon a cane as he walked. On the last Sunday of 1888 he went in the afternoon with three companions to enjoy a time of quiet meditation in a nearby villa. In descending a stair, as he placed the end of his cane on a smooth marble step, it slipped, and he fell headlong. His secretary, Joseph Harrald, tells us:

Neither he nor his friends realized at first how much he was injured. In his descent he turned a somersault, shook some money out of his pocket into his boot, knocked out two teeth that he was glad to lose, and as he picked himself up he smilingly told his alarmed companions that it was "painless dentistry, with money to boot."[5]

But although he thus joked, upon being helped back to the hotel he was put to bed in pain and was soon forced to realize that the accident had been severe indeed. In a letter to the people of the Tabernacle he stated:

> My injuries are far greater than I supposed. It will be some time before foot, mouth, head and nerves can be right again. What a mercy that I was not smashed quite up . . . another stone would have brought me to mine end. . . . May I be spared to keep my own footing to the end, and let the down-graders know how terrible is a fall from the high places of the Lord's truth. Yours very truly,
>
> C. H. Spurgeon.[6]

The recuperation from the fall was slow. After being laid up nearly four weeks he told the deacons, "As soon as I can stand through a sermon and walk without pain I will take it as my order [to return] home. Soon may that glad token be given me, for I long to be among you, after these months of weakness, interset with pain."[7]

When he arrived back at the Tabernacle (February 24, 1889) after a two-month absence, he was greeted by an immense congregation. During his absence the pulpit had been supplied by a young Scottish preacher, John MacNeill, a Presbyterian of such eloquence that he was often referred to as "a second Spurgeon." The work had been well maintained, but the people were overjoyed in having the pastor back. The deacons, however, earnestly suggested to Spurgeon that he refuse the many calls he received to preach elsewhere and that he husband his strength for the many duties of the Tabernacle.

Spurgeon was soon as busy as ever. In May he addressed the College Conference, speaking on "Our Power, and the Conditions

---

5. *The Sword and the Trowel*, 1892, p. 557.
6. Pike, *Life and Work*, 6:309.
7. Ibid.

of Obtaining It," and the collection for the work of the College amounted to £2,800.

He accepted an invitation to speak at an afternoon meeting among his old congregation at Waterbeach. But he refused to stay for the evening meeting, saying, "I am now over-pressed with many labours, and to remain at Waterbeach all night involves losing the next day. If I am home at night, I get a good night's rest in my own bed, which is everything to a feeble man, and then I have the day before me. I am sorry it is so, for I should like to have seen more of my old friends."[8]

"In June a party of sailors had a sermon [from him] at the Tabernacle; and during that same month he addressed a large assembly who met to hear some of the old fugal tunes of other days. . . . In July he paid a memorable visit to [the island of] Guernsey, where a number of special services were held in connection with the ministry of [a former student] Mr. F. T. Snell."[9]

During October a missionary conference was held at the Tabernacle. Spurgeon, Dr. Maclaren, and Mr. McNeille were the speakers, and the occasion was marked especially by a farewell to several men, mostly from the College, who were leaving for the foreign field. Spurgeon had long been closely friendly with Hudson Taylor, the founder of the China Inland Mission, and he had led the Tabernacle to give toward this excellent work. And on this occasion, "the scene was one of great enthusiasm when Spurgeon descended from the upper to the lower platform to shake hands with a number of young men and women who were going out to China."[10]

In the same month he had tea with the Primate of the Church of England. In a letter in which he refused an invitation to a banquet sponsored by the Master Cutler:

> I am so taken up with my work that I must not leave home. Really, I am not a man for a feast, even if I could come. Our Lord Mayor pressed me to meet the Archbishop and bishops at a banquet, but I could not bring my soul to it—the banquet. I had no objection to the bishops. Last week I had tea with the Archbishop and luncheon with the Bishop of Rochester; but the banquet was out of my line. I am best at work—my own work. Still, God bless you, and the Master, and all the good folk![11]

8. Ibid., p. 311.
9. Ibid.
10. Ibid.
11. Ibid., p. 312.

By the middle of November (1889) his strength was spent. As he preached "his shoulder was drawn up as if by sharp hitches of pain," and he had no choice but to escape England's winter by returning to Mentone. During his absence the pulpit was to be supplied by an American, Dr. A. T. Pierson, and an evangelistic team was to hold a gospel campaign. Spurgeon urged the people to "gather up the fruits of the special mission, that we may have a large increase to God's glory."

During his previous stays at Menton he had made it his practice, if he was well enough to hold a pen, to devote himself to his writing. This time (December 1889 through January 1890) he gave himself over to working on a commentary on Matthew, *The Gospel of the Kingdom*. His days in the warmth proved profitable, and he was able to return at the end of two months renewed in both body and spirit.

Again he threw himself into the work. But within a month, in refusing an invitation to preach again at Waterbeach, he stated, "I wish I could be constantly out but I do not get any stronger and every year I have more to do. . . . I have been laid up three days with swollen left hand and pain. . . . Still, I shall hold up as long as I can."[12]

But although he could not go to Waterbeach or numerous other places that wanted him, he did minister frequently in and around London—this in addition to his constant labor at the Tabernacle.

He now suffered a further attack concerning the action he had taken in the controversy. This came from none other than Dr. Joseph Parker—an open letter in which Parker strongly criticized Spurgeon's complaints against the departure from the faith. He especially opposed Spurgeon's action in withdrawing from the Union. Parker had long exercised a very acceptable ministry, but unlike Spurgeon he had never been a doctrinal preacher, and he could now easily condone those who denied the Scriptures. Spurgeon made no reply to the open letter, yet he undoubtedly felt its effect, not only because of the criticism of himself but also because of Parker's favor toward the New Theology men and his failure to stand with the evangelicals. Parker's action shows how unthinkingly good men were influenced by the gradual manner in which modernistic teaching was introduced into England.

Despite his steadily worsening physical condition, Spurgeon's

12. Ibid., p. 313.

zeal for souls remained as warm as ever. This is evident in the following letter which he wrote to a young boy.

O Lord, bless this letter.   Norwood, July 1, /90

My Dear Arthur Layzell,

I was a little while ago at a meeting for prayer where a large number of ministers were gathered together. The subject of prayer was "our children." It soon brought the tears to my eyes to hear those good fathers pleading with God for their sons and daughters. As they went on entreating the Lord to save their families my heart seemed ready to burst with strong desire that it might be even so. Then I thought, I will write to those sons and daughters, to remind them of their parents' prayers.

Dear Arthur, you are highly privileged in having parents who pray for you. Your name is known in the courts of heaven. Your case has been laid before the throne of God.

Do you not pray for yourself? If you do not do so, why not? If other people value your soul, can it be right for you to neglect it? See, the entreaties and wrestlings of your father will not save you if you never seek the Lord yourself. You know this.

You do not intend to cause grief to dear mother and father: but you do. So long as you are not saved, they can never rest. However obedient and sweet and kind you may be, they will never feel happy about you until you believe in the Lord Jesus Christ, and so find everlasting salvation.

Think of this. Remember how much you have already sinned, and none can wash you but Jesus. When you grow up you may become very sinful, and none can change your nature and make you holy but the Lord Jesus, through His Spirit.

You need what father and mother seek for you and you need it NOW. Why not seek it at once? I heard a father pray, "Lord, save our children, *and save them young.*" It is never too soon to be safe; never too soon to be happy; never too soon to be holy. Jesus loves to receive the very young ones.

You cannot save yourself, but the great Lord Jesus can save you. Ask him to do it. "He that asketh receiveth." Then trust in Jesus to save you. He can do it, for he died and rose again that whosoever believeth in him might not perish, but have everlasting life.

Come and tell Jesus you have sinned; seek forgiveness; trust in Him for it, and be sure that you are saved.

Then imitate our Lord. Be at home what Jesus was at Nazareth. Yours will be a happy home, and your dear father and mother will feel that the dearest wish of their hearts has been granted them.

I pray you think of heaven and hell, for in one of those places you will

live forever. *Meet me in heaven.* Meet me at once at the mercy-seat. Run
upstairs and pray to the great Father, through Jesus Christ.
  Yours very lovingly,

C. H. Spurgeon.[13]

Although sick, tired, and very busy, Spurgeon took time to write
to a boy—one whom he had never met and of whom he had learned
only through the prayers of his parents.

His earlier correspondence had been remarkable for its excellent
orthography, but in this letter the writing is rough and irregular.
Undoubtedly, his hand was swollen and probably painful as he held
the pen, and we must assume that he wrote to each of the children
for whom the parents had prayed at that meeting. Yet how worthy
were the results, for this letter was used of the Lord to bring young
Arthur Layzell to Himself. Very likely the other letters were equally
fruitful in other young lives.

After three more months of struggling, Spurgeon returned to Menton. This was in October 1890, and although he frequently suffered
pain and weakness during his stay there, he returned to England in
February 1891 in good spirits. There was some slight measure of
strength in his step, and both he and the people were encouraged
and felt he might be on the verge of a new lease on life.

But such was not the case.

The annual church meeting was soon held, and it proved to be
the last time he would conduct the church's business. The reports
provided great cause for thanksgiving: the membership was 5,328;
the church had 127 lay ministers serving in and around London; the
people of the Tabernacle conducted 23 mission stations, these having 4,000 seatings, and they operated 27 Sunday schools, with 600
teachers and 8,000 scholars. Two years earlier Spurgeon had built,
at his own expense, a fine new church at Thornton Heath (not far
from his home) and now a new building seating 1,000 was about to
be opened near the Surrey Gardens and was a memorial of the years
in which he had preached in the great Music Hall there.

Likewise *The Sword and the Trowel* reported, "The month of
March has been a memorable one. . . . Pastor C. H. S. continued to
see persons who wished to join the church, and out of these he had

13. Original letter owned by George Layzell of Cambridge, Ontario, Canada, a son
    of Arthur Layzell.

eighty-four to propose for fellowship [baptism and membership]. How much of joyous labour all these involved is best known to the Pastor and to the sympathizing reapers who shared his delightful toil."[14]

The College Conference followed. Spurgeon's soul was deeply stirred by the fact that a handful of the men had departed from the faith and had withdrawn from fellowship during the controversy. But a very large majority had remained, and he spoke with great vigor and conviction in urging them on in zealous labor and defense of the truth. The effort, however, proved more than he could bear. On the following Sunday evening, as he entered the pulpit he was so overcome by nervousness and weakness that he could not remain. This was the first time in his forty years of ministry that he had been forced to leave the pulpit by what he called "overpowering nervousness." Nevertheless, he rallied and for a month labored with great diligence, preaching at several churches as well as conducting his ministry at the Tabernacle.

On June 7, 1891, Spurgeon stood before his people for the last time. That platform had been his "pulpit throne from which he had proclaimed the Gospel to at least twenty million hearers,"[15] but now the great congregation was to hear his voice no more.

Undoubtedly because he knew the end of his labor was near he set out the next morning, against strong advice not to do so, for Stambourne. He wanted to visit again some of the scenes of his childhood,[16] but he proved too weak for such travel, and after four days he returned, utterly exhausted and in pain.

For the following three months he was completely laid aside.

He was given all that medical skill and careful nursing could provide, but he remained seriously ill. Prayer was made for him "by believers all over the world and the Tabernacle Church, beginning with a whole day of intercession, continued to meet morning, noon and night to plead for his recovery."[17] He was remembered in prayer by the chief Jewish rabbi, by certain clergy of Westminster Abbey and St. Paul's Cathedral, and by the ministers of churches of all denominations. Reports of his condition were carried repeatedly in the secular and religious press, and messages of sympathy were sent by the Prince of Wales, by Mr. Gladstone the former Prime

14. Iain Murray, ed., *The Full Harvest* (London: Banner of Truth, 1973), p. 497.
15. Ibid., p. 499.
16. He had photos taken of several of these scenes, and they were reproduced in his *Memories of Stambourne,* which was published after his death.
17. Murray, *The Full Harvest,* p. 500.

Minister, by several members of the aristocracy and of Parliament, and by numerous others from all walks of life.

As the weeks came and went he experienced a series of hopeful advances that alternated with disappointing relapses, and his condition showed no thorough improvement. As the winter approached it was evident he must go to Mentone, if he could bear the strain of the travel. Accordingly, on Monday, October 26, 1891, accompanied by his brother, his secretary, and Mrs. Spurgeon, he set out on the thousand miles' journey. This was the first time Mrs. Spurgeon had ever been able to be with him at Mentone, and it was a delight to both of them that she was well enough to accompany him now.

Upon reaching the warmer air he improved somewhat. He was able to work toward completing his commentary on the Gospel of Matthew, and he was also able to be outdoors much of the time, sitting or being wheeled in a wheelchair.

On New Year's Eve he gave a short address to a number of friends who gathered in his apartment at the hotel, and he did the same on the following morning. He wanted to attempt to speak on the two following Sundays but was persuaded not to do so. On January 17, however, he gave out the hymn that closed the little service, and that also closed his active participation in the ministry of the Lord. Very fittingly it was:

> The sands of time are sinking,
> The dawn of heaven breaks,
> The summer morn I've sighed for,
> The fair sweet morn awakes.
> Dark, dark hath been the midnight,
> But dayspring is at hand,
> And glory, glory dwelleth
> In Immanuel's land.

> O Christ! He is the fountain,
> The deep sweet well of love;
> The streams on earth I've tasted,
> More deep I'll drink above:
> There to an ocean fullness
> His mercy doth expand,
> And glory, glory dwelleth
> In Immanuel's land.

During the days that followed he was much of the time only partly conscious. It was evident to Mrs. Spurgeon and to the doctor that he was fast sinking away. On January 28 he became totally unconscious, and despite all that could be done this remained his condition till, on the evening of Sunday, January 31, 1892, his earthly journey came to its close, and he "departed to be with Christ" which, as the Scriptures assure us, is far better.

At the close of his sermon on Lord's day evening, December 27, 1874, Spurgeon said, "In a little while there will be a concourse of persons in the streets. Methinks I hear someone enquiring, 'What are all these people waiting for?' 'Do you know? He is to be buried today.' 'And who is that?' 'It is Spurgeon.' 'What! the man that preached at the Tabernacle?' 'Yes; he is to be buried to-day.'

"That will happen very soon; and when you see my coffin carried to the silent grave, I should like every one of you, whether converted or not, to be constrained to say, 'He did earnestly urge us, in plain and simple language, not to put off the consideration of eternal things. He did entreat us to look to Christ. Now he is gone, our blood is not at his door if we perish.' "

The Full Harvest, ed. Iain Murray

21

"With Christ, Which Is Far Better"

Secretary Harrald immediately sent a telegraphed message to the Tabernacle in London. It read:

"Our beloved Pastor entered heaven 11.5 Sunday night." Previous telegrams had reported Spurgeon's increasingly serious condition, but this one proved a sudden and terrible shock for the Tabernacle people.

The news became the chief subject of the Monday papers in London, and so heavy was the demand for copies that it was soon difficult to find one left for sale anywhere. Papers in other lands throughout much of the world likewise carried the report, and messages of condolence came to Mrs. Spurgeon with such abundance that the telegraph wires at Mentone could carry but a small portion of them.

The body, placed in an olive-wood casket, was taken to the Presbyterian Church in Mentone.[1] A year earlier Spurgeon had preached at the opening of this church's new building, and he had long enjoyed rich fellowship with its minister, a warm evangelical. Many persons from various parts of southern France gathered there for a

---

1. French law required that a body should not be left at a hotel more than twenty-four hours.

service on the morning of Thursday, February 4, and then the casket
was placed aboard a train for its four-day journey to London.

Meanwhile, at the Tabernacle there were days of tear-filled prayer
and solemn remembrance. The Monday had been previously
planned as a day of intercession regarding the influenza epidemic
that was then raging in the city, but to those petitions there were
now added those on behalf of Mrs. Spurgeon and the bereaved
church. The deacons, with congregational approval, asked James
Spurgeon to continue as Pastor in Charge and Dr. Pierson to accept
the office of Officiating Minister, and on the following Sunday these
men ministered to crowds that packed the building itself and also
overflowed with a host of saddened men and women flooding a
large area outside the doors.

The next morning, (Monday, February 8) the casket reached London. It was placed first in the Common Room of the Pastors' College, and throughout the day a steady stream of people, estimated
to number as many as 50,000 passed by. On the Tuesday it was
carried into the Tabernacle where two or three front seats had been
removed to provide an open area in which it could be placed.
Flowers surrounded it, and over it there waved several palm
branches which Mrs. Spurgeon had chosen in Menton as emblemat-
ic of the palms spoken of in the book of Revelation. Around the
railing of the upper platform there ran the sentence "Remember the
words that I said unto you, being yet present with you," and around
the lower, "I have fought a good fight, I have finished my course, I
have kept the faith."[2]

It was recognized that the Tabernacle, despite its great size,
would not contain all the people who would want to attend the
funeral service, and therefore five services were planned. The first
was held on the Wednesday morning and it was "For Members of the
Church." The second, "For Ministers and Students," was at three in
the afternoon; the third, "For Christian Workers," at 7:00 in the
evening; and the fourth, "For the General Public," was at the late
hour of 10:00 P.M.

A number of men took part in these services. All spoke of Spurgeon's great devotion and extraordinary abilities, and all expressed

2. In several biographies that appeared after Spurgeon's death it was said that he
   had used these words as descriptive of his life and that he uttered them just
   before he died. Mr. Harrald emphatically denied this, stating that Spurgeon's
   attitude was one of utter humility, and that he never would have applied these
   statements to himself.

profound sorrow at his passing. Their full remarks are worthy of being repeated, but we can notice merely a few.

J. W. Harrald, reporting many details of Spurgeon's last few months on earth, made mention of the Christian fortitude manifested by Mrs. Spurgeon. He told how the five persons who were with Spurgeon during his final moments, upon realizing that death had come, knelt at the bedside. Mrs. Spurgeon broke forth in prayer, and Harrald says, "We were touched beyond all expression . . . to hear the voice of the loved one, so sorely bereaved, thanking God for the many years that she had had the unspeakable joy of having such a precious husband lent to her. . . . Seven months ago she gave her husband up to the Lord [during his extreme sickness in London] but the Lord lent him to her a little longer."[3]

Deacon T. H. Olney also spoke, and after enlarging on Spurgeon's many qualities, told of the leadership he exercised among the deacons and elders and in turn throughout all the church.

> I must also bear testimony that he inspired very great confidence in us all. Whatever he recommended we accepted at once. I can remember the building of this great Tabernacle, the opening of the Stockwell Orphanage and other things that we have not time to refer to. Many of the great undertakings might at first have seemed imprudent, but his plans were always well matured. They were always thought over beforehand, and prayed upon, before they were introduced to us. We, as Deacons, had very little to do but back him up.[4]

Elder J. T. Dunn, who had been a chief helper to Spurgeon since his early days in London, spoke especially of his ability and delight in leading souls to Christ.

> When persons came to enquire concerning salvation, or to confess their faith in the Lord Jesus Christ, how his eyes would brighten; and how heartily he would welcome them. It mattered not to him what the character of the clothing, or what the age of the candidate. He could always meet their condition and tenderly sympathize with them. Many a one I have seen go into that vestry with a tearful eye, who has returned with joy on the countenance. The Lord has struck the fetters from many a sin-bound soul while upon his knees in that hallowed room.[5]

3. A. T. Pierson, *From the Pulpit to the Palm-Branch* (New York: A. C. Armstrong, 1982), p. 110.
4. Ibid., p. 119.
5. Ibid., p. 121.

Another member of the Olney family, Deacon William Olney, stated:

> I have been asked to speak on behalf of the many missionary workers. Our dear Pastor, whom God has taken to Himself, had a remarkable power of infusing his own love for souls into the hearts of others. In response to his "Trumpet calls to Christian Energy" from this platform men went out of this congregation in hundreds, to fling themselves into the slums of the south of London, and bring in members to this church out of some of the lowest parts of the neighbourhood. As a consequence of this there are to-day twenty-three mission stations and twenty-six branch schools, and at these places there are every Sunday evening about one thousand members of this church working for the Lord Jesus Christ amongst the poor.[6]

Several of the leading figures of the Baptist Union, though they had failed to agree with Spurgeon's withdrawal from that body, had continued to express the love and admiration in which they held him. The major figure among these men was Dr. Alexander Maclaren, and as one of the speakers at the funeral services he said:

> Thinking of C. H. Spurgeon's life, I have learned what is *the staple of a successful ministry.* . . . I would make allowances for divergencies of natural temperament and for differences of audience to whom we have to speak; but making all allowances for these, and remembering that no one man is capable of all things, I still point to that coffin and say that, to myself, it proclaims that if a man desires to reach, and to hold, and to bless, the largest number of his fellow-men, he must keep fast to the great verities of the Christian faith—salvation through Jesus Christ, the Incarnate Lamb of God; life through the Divine Spirit; faith in Christ, the uniting bond.[7]

Representatives of all the Protestant denominations took part in these services—the moderator of the Presbyterian Synod, the president of the Congregational Union, and certain members of the Church of England clergy. We notice, however, an especially perceptive paragraph from Dr. Stephenson, president of the Wesleyan Conference.

> I venture to suggest to you in reference to our dear friend who has gone . . . he rendered a great service to his age, and to the coming age

6. Ibid., p. 122.
7. Ibid., p. 126.

also, in that he upheld during so long a time the majesty of preaching. Men say that preaching is played out and that the pulpit is superfluous. The editor is to be the great minister of God in the future, and people are to get the Gospel from the newspapers. . . . But with that coffin before us, none of us can doubt that the pulpit is the power in the world still—that still by the foolishness of preaching God is pleased to save men.

I am quite sure that in the fact that from this place there rolled forth over the world a voice which it was willing to hear, and which it listened for—yes, listened for, even through the strife and din of politics, of commerce and pleasure—there has been maintained a testimony to the power of the simple preaching of the Gospel, the value of which it is impossible for us to estimate now.[8]

At the time of Spurgeon's last illness Moody and Sankey had been conducting an evangelistic campaign in Scotland. Upon learning of Spurgeon's death Moody wanted to hasten to London to stand, he said, "by the grave of him who has done so much for me." But it was impossible for him to be absent from his meetings, and therefore he asked Sankey to go and to represent them both. Sankey spoke at the service for Christian workers, saying:

I feel it a great privilege to meet here with the thousands who gather around this bier, to pay some little note of homage to one who has done so much for me. That voice is silenced forever on earth, but who of us cannot recall its clarion tones as it has moved us from time to time in this great temple. It has always been my custom, when coming from my own land to this country, to visit this Tabernacle to have my torch lighted anew. . . .

When darkness seemed to be spreading over the religious world we would often cast longing eyes to London and watch what this great captain was saying and doing. We always found inspiration from this pulpit, and always felt that in him we had a friend who would stand against all foes, a friend we could safely follow. Many a prayer has come across the sea for him, from those who never had the joy of hearing his magnificent voice. Our land loves Charles Haddon Spurgeon.

I learned from the Pastor of this church how to use the voice that God had given me, that I might preach to the thousands who have assembled in our great congregations. . . . I might almost say that he taught me how to sing the praises of God. I have held him up as an example . . . as a man who could inspire his people to worship in hymns of praise by devoting

8. Ibid., p. 141.

time to the reading of the hymn, and then standing and singing with the people. . . . The praise of God is a part of the worship and should not be slighted. . . .

I will sing a little hymn that I think is appropriate for this occasion.

Mr. Sankey then sang, with exquisite feeling, the hymn beginning,

> Sleep on beloved, sleep and take thy rest,
> Lay down thy head upon thy Saviour's breast;
> We love thee well, but Jesus loves thee best,
> Good night! Good night! Good night![9]

The final funeral service and the interment were held the following day, Thursday, February 11. Two of the men who had attended the Pastors' College and whose subsequent ministries had won the warm approval of Spurgeon—William Williams and Archibald Brown—took part first, the former leading in prayer and the latter reading the Scriptures. The sermon was preached by Dr. Pierson, and he spoke of Spurgeon as "a genius in the intellectual sphere," "a genius in the moral sphere," and "a genius in the spiritual sphere." He closed with the words

The eyes now closed in death, that twinkled like two stars in a dark firmament, and brought light and joy to many bereaved and saddened hearts, have lost their light forever. The voice that spoke in tones so convincing and persuasive is hushed in death. The hand whose grasp uplifted many a fallen one, and gave new strength and encouragement to many a stricken one, will never again take our hands within its holy embrace. We bless God for thee, my brother. We are glad that heaven is made richer though we be made poorer; and by this bier we solemnly pledge that we will undertake, by God's grace, to follow thy blessed footsteps, even as thou didst follow thy blessed Lord![10]

The service closed with the singing of a hymn which had been a favorite with Spurgeon.

> Forever with the Lord!
> Amen, so let it be:
> Life from the dead is in that word,
> 'Tis immortality.

9. Ibid., pp. 161-63.
10. Ibid., p. 203.

Here in the body pent,
Absent from Him I roam,
Yet nightly pitch my moving tent
A day's march nearer home.

My father's house on high,
Home of my soul, how near
At times, to faith's foreseeing eye,
Thy golden gates appear!
Ah! then my spirit faints
To reach the land I love,
The bright inheritance of saints,
Jerusalem above.

So when my latest breath
Shall rend the veil in twain,
By death I shall escape from death,
And life eternal gain.
Knowing as I am known,
How shall I love that word,
And oft repeat before the throne,
"Forever with the Lord!"

Following the benediction, "Thousands of handkerchiefs were raised to tearful eyes, as they took a last loving look at the casket that contained all that was mortal of him to whom all owed so much."[11]

The hearse bearing the casket, with several funeral carriages, set out on its five-mile journey to the Norwood Cemetery. People lined the streets in great numbers all the way, the bells of churches were sounded as the procession passed, and even the pubs along the route were closed. "At the Orphan House a covered platform had been erected; and in deep mourning the children sat there, supposed to be singing, but most of them weeping . . . for Mr. Spurgeon had taken them all to his heart."[12]

At the cemetery "The near relatives of the departed Pastor gathered first around the tomb . . . then over a thousand mourners assembled within the barriers, and many thousands crowded beyond."

The service at the graveside was taken largely by Archibald

11. Ibid., p. 204.
12. Ibid., p. 206.

Brown. Looking down upon the casket and thinking of the dear form it carried, he said:

> Beloved President, Faithful Pastor, Prince of Preachers, Brother Beloved, Dear Spurgeon—we bid thee not "Farewell" but only for a little while "Good-night." Thou shalt rise soon at the first dawn of the Resurrection-day of the redeemed. Yet is not the good-night ours to bid, but thine; it is we who linger in the darkness; thou art in God's holy light. Our night shall soon be passed and with it all our weeping. Then, with thine, our songs shall greet the morning of a day that knows no cloud nor close; for there shall be no night there.
>
> Hard worker in the field! thy toil is ended. Straight has been the furrow thou hast ploughed. No looking back has marred thy course. Harvests have followed thy patient sowing, and heaven is already rich with thine ingathered sheaves, and shall be still enriched through years yet lying in eternity.
>
> Champion of God! thy battle, long and nobly fought, is over; the sword which clave to thy hand, has dropped at last; a palm branch takes its place. No longer does the helmet press thy brow, oft weary with its surging thoughts of battle; a victor's wreath from the great Commander's hand has already proved thy full reward.
>
> Here for a little while shall rest thy precious dust. Then shall thy Well-Beloved come; and at His voice thou shalt spring from thy couch of earth, fashioned like unto His body, into glory. Then, spirit, soul, and body shall magnify thy Lord's redemption. Until then beloved sleep. We praise God for thee, and by the blood of the everlasting covenant, hope and expect to praise God with thee. Amen.[13]

Thus, while the soul of Charles Haddon Spurgeon was in the presence of the Lord, his body was placed within its tomb, there to await, as Archibald Brown had so beautifully stated, the dawn of the resurrection morning.

And the people returned to London, to take up their duties in the Tabernacle, the college, the almshouses, the orphanage, and the numerous missions and schools, to labor with fervor and patience as they had done for years, but yet to feel a sad difference, for the leader, the pastor they had loved, was no longer there.

How rich his life had been. He had walked with God and lived in prayer. Nothing in his actions was merely put on, but all was wonderfully real. His one purpose had been to "preach Jesus Christ and Him crucified," and in this determination he had devoted all his

13. Ibid., p. 210.

talents—the extraordinary memory, the great powers of public speech—and his joy had been found in bringing glory to the Savior and in leading souls to know Him. Early in life he had lost all consideration of his own self, and his prayer that he might be hidden behind the cross, that Christ alone might be seen, had expressed his heart's chief purpose.

Spurgeon used to declare that when he reached heaven he "would stand at the corner of one of the streets and proclaim to the angels the old, old story of Jesus and His love."[14] Whether or not such a privilege will be granted any saint we do not know, but we may be sure that as the redeemed multitude before the throne sings "Worthy is the Lamb that was slain," lifted among them with eternal enthusiasm will be a voice that delighted to praise the Lamb here upon the earth—the voice of Charles Haddon Spurgeon.

14. Ibid., p. 44. This was Spurgeon's interpretation of Ephesians 3:10.

Appendix:

Subsequent History of the Metropolitan Tabernacle

At the time Spurgeon died, the Tabernacle and its institutions were all in strong operation. The church was as well attended as ever, the financial support came in regularly, and the prosperity of all seemed assured for several years to come.

But needed was a pastor who would maintain the work in Spurgeon's manner. A few years earlier Dr. Pierson had described the services of the Tabernacle, saying, "Here is nothing to divert the mind from the simplicity of worship and the Gospel. . . . A precentor leads congregational song without even the help of a cornet; prayer and praise, the reading of the Word of God with the plain putting of Gospel truth—these have been Mr. Spurgeon's life-long 'means of grace.' "

For the time being Dr. Pierson continued to serve as Officiating Minister and James Spurgeon as Pastor in Charge. This arrangement could only be temporary, as Dr. Pierson, being a Presbyterian, did not accept the doctrine of believer's baptism. He was also a dispensationalist—a position Spurgeon had vigorously rejected. In four months it was necessary for Dr. Pierson to fulfill an engagement in America, and Thomas Spurgeon, who had recently returned from New Zealand, was asked to supply the pulpit.

After another four months Dr. Pierson was able to return, but the congregation was divided about having him resume the duties of Officiating Minister. By that time Thomas Spurgeon had returned to New Zealand, and more than 2,000 members of the church voted to have him come back to England and accept the pastorate of the Tabernacle.

Thomas accepted the call. He possessed something of the voice and pulpit manner of his father, but he was a much weaker preacher. Throughout the 1890s, though several of the older officials and members of the Tabernacle passed away, the congregation continued to be numbered in the thousands, and the several institutions were generally maintained. Nevertheless, there was a noticeable lack of the fervor that had formerly characterized the work.

In 1898 the Tabernacle was destroyed by fire. The services were held in temporary quarters, and many people began to attend other churches. After three years the building was reconstructed but with a reduced seating capacity. During this period Spurgeon's invaluable library of 12,000 volumes—many of them rare items from Puritan times—was put up for sale and was purchased by the William Jewel College of Liberty, Missouri.

In 1907 Thomas Spurgeon's health caused him to resign the pastorate. He was followed by Archibald Brown, an able preacher and a man much like Spurgeon in doctrine and methods. But Brown also was not in good health, and he remained only three years.

At the suggestion of Dr. Pierson the Tabernacle then called another American, Dr. A. C. Dixon. Dr. Dixon's methods were quite different from those of Spurgeon. He installed a piano and formed a choir, and under his rather sensational type of ministry there were numerous professions of faith, but the church showed a decline in attendance and zeal. Moreover, it was while he was at the Tabernacle that the First World War took place, taking many men into the services and disturbing the work of the church. In 1919 Dixon left the Tabernacle, and it was then a very different church from what it had been under C. H. Spurgeon.

Dixon was followed by H. Tydeman Chilvers. Mr. Chilvers was a more Spurgeonic type of man, and although under his ministry an organ was installed in the church, he endeavored to bring the work back to the simplicity and the Calvinistic doctrine of former days. He also took a strong stand against liberalism and worldliness, and under his ministry, which lasted till 1935, the attendance was increased, and the church became generally strengthened.

After two years without a pastor, in 1938 a call was extended to

Dr. Graham Scroggie. Dr. Scroggie was a Scotsman and was widely known as a preacher and an author. His ministry, however, was hindered by the Second World War, for not only was the congregation scattered by the removal of numerous persons out of London, but the Tabernacle received a direct hit in a bombing attack in 1941 and was again destroyed. Services were held in the basement, with the ruined remains overhead, and although Dr. Scroggie labored faithfully, by 1943 his age and poor health caused him to resign.

By this time changes had come about also in Spurgeon's institutions. In 1923 a fine estate at the edge of London was made available to the Pastors' College, and the College, disassociated from any management by the Tabernacle, was removed there. In later years a new library and other buildings were added to the original large stone mansion. During the Second World War the children in the orphanage were taken to safety in a town to the south of London, and at the end of the war the trustees—who no longer needed to be members of the Tabernacle—had a new building constructed in the town of Birchington in Kent.

After Dr. Scroggie's resignation two ministries carried on the work under the difficult circumstances of the much reduced congregation and the bombed-out building. A period without a pastor followed, and the church rejoined the Baptist Union.

In 1954 Eric W. Hayden accepted the pastorate and led the people in the work of reconstruction. A considerable sum of money (£224,500) was provided by government agencies, and a new Tabernacle that incorporated the front entrance from the original building was erected. It seated about 1,800, but by this time the area had changed, the days of Spurgeon were long forgotten, and an auditorium that would have accommodated 300 or 400, with suitable Sunday school accommodations, would have sufficed.

Mr. Hayden remained for five years, but a time of depressed conditions followed. The area proved difficult to reach, *The Sword and the Trowel* ceased publication, and the congregation became so small that in 1965 the new pastor, Dennis Pascoe, stated, "Our membership can now be accommodated in a few pews."

Then, in 1970 Dr. Peter Masters accepted a call to the Tabernacle. Dr. Masters was Spurgeonic in doctrine and methods, and under his ministry, despite the difficulty, the work began to grow. He led the work out of the Baptist Union, began to republish *The Sword and the Trowel,* and used busses to pick up children for the Sunday school. He established a School of Theology, which guides men's studies throughout the year and conducts a week of lectures during the summer with an attendance of some 350. In recent years the size of the auditorium has been reduced by the construction of a wall that cuts off a third or so of the building and renders it more suited to the present congregation of some 300 hearers.

Thus the theology that Spurgeon held is still preached at the Tabernacle, and although the institutions are gone, in an England that is very largely given over to agnosticism, the work Spurgeon began is still being conducted after the pattern he set for it.

Annotated Bibliography

In *A Baptist Bibliography*, edited by Edward C. Starr and published by the American Baptist Historical Society, Rochester, New York, the section on C. H. Spurgeon covers 64 pages and lists 1135 items. This is an exhaustive survey.

Spurgeon wrote some 140 works. Most of these are no longer in publication and are difficult to obtain in the second-hand market. Some, however, have more recently been produced, the chief of which are:

The New Park Street Pulpit, 1855 to 1860, and *The Metropolitan Tabernacle Pulpit*, 1880 to 1890, published by the Banner of Truth Trust, London and Edinburgh.

The New Park Street Pulpit, 1855 to 1860, and the *Metropolitan Tabernacle Pulpit*, 1861 to 1917, published by the Pilgrim Publications of Pasadena, Texas. Pilgrim Publications has also republished everything that came from Spurgeon's own pen in *The Sword and the Trowel* from the beginning of the magazine in 1865 till his death in 1892.

A brief selection of other works by Spurgeon, some obtainable only in their original form and others that have been more recently republished, may be listed as follows:

All of Grace. An earnest word with those who are seeking salvation.

An All-Round Ministry. Addresses to ministers and students.

Cheque Book of the Bank of Faith. Precious promises arranged for daily use.

Commenting and Commentaries. Two lectures to the Pastors' College, together with a catalogue of commentaries with Spurgeon's appraisal of each one. Republished 1969, by the Banner of Truth Trust, with also a Complete Textual Index to all Spurgeon's sermons.

Feathers for Arrows. Illustrations for preachers and teachers.

Grace Triumphant. A series of unpublished sermons printed after Spurgeon's death.

John Ploughman's Pictures and *John Ploughman's Talk,* Plain advice and plain talk for plain people.

Lectures to My Students. Three volumes of advice on the work of the ministry, republished numerous times.

Morning by Morning and *Evening by Evening.* Devotional readings with which to begin and end the day.

Sermon Notes. Outlines prepared from some of Spurgeon's sermons.

Speeches at Home and Abroad. Discourses on various subjects.

The Clue to the Maze. The so-called "honest doubt" of the New Theology answer by Spurgeon with "honest faith."

The Greatest Fight in the World. Addresses in opposition to the Down-Grade movement.

The Gospel of the Kingdom. Spurgeon's last work, his commentary on the Gospel of Matthew.

The Saint and His Saviour. Spurgeon's first book.

The Salt Cellars. Two volumes of collected Proverbs.

The Soul Winner. "How to lead sinners to the Saviour."

The Treasury of David. Spurgeon's seven-volume commentary on the Psalms.

Trumpet Calls to Christian Energy. Sermons to arouse Christians to greater labors for Christ.

The biographies of Spurgeon are numerous. Following his death in 1892 they appeared for the next two or three years at the rate of about one a month. Many of these were written hurriedly to meet the need of the hour. Others were produced during later years, and the best may be listed as:

G. Holden Pike, *The Life and Work of Charles Haddon Spurgeon.* A six-volume work, by the assistant editor of *The Sword and the Trowel.* 1898.

C. H. Spurgeon's Autobiography, compiled after Spurgeon's death by Mrs. Spurgeon and Spurgeon's secretary, J. W. Harrald. Four volumes. 1897.

The Early Years and *The Full Harvest.* A condensation of the *Autobiography* into two volumes, edited by Iain Murray and published by the Banner of Truth Trust. 1962, 1973.

E. W. Bacon, *Spurgeon—Heir of the Puritans.* 1967.

J. C. Carlile, *C. H. Spurgeon—An Interpretative Biography.* 1933.

James Douglas, *The Prince of Preachers.*

W. Y. Fullerton, *C. H. Spurgeon.* 1920.

J. W. Fulton, *Spurgeon, Our Ally.*

Iain Murray, *The Forgotten Spurgeon.* 1966.

Charles Ray, *The Life of Charles Haddon Spurgeon.* 1903.

Robert Shindler, *From the Usher's Desk to the Tabernacle Pulpit,* and *From the Pulpit to the Palm Branch.* 1892.

William Williams, *Personal Reminiscences of Charles Haddon Spurgeon.* 1895.

A number of books on Spurgeon have been written by the Rev. Eric W. Hayden and published by Pilgrim Publications. Among them are the following: *A History of Spurgeon's Tabernacle, Searchlight on Spurgeon, A Pictorial Biography of C. H. Spurgeon,* and *A Traveller's Guide to Spurgeon Country.*

General Index